C000110599

KENT

A Chronicle of The Century

Volume Three: 1950-1974

by Bob Ogley

The third volume of Bob Ogley's *Chronicle of the Century* embraces the memorable years of the fifties — the birth of the teenager and Rock 'n Roll — when we were ushered into the New Elizabethan Age with an optimism that was quickly confirmed. It continues through the sixties — mini skirts and mini cars, youth culture and flower power, student protest and the 'permissive society' — a decade of well-being and unprecedented change. It ends with the less exciting early seventies — strikes and three-day weeks, wage restraint and a growing disquiet in the workplace. Here are Kent's principal players, archaeological discoveries, engineering achievements, dramas, scandals and disasters. With the help of almost 200 illustrations, they will take you back in time.

Froglets Publications

Froglets
Publications Ltd
Brasted Chart,
Westerham,
Kent TN16 1LY
Tel: 01959 562972
Fax: 01959 565365

Volume One
ISBN Hardback 1 872337 24 4
ISBN Paperback 1 872337 19 8

Volume Two
ISBN Hardback 1 872337 84 8
ISBN Paperback 1 872337 89 9

Volume Three
ISBN Hardback 1 872337 16 3
ISBN Paperback 1 872337 11 2

Front cover illustrations

Meteor 8, Cars en route for the first F1 meeting at Brands Hatch 1960, Mick Jagger & Marianne Faithfull, Colin Cowdrey, and early trials of the hovercraft at Dover.

Originated by Froglets Publications Ltd. Scanning by CK Litho, Whitstable. Printed and slot bound by Thanet Press, Margate. Casebound by Green Street Bindery, Oxford.

Jacket design and additional artwork by Alison Clark

FOREWORD

Was it bravery or recklessness that led me to promise, in 1996, that I would write four volumes about the county of Kent, all its principal players and all its exhilarating historical moments in time for the millennium? I suggest the latter.

But, remarkably, I am now three quarters of the way towards my goal and having a wonderful time. Little wonder. Like most people aged between 50 and 70 the sixties and, especially the fities, was my era and by collecting stories, memories and those evocative photographs I have experienced a delicate resurrection of my own youth. If writing a book can bring about this reincarnation I sincerely hope that reading it can, also! Nostalgia is a wonderful tonic.

My thanks as usual to the critics who have been so kind and to all those who have been involved in this publication. Fern Flynn, who masterminds the Froglets empire, has once again been involved in all stages of production and Avril Oswald and Mark Laver have read and corrected the text and made many useful suggestions.

Local history departments of Kent Libraries, heritage centres, museum curators and local editors have given great help in the gathering of information. So have the readers of many newspapers. There are too many to name individually but they know I am grateful.

However, I would particularly like to thank the following: David Witherspoon, Bob Hollingsbee, Gordon Luck, Frank Chapman, Gordon Anckorn, Chris Taylor, the Kent cricket archivist, Tom White of Kent's Fire Brigade museum, John Endicote of the police museum, Colin Triggs from Gillingham FC, all from the Pat Marsh Show on Radio Kent and the helpful staff of Topham Picturepoint.

Next year I have the most difficult task of all — to study the modern years, between 1975 and 1999, and pick out the events that form a momentous part of Kent's fascinating, ongoing story. I hope readers will appreciate that, on this occasion, I will not have the advantage of hindsight which has helped me to put events and personalities into a historical perspective. The choice is vast; readers will have to trust my editorial judgement.

Bob Ogley

PHOTOGRAPH CREDITS

We are grateful to the following for the use of their copyright photographs. In some cases we have been unable to trace the copyright holder but have made every effort to do so. **Topham Picture Source:** 4-5,6 (bottom), 9, 10, 12, 14, 17, 25, 28, 30-31, 33, 34, 35, 37, 44, 46, 51, 52, 53, 54, 55, 58, 60, 62, 63, 65, 66, 75, 78, 79, 80, 81, 82, 83, 84, 85, 86, 88, 89, 90, 95, 96, 98, 99, 104-5, 108, 109, 114, 115, 116, 124, 127, 130, 132, 140, 144, 151, 160, 165, 172, 182, 185, 187, 189, 193. **Kentish Times:** 36, 56, 94, 138, 152, 194 (bottom), **Kent County Council Arts and Libraries:** ***Folkestone*** 27, 157. ***Ramsgate*** 50, 131, 153. ***Gravesend*** 107. **Medway News:** 32, 47, 100, 129. **Sevenoaks Chronicle:** 18, 29, 97, 133, 134, 135, 142, 149, 155, 161, 170-171, 177, 181. **Chris Taylor** (Kent County Cricket Club): 39, 49, 139, 141, 183 (bottom). **Kent Messenger:** 87, 158, 166.**Fern Flynn:** 69-70, 74, 91, 125, 137, 167, 168, 175, 179, 180. **Imperial War Museum:** 43, 146. **Kent County Fire Brigade Museum:** 22, 24, 40, 64, 118, 123, 162-163, 194. **Kent Police Museum:** 15, 21, 20, 59, 61. **Dover Museum:** 48. **National Railway Museum:** 13. **Bob Hollingsbee:** 178, 190. **Author's collection:** 41, 42, 45, 68, 71, 77, 103, 110, 116 (bottom), 119, 136, 145, 169, 174, 186, 188. **National Trust (Scotney):** 159. **Rochester-upon-Medway Local History Dept** 126. **Bromley Library:** 154, 173. **Samuel Whitbread Ltd:** 7. **Roger Triggs:** 11. **Gordon Anckorn:** 16, 57. **Frank Chapman:** 156. **G.E.Hall:** 148. **D.Witherspoon:** 134. **Miss M.G. Nunn:** 122. **Cobtree Trust:** 111. **Leeds Castle Foundation:** 192 (both).**Mayfair Cards:** 121.**Pictorial Press:** 136

The New Elizabethan Age brings a wave of optimism

THE FIFTIES began in Kent with much that remained from the pre-war days. There were promenade concerts at Folkestone, trams ran to Woolwich, Les Ames was playing cricket, steam trains puffed along the light railway lines at Headcorn and Tilmanstone and the RAF still flew from Hawkinge and Biggin Hill.

Elsewhere echoes of the past reverberated. Gillingham were on their way back to the Football League and the sophisticated Noel Coward was on his way from Romney Marsh to Bermuda. Dr Hewlett Johnson, the Red Dean of Canterbury, was still pleading the Communist cause and Churchill was condemning Labour's indifference to a United Europe. George VI, who had shouldered a burden as heavy as any in the land, was still a much-loved King.

His death in 1952, like that of his great grandmother, 51 years earlier, ushered us into another era. The New Elizabethan Age heralded an optimism that was quickly confirmed. A British Expedition conquered Everest, England won the Ashes and Neville Duke from Tonbridge broke the sound barrier. By now Churchill was back at number 10 and among his proteges were the members for Bromley and Bexley respectively — Harold Macmillan and Edward Heath.

Although the great European war was now well in the past, conscription in the early fifties was sending our youths to fight in Korea, Malaya, Kenya and Cyprus and to safeguard West Germany and the Suez Canal. This was also the decade of the teenager — to coin a new word — to whom heroes were not Monty, Winston or Clem but Bill Hayley and James Dean, Cliff and Elvis. They enjoyed parties, rock n' roll, skiffle and possessed a new, more casual attitude to life, later to be known as the "opening of the generation gap".

There was another kind of youth in the early 1950s. They stood in groups on the streets of Maidstone or Tunbridge Wells or Dartford. The males had hairstyles like spokes, laminated with Brylcreem. They were bejewelled and crimped and wore stove-pipe trousers, long coats, black string ties and flowery waistcoats. The magistrates, who got to know many of them well, called them spivs or drones but they saw themselves as Teddy Boys and Teddy Girls.

There were better role models for the kids of Kent to admire, both fact and fiction. Dick Barton, from Brenchley, where his creator lived, was a wireless hero and so was Frank Muir, from Ramsgate, who collaborated so brilliantly with Dennis Norden, while, on the stage, Dame Sybil Thorndike held the world of theatre spellbound.

Young sportsmen admired Gillingham's determination to get back into the Football League. They hero-worshipped a young Colin Cowdrey who moved from Tonbridge School, to Oxford, to Kent and to the England team in Australia in a few sensational summers of admirable strokeplay. They were fascinated by the skills of ice queen, Jeannette Altwegg from Downe, the destructive power of the Dartford destroyer, Dave Charnley and 'Our 'Enery' (Henry Cooper) and they mourned the death of Anthony Mildmay, the greatest amateur steeplechaser of them all.

Kent took a prominent role in the Coronation junketings. After all the young Queen was well-known in Kent and so was her outspoken cricket-playing consort who turned out on occasions at Mersham where his cousins lived. Proprietors of electrical shops who sold the magic boxes were delighted when the date of the Big Day was announced. This was the incentive they, and television, needed to persuade thousands to buy a set for the first time.

When Archbishop Fisher's starring role was over there were more Kentish heroes to watch. Muffin the Mule (the voice and creation of Annette Mills), Noddy in his Toyland (Enid Blyton) and the avuncular East End ("evenin' all") copper, Jack Warner from Thanet, who solved a crime each week at Dock Green.

There was sadness in the early 50s. A double-decker bus ploughed into a marching column of cadets at Chatham, a tidal surge inundated every town, village and hamlet from Woolwich to the North Foreland, a Thunderjet thundered onto Lloyds Bank in Broadstairs and later on two express trains collided in the fog at Lewisham.

It was our literary characters who cheered us up. Somerset Maugham (Canterbury), Herbert Edward Bates (Little Chart, near Pluckley), Ian Fleming (Sandwich), Vita Sackville-West (Sissinghurst), Richard Church (Goudhurst), Richmal Crompton (Bromley Common) and also Trottiscliffe's Graham Sutherland who painted Winston Churchill, incurred the wrath of the old man, and moved smartly to a more evocative commission at Coventry.

The fifties, often dismissed as a difficult period, paved the way to the more memorable years to follow. No other decade had a greater effect on popular modern culture than the sixties and they permeated every level of society — particularly here in "swinging Kent".

August 10th, 1950 *and a scene that is familiar all over Kent in the apple picking season.*

This could be the great fruit belt between Sittingbourne and Faversham, it could be the orchards of the Weald where apples compete with hops, it could be the fertile valleys between Edenbridge and Tonbridge or even the rich loams of east Kent. In fact this is Scadbury Farm, Sidcup, near the home of the man who took the picture, John Topham.

Such orchards have thrived in Kent since the middle of the nineteenth century when an increasing demand from urban centres and from jam factories encouraged farmers with sufficient capital and foresight to plant the trees.

As London grew, so did its appetite for fruit, sent there by water from the Kentish villages or by oxen which was superseded by the horse and then by the combustion engine.

Kent is called the Garden of England, not for its pretty flowers or formal landscapes, but for its market produce.

The future, however, looks grim, for the greatest menace to the survival of the Garden of England is the pressure of population, expanding industry and the need for new roads. If development continues at the present rate it is possible that the finest orchards in England will soon disappear for ever.

Many problems have faced Kent Education Committee since the end of the war. One has been the deterioration of buildings — many damaged by bombs — and another, the greatly increased birth rate which has resulted in bigger classes and the urgent need for new schools. The village of Stansted has none of these problems. Not only is it the one of the smallest schools in the country but the building survived the war intact. Here is the headmistress, Mrs G.P. Murphy, taking the entire school home (minus two pupils who were absent).

The Women's Institute continues to be one of the most successful organisations in Kent. Here is a typical village hall scene — members of Birling WI learning how to make baskets.

'You can hear every word he sings which is a pity, considering his material. It's like being force-fed with treacle' — London critic on Frank Sinatra's debut concert in England.

1950

January 31st: The American Atomic Energy Commission is to produce a hydrogen bomb, 100 to 1,000 times more powerful than the atom bombs dropped on Hiroshima and Nagasaki. Research is already well under way into the new weapon.

February 15th: Russia and China have formed a friendship pact. The two great Communist nations will now have a united front against the world.

February 24th: Twenty out of a record 126 women candidates have won seats in Parliament. The Liberals have lost 314 election deposits and the Party is in disarray.

March 18th: Roger Bannister today ran the mile in a record four minutes 1.48 seconds.

April 24th: King Abdullah of Jordan has created a new kingdom by annexing Arab Palestine. Other Arab states are furious; they see the West Bank territory as Palestinian homeland.

Mr Nevill Christopherson, a member of the Free Foresters and Band of Brothers, has been appointed general manager and secretary of Kent Cricket Club.

May 26th: Petrol rationing has ended after ten years. Kent seaside resorts are now preparing for the biggest Whitsun invasion they have ever known.

May 29th: The war-damaged Central Cinema, Canterbury, has been converted into a theatre, The Marlowe. It opened today with the showing of *The Chiltern Hundreds.*

WHITE HORSE
Chilham

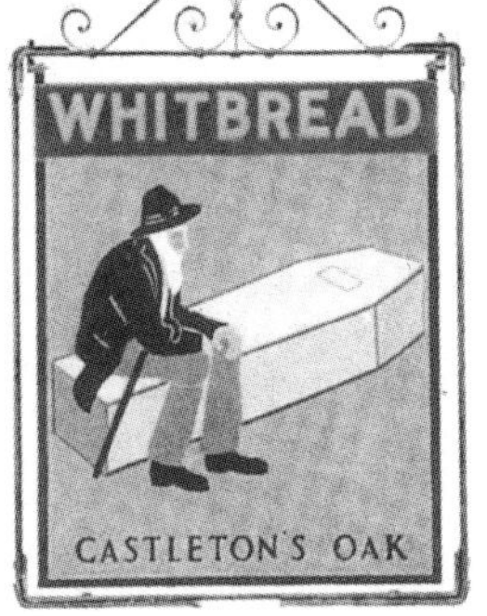

CASTLETON'S OAK
Biddenden

A new and fascinating hobby, introduced by Whitbread Brewery, is the reproduction in miniature of many of Kent's famous and historic taverns. Two sets of 50 of these aluminium signs are available and are proving an irresistible challenge among thousands of visitors to the Garden of England. The signs are made at the Wateringbury Brewery.

May 31st: Ten mile queues stretched from London city centre into Kent yesterday as motorists returned from their Whitsun excursion, having enjoyed ten hours of sunshine. An AA official in Kent said there was a solid mass of traffic through most towns.

June 25th: The independent nation of South Korea has been invaded by Communists from the north. Troops and tanks crossed the 38th Parallel, the agreed border between the two states.

June 28th: England has lost its first round World Cup match to the United States. Joint favourites with the home side Brazil to win the trophy, they were beaten one-nil in a shock result.

July 6th: Queen Elizabeth arrived by special train on the small branch line to Cranbrook today and enjoyed an afternoon in the Weald of Kent chatting to scores of local people.

July 26th: British troops are being sent to Korea under the orders of the United Nations. US troops are already supporting the South Koreans.

July 31st: A self-service shopping store has opened in Croydon. J. Sainsbury's believe more such stores will open in the future.

June 22nd: Those early flying pioneers, who won their wings with the Royal Aero Club at Stanford Hill, Eastchurch, will be astonished to learn that this historic site has been converted into an open prison.

After lying derelict for more than three years, the permanent camp buildings — once the headquarters of naval aviation — have been taken over by the Home Office.

The field which saw those early fragile biplanes piloted by the likes of the Hon Charles Rolls and Francis McClean is to return to agriculture.

It was not uncommon for a flyer or technician to complain about the isolation of Eastchurch. Now it is the turn of inmates to experience the solitary remoteness of this corner of Sheppey. Several miles from the nearest town and surrounded by marshland it is the ideal site for an experimental open penal settlement.

August 5th: Florence Chadwick, an American, has cut an hour off the best time for a Channel swim. She came ashore at Dover in 13 hours 23 minutes.

August 8th: Fearing that lions may escape from their cage in the zoo, police stood by with rifles early today as a huge fire spread through Dreamland at Margate. Reinforcements from all over Kent were drafted in to bring the flames under control.

August 15th: Princess Elizabeth has given birth to a daughter — her second child. She will be christened Anne Elizabeth Alice Louise.

A 17-year-old Tonbridge schoolboy, Michael Colin Cowdrey made his debut for Kent today scoring 15 and 26 against Derbyshire. His father had given him the initials MCC hoping one day he would play for England.

October 24th: What remained of the ill-fated Crystal Palace has been destroyed in another great conflagration. 25 firefighters and 100 appliances fought the blaze which could be seen for many miles.

November 2nd: George Bernard Shaw, the successful Irish playwright with subversive opinions, died at his home today at Ayot St Lawrence, Hertfordshire. He was 94.

December 25th: The Coronation Stone has been stolen from Westminster Abbey where it has lain for 650 years. Scottish nationalists are believed to be responsible, claiming that it belongs to Scotland.

December 31st: This has been the year of the bus. Maidstone and District ran 900 vehicles for 29 million miles and carried 165 million passengers during 1950.

GREAT HITS OF 1950

I've Got A Lovely Bunch of Coconuts

Mona Lisa

Europe decision angers the member for Bromley

February 24th: In the closest general election for 100 years Labour remains in office with 315 seats against the Tories' 298 and Liberals' nine.There is a big switch in the public mood and it appears the nation wants no further Labour nationalisation but is well satisfied with its Welfare State.

One politician, exasperated by Labour policy, is the member for Bromley, Harold Macmillan, who wants Britain to join the nations committed to reconstruction and reconciliation in Europe. One plan, supported by France and Germany, is to pool coal and steel production as a "rock for an economic community".

Macmillan told his constituents in Bromley last week that the Labour Cabinet had never even discussed the issue and the only meaningful comment was made by Herbert Morrison when he was tracked down in the Ivy Restaurant. "It's no good", he said. "We can't do it, the Durham miners won't wear it".

In his Bromley speech, Macmillan said: "This has been a black week for Britain, for the Empire, for Europe and for the peace of the world...without British participation, Franco-Germany unity may be a source, not of security, but danger."

Most of Kent's Conservative members increased their vote while a 24-year-old chemistry graduate, Margaret Roberts, made great inroads into the huge Labour majority at Dartford.

Opposition leader, Mr Winston Churchill, speaking from Chartwell, said: "Parliament is unstable. It's stalemate."

Medway Towns stricken by disaster at sea

January 14th: After 30 hours of unbearable suspense it has been confirmed that 16 Chatham Dockyard technicians died when the British submarine *HMS Truculent* was accidentally rammed in the Thames Estuary on Thursday (January 12th). Altogether 60 seamen are feared dead in the worst submarine disaster the country has known since the *Thetis* went down in 1939.

Today (Saturday) the 1,575-ton *Truculent* is lying in 54 feet of water as navy divers continue to search for likely survivors. There is now little hope that they will be successful.

The submarine, which was on its first journey to sea after a refit at Chatham, was struck by a Swedish ship weighing just 643 tons but strengthened for ice-breaking.

Of the civilians aboard the *Truculent* two of them — Roy Edward Stevens, aged 38, an inspector of engine filters from Rainham and Dennis Albert Griffiths, 22, a ships' fitter from Gillingham — were saved.

The great Royal Dockyard, founded in the days of Elizabeth 1, has known tragedy before and its fortitude has been tested many times but never before has disaster occurred so near nor the suspense of uncertainty been so prolonged.

The submarine left Chatham on Thursday for a trial run across the estuary and it was on the return journey that she was hit by the *Divina* which possessed specially reinforced bows for ice breaking. Four officers and a seaman in the conning tower were thrown into the water and rescued by a Dutch steamer. Twelve other men were quickly picked up.

Immediately after the news came through there was frantic activity at Admiralty House, Chatham. The C-in-C of The Nore, Admiral Sir Henry Rethven Moore sent a distress signal to all shipping in the vicinity "Keep silence for distress calls on all ship-to-shore wavelengths."

Admiralty rescue vessels, lifeboats from Margate and Southend and divers and salvage experts from Portsmouth went to the aid of the stricken submarine.

Hampered by fog they worked without sleep for 30 hours and today most of them are still out to sea — knowing in their hearts that all hope can now be discounted.

The mayors of Chatham, Rochester and Gillingham have opened a Three Towns' Fund to help the dependants of the local victims of the *Truculent* disaster.

A magnificent watercolour by Joseph Mallord William Turner has been acquired by Deal Borough Council and will hang proudly in the council offices. It shows the town in the foreground with a wrecked vessel on the Goodwins in the distance. There are dilapidated buildings on shore with Dutch gables, the sails of the luggers and the tiny silhouette of Sandown Castle. This painting (circa 1824) helped to enhance Turner's reputation as England's greatest marine artist.

Kent celebrates this year the 500th anniversary of the death of Jack Cade — the Ashford rebel who, aggrieved at the tyranny practiced by tax collectors, led 20,000 men into battle against the Henry VI's forces and beat them at Sevenoaks. Although pardons were granted to those who took part in the uprising, Cade went into hiding. He was tracked down by Alexander Iden, High Sheriff of Kent, who found the rebel playing bowls at an inn in Newick. Resisting arrest, Cade was shot and, true to tradition, his head was displayed on London Bridge.

June 20th: *Princess Elizabeth, as Godmother, holds Michael John, the youngest son of Lord and Lady Brabourne after his christening in Mersham Parish Church. Lady Patricia Brabourne (extreme right) is the daughter of Earl Louis Mountbatten, the King's cousin, who is pictured here with his son-in-law, Lord Brabourne, admiring his new grandson. The link between the Royal Family and the Brabournes has led to a number of private visits to their charming home in Mersham, near Ashford.*

Lord Mildmay with Cromwell at Liverpool before the dramatic Grand National in 1948.

Royal family devastated as Lord Mildmay drowns

May 12th: The great steeplechase jockey, Lord Mildmay of Flete — who has done more to elevate the sport of jumping over fences from a rough minor pastime into a national sport — has drowned in the sea near his Devon estate

There are few details available. Apparently the man affectionately known as "the last of the Corinthians" left his home at Mothecombe just before breakfast for a dip in the sea and never came back. His body has not yet been recovered.

Anthony Mildmay was 41 and, in the National Hunt season not yet ended, again the leading amateur — as he has been for the last four years.

Few racegoers will forget the 1948 Grand National when Mildmay was up with the leaders on the great horse Cromwell. With less than a mile to go His Lordship was suddenly racked with cramp. Slumped over the mane he somehow held on as Cromwell jumped the last few fences to finish third.

Mildmay rode for Peter Cazalet whose stables are at Shipbourne, Tonbridge. A great friend of the Royal Family, he recently persuaded Queen Elizabeth and Princess Elizabeth to buy a racehorse.

The Queen thought this would amuse her horse-mad daughter so they commissioned Mildmay's great friend Cazalet to find a suitable horse. He recommended an Irish-bred steeplechaser called Monaveen and a new racing partnership developed.

Lord Mildmay was a legendary figure in the racing world. A banker by profession, he gave up working in the City in 1933 to start a market garden business on his father's estate at Shoreham, Sevenoaks. This gave him the time to become an amateur jockey and he rode many winners for Cazalet.

The Queen and Princess are devastated by the death of the 6ft 2in jockey, as is the whole racing world.

Troubled colliery railroad finally closes

December 6th: This is a sad day for railway enthusiasts. The East Kent Light Railway line between Tilmanstone and Wingham — which had opened amid great excitement earlier in the century primarily for the transport of coal — finally closed today.

The company has been plagued by financial difficulties for years but the demise of the EKLR became inevitable when railways were nationalised in 1948 and passenger services ceased.

Older miners can recall the completion of the line in 1912 and how thousands of tons were carried to and from the pits. They also remember the great clamour among shareholders for part ownership in a railway company promising rich reward in the "coming Kent coal boom". It never materialised.

EKLR is not the only line in Kent to close. The Sheppey Light Railway between Leysdown and Queenborough met the same fate this month.

The Gillingham team of 1950-51: Back row (l to r): Skivington, Boswell, Henson, Marks, Ayres, Burke, Gage, Kingsnorth, Armstrong, Williams. Middle row: Edmed, O'Donnell (trainers), Collins, Russell, W. Burtenshaw, Veck, Lewin, Jenkins, Wright, Briggs, Piper, Day. Seated: McGuire, E.Fletcher (secretary), S.Martin, A.Weller, C.Cox and H.Wood (directors), A Clark (manager), R.Swan (ass sec), Dorling, Griffiths (trainer). Front: Nobbs, Hales, Carr, Poulton, C.Burtenshaw, Warsap, Trumper, Humphreys.

Ecstatic 'Gills' return to the Football League

March 28th: The Gills are back on the soccer map at last. After 12 years in the wilderness and months of great tension they have been readmitted to the Third Division of the Football League.

The decision came late last night after a meeting of high drama at the Cafe Royal, London, where the league mandarins were considering a proposal that two extra clubs should be take into each section of the Third Division.

Hundreds of Gillingham supporters, carrying billboards declaring their team was worthy of league status, picketed outside as a ballot was held. When they heard the result they were ecstatic. Gillingham, 44 votes, and Colchester, 28, were the successful teams.

The decision to readmit the Gills is fully justified. In the last five seasons in the Southern League they have won the title twice, been runners-up once and scored more than 300 goals. Great improvements have been made to Priestfield Stadium and an incredible £10,000 spent on acquiring five new players.

Manager Archie Clark and chairman Charles Cox will be aiming for promotion to Division Two and then, who knows, a place among the giants of the game. They certainly anticipate crowds in excess of 20,000.

1950

The sight of a man with a red flag walking in front of a steam train pulling freight wagons may seem a little bizarre to visitors. But for the people of Dover the Promenade Railway, which runs between the Harbour and the Eastern Docks, is part of the everyday scene —albeit a hazardous one. Before the war a fence ran alongside the side of the line but this was removed to allow vehicles to use a larger area. Now a flag-carrying guard walks a few yards in front.

The grey, lumpy, hard limestone known throughout the country as Kentish Rag is to be used to repair the Tower of London. Quarrymen at Brishing Court, Boughton Monchelsea are already dressing the stone which has been chosen for its strength and durability.

The use of ragstone in building has declined dramatically in recent years and many pits have closed but the Tower of London was built, mainly of ragstone, by the Normans, as were the great castle keeps at Rochester and Dover — and occasional repairs are necessary.

Kentish Rag was actually quarried by the Romans several centuries earlier and in the years that followed it became the natural material for many of the county's finest buildings including Knole, Cobham Court, the Westgate at Canterbury, Ightham Mote, the mediaeval bridges over the Medway and numerous churches.

It began to lose favour as a building material in the 16th century but was employed in the building of Sevenoaks School, Archbishop's Palace and the prison at Maidstone and many hospitals, almshouses, national schools and villages, particularly in the hills between Sevenoaks and Maidstone

Although ragstone is quarried in the ridge of the Lower Greensand formation which extends from Hythe to Petersfield in Hampshire it is rarely found west of the Kentish border near Westerham.

'The festival style is clean, bright and new. It's looks neither to classical Athens, nor imperial New Delhi, nor chromium-plated New York but to modest Scandinavia' — author Peter Vansittart.

1951

January: It has just been announced that Kent and England leg spin bowler, Doug Wright, netted £5,253 in his benefit year which is a a county record.

January 27th: Britain's meat shortage is such that three ration books would be needed to buy a pound. The meat shortage has created a growing blackmarket.

January 28th: The United States went ahead today with a second nuclear bomb test in the Nevada desert. The flash could be seen from Las Vegas, 45 miles away.

February 1st: Robert Dougall and Alvar Liddell are among eight new newsreaders appointed by the BBC. No women or men with "dialect" voices have been appointed.

February 28th: England today won the fifth and final Test Match in Australia but lost the series 4-1. Two Kent players, Doug Wright and Godfrey Evans are in the tour party.

March 24th: The University Boat Race was called off today after the Oxford boat sank.

March 30th: The Commander of the UN forces in Korea, General Douglas MacArthur, demanded that his troops should attack China and destroy the Communist regime there.

April 11th: General MacArthur has been sacked from all posts by President Harry Truman who said: "It would be tragically wrong for the United States to take the initiative in extending the war."

May 6th: Residents of Borstal village are being terrorised by boys who abscond from the nearby institution. One man told the local council that his home had been entered six times in five years.

May 9th: The Government has changed its mind over the ages at which men and women should receive old age pensions. It is now 65 and 60 instead of 70 and 65.

May 11th: King Frederick and Queen Ingrid of Denmark inspected The Buffs at Dover at the start of their four-month State visit of England. 18 RAF meteors swept low over the harbour and the mighty battleship *Vanguard* opened up with a 21-gun salute in honour of the distinguished guests.

Goods trains continue to run on the line between Whitstable and Canterbury, where Stephenson introduced his famous Invicta in 1830. The main load is grain, brought to Whitstable by barge, while coal often travels in the opposite direction. It is unlikely to last. Roads are now handling most haulage and the line is another candidate for closure. Picture shows an engine approaching Tyler Hill —England's first railway tunnel.

May: Les Ames, one of Kent's greatest players, has retired from the game after collapsing from back trouble in a match at Gillingham. In recognition of his services to cricket he will be made a life member of both Kent Cricket Club and the MCC.

June 1st: Coffins containing the body of Mrs Harriet Cobb and her son who died more than 100 years ago, have been destroyed in a fire at a burial vault in Emmanuel Church cemetery, Margate. It is believed children dropped lighted matches into the chamber.

June 9th: Princess Elizabeth officiated at the Trooping of the Colour today as her father is unwell.

June 16th: It has been confirmed that the entire crew of a British submarine died in the English Channel. *HMS Affray* was found in 258 feet of water.

July 11th: The Queen today laid the foundation stone of the National Theatre.

The Grain to Port Victoria railway line has finally closed.

August 10th: Hellfire Corner honoured Winston Churchill by bestowing upon him the Freedom of Dover and Deal. Various tributes were made to which Churchill replied: "How easy it would have been for five or six thousand Germans from Calais to mount a tip-and-run raid, seize Dover Castle and destroy the big guns mounted here. How foolish we would have looked if that had happened. I took great pains about those guns. I was always very anxious."

August 24th: A secret and sinister African organisation called the Mau Mau has been linked to a big increase in burglaries in the white suburbs of Nairobi, Kenya.

September 14th: Traditional scenes and methods of hop-picking will eventually disappear if recommendations from the Hop Picking Productivity Council are ever adopted by Kent growers. They suggest that picking can be accomplished by machine and this method is widely used in America.

September 23rd: The King's left lung was removed in a successful operation at Buckingham Palace yesterday. Because of the King's illness the Prime Minister Clement Attlee has cut short his holiday and returned to London.

October 3rd: Britain's first atomic bomb has been tested in the Indian Ocean.

October 31st: More and more Britons are buying television sets. Last year's figures of 344,000 is certain to be bettered.

November 15th: Terrorist threats have halted work on 16 rubber plantations in Malaya.

November 20th: British families have been evacuated from Egypt following growing tension over the Suez Canal rights.

OBITUARY

Henry Iles, the man who brought Dreamland to Margate and achieved more than any other person in developing the area as a tourist attraction has died, aged 78.

GREAT HITS OF 1951

If

Shall We Dance

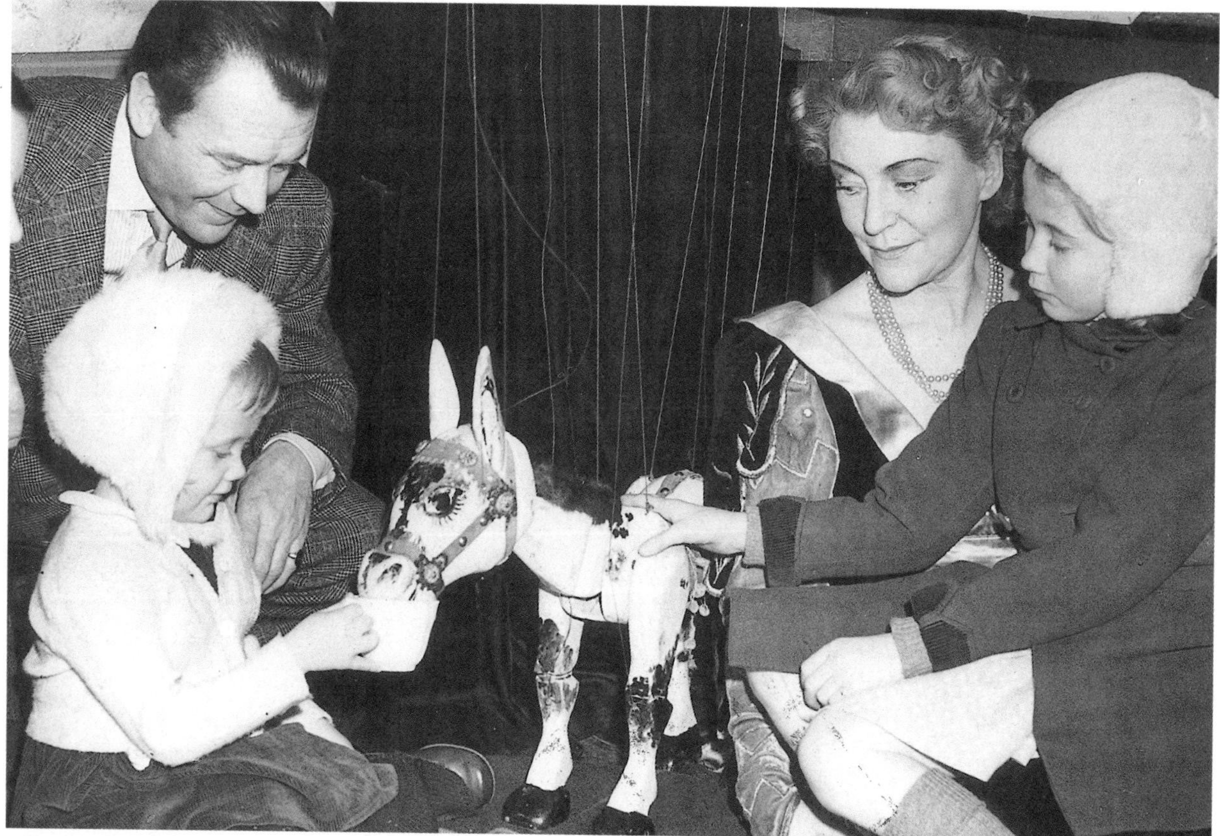

January 11th: *Screen star John Mills, who lives at Cowden, near Edenbridge, took his two daughters Hayley and Juliet to Wimbledon Theatre last night to see his sister, Annette, and her puppet, Muffin the Mule, who is delighting children all over the country and even has his own television show. Picture shows John and Hayley (left) giving Muffin a drink while Annette and Juliet look on.*

Kent catches the festive mood

May 4th: Thousands of Kent commuters who travel on the Charing Cross line to London have been watching, with growing fascination, as 27 acres of a derelict, bomb-damaged area at Waterloo is transformed into the Festival of Britain exhibition site.

Yesterday many of them congregated on the South Bank of the Thames to watch the King and Queen officially declare the festival open.

It is not the end of austerity but a clear sign that a brighter future awaits a country still suffering from the ravages of a long war and the difficult years which followed.

The Dome of Discovery, the new pleasure gardens and the Festival Hall — the only permanent building — have been designed by a team of architects led by Hugh Casson. The project, which cost £8 million, has been described by Herbert Morrison as "the people giving themselves a pat on the back". Many newspapers have criticised the cost, describing it as "Morrison's folly".

Certainly the mood of fun, symbolised by the floating, floodlit, aluminium Skylon which towers above the site with no visible means of support, is making its mark in Kent and most towns are organising festival weeks.

The people of Ashford have erected a triumphal archway over the High Street and a carnival will take place in a few weeks' time. Canterbury will hold a music and religious drama with a special guest reading by Dame Sybil Thorndike while Charles Dickens, Mr Pickwick and all his friends will live again in Rochester.

Tenterden will give homage to William Caxton with a printing exhibition. "I was born in the Weald of Kent", said Caxton, "where English is spoken, broad and rude".

Organisers of the Kent Agricultural Show at Mote Park will hold a special display of fruit and flowers "as fine as anywhere in Britain" and the RAF will open aerodromes at Biggin Hill, Hawkinge, Manston and West Malling in celebration of that epic victory in the air.

Some of the detectives, soldiers and uniformed policemen in Symons Avenue, Chatham, close to where the armed Alan Poole is holding out alone. In the fields round the back of the house and further up the road more policemen are attempting to flush out the man they suspect of killing their colleague, Pc Alan Baxter.

Chatham Pc murdered by army deserter

June 8th: Alan Derek Poole, a 20-year-old army deserter — wanted for the murder of a policeman — was himself killed today in his parents' home at Symons Avenue, Chatham, following scenes that were reminiscent of the famous seige of Sydney Street.

Poole, crazy about knives and weapons and American gangster magazines, was shot by the armed police who were attempting to "flush him out".

So ended one of the most intensive manhunts the Medway Towns had ever known. Two days earlier — on Monday evening — Poole had gunned down Pc Alan Baxter in cold blood.

The policeman, a 31-year-old married man, had responded to a 999 caller who said that a gunman, with two girls, was hiding out in a corporation rubbish dump at Luton.

Alan Baxter, accompanied by his sergeant, William Langford and Pc Brown, found Poole at the dump with a Sten gun. He fired first at Langford but missed and then at Baxter who was sitting in the Chatham squad car.

The policeman, bleeding profusely from bullet wounds, was taken immediately to St Bartholomew's Hospital. He died the following day.

The police found the two girls who had themselves escaped from a remand home and were living with Poole in the open and helping him steal food from nearby homes.

This morning 200 policemen together with soldiers, sailors and firemen surrounded the two-storey council house in Symons Avenue. Poole was alone, having already ordered his mother, father, brother and sister out of the house.

He was asked to give himself up but refused. Tear gas bombs were thrown and powerful jets of water pumped into the house by firemen. Every so often Poole would unleash a further round. The snipers outside responded.

When the shooting stopped the police waited for two hours before entering the house. Poole was found to be dead.

Pc Baxter's widow is seriously ill in All Saint's Hospital, Chatham. The murder of her husband coincided with the arrival of the couple's baby who lived for only a few hours.

The heroic policeman was born in Maidstone in 1917 and joined the police force a year before the outbreak of war.

West Kents ambushed in Malaya: 12 killed

October 27th: An officer and 11 men were killed yesterday when two platoons of the Royal West Kent Regiment were ambushed in the jungles of Malaya. Several others are in hospital, seriously wounded.

An account of the ambush from Kuala Lumpur states that the Royal West Kents, commanded by Lt-Col A. Martyn, were rushed to a rubber plantation near Selangor where the bandits were hiding. The plan was to flush them out.

The rebels, however, were lying in wait on a high cutting on the estate and as soon as the 25 men of the West Kents with two Iban trackers came in sight they charged with bloodcurling yells.

The battle lasted for an hour and only two West Kents survived unscathed. Of the 18 dead, six were bandits including Ah Leong, a section leader.

When the manager of the plantation, Mr F.W. Pearse, drove into the battle in a small armoured truck, the bandits thought reinforcements had arrived and fled.

The ambush highlights the seriousness of the situation in Malaya where British troops and police are attempting to defeat insurgents committed to set up a Communist state. Already a network of hide-outs near Kuala Lumpur has been wiped out and the RAF has joined the attack. Earlier this month Sir Henry Gurney, High Commissioner for Malaya, was killed in a Communist ambush. More recent threats has halted work on 16 rubber plantations.

Among the survivors from the Selangor ambush are two young soldiers from Northfleet, L/Cpl John Clarence Martin and Private Peter Pannell.

Martin, 19, was the only effective officer left when the bandits ripped into the patrol. He took over until he too fell badly wounded. As he rolled over and feigned death, Private Pannell assumed charge.

Remains of the Meteor which crashed on a bungalow

3 Meteors crash at Biggin Hill

June 18th: **Three RAF pilots were killed this evening at Biggin Hill when the aircraft they were each flying crashed within 100 yards of each other in a dramatic chain of events. Two residents were taken to hospital after their home had been hit and an ambulance overturned on its way to the scene.**

An hour earlier Mr Winston Churchill had been inspecting 615 (County of Surrey) Squadron of which he is Honorary Air Commodore.

The fighters which crashed all belonged to the Biggin Hill based 600 Squadron. Onlookers saw the first, a Meteor VIII, falter in mid-air and then pieces of the superstructure break up. It plunged to earth and crashed onto the roof of a bungalow.

Two Mark IV Meteors circling over the wreckage then collided and crashed into the valley below the aerodrome. The pilots were killed and one aircraft hit the home of Mr Frank Buley, who was injured.

Noel Coward, prolific playwright, will return to Goldenhurst

July: The elegant and slightly outrageous playwright-actor, Noel Coward, who has been living in a house on the seacliffs between Dover and Folkestone, has decided to move back to Goldenhurst on the boundaries of Romney Marsh saying "it is my own land and so much quieter. I shall miss the sea and the ships but I shall have the marsh and the trees, the orchard and the croquet lawn".

Coward, who travels around in a Rolls Royce, has proved himself an accomplished cabaret performer singing his own lyrics at the piano. He achieved great acclaim during the war with his films *In Which We Serve* and *Brief Encounter* and many of his finest stage successes have been written while living in his country homes in Kent.

He now plans to remodel and extend Goldenhurst and furnish it with antiques purchased from nearby towns.

The visitors' book at Goldenhurst contains such names as David Niven, Charlie Chaplin, Evelyn Waugh, Sir Frederick Ashton and other celebrities from the entertainment world.

November 11th: Three of a kind. During a Conservative victory dance, held at Sidcup on Saturday, Edward Heath (Bexley) shares a joke with his great friends, Pat Hornsby-Smith (Chislehurst) and Margaret Roberts (Dartford).

ELECTION DAY, '51 — TORIES BACK IN POWER: CHURCHILL FORMS GOVERNMENT

Defeat for Miss Roberts — but she wins a husband!

October 26th: By the narrow margin of just 26 seats, the Tories have won the general election and Winston Churchill, at 77, is forming his first peacetime government. The final score in yesterday's polling is Conservative 321 seats, Labour 295, Liberals, six, others three.

Kent is almost an exclusively Conservative county again with the exception of Dartford, where the competent Margaret Roberts polled 27,760 votes and cut the once-massive Labour majority to less than 13,000.

Miss Roberts, aged 25, may not have won Dartford but it looks as if she has won a husband. On election day she and Denis Thatcher, managing director of the Atlas Paint Company at Erith and 10 years her senior, announced their engagement. They intend to marry at the Wesley Chapel in the City in December. Miss Roberts says she will not wear white and there will be no bridesmaids.

Dartford Conservative Association were hoping the young chemistry graduate would continue to act as prospective parliamentary candidate but Miss Roberts whose simple sincerity endeared her to many people said she has no intention of giving up her political or legal aspirations but will not contest Dartford again

For several months now she has been lodging at Knole Road, Dartford, and working as an analytical chemist at J. Lyons and Company in Kensington.

Mrs Margaret Phillimore, a member of the Association, said: "She used to get up at 6.30 and go to work, come home during the rush hour, change, have a quick meal and go to an election meeting. She worked tirelessly."

To the delight of Miss Roberts, her great friends Ted Heath and Pat Hornsby-Smith did win their seats — at Bexley and Chislehurst respectively — with increased but still slender majorities.

1951

Hundreds of people gathered outside the Constitutional Club in Sevenoaks to hear Winston Churchill support his own Conservative parliamentary candidate, John Rodgers.

Photograph shows Churchill's view of the assembled crowd from the window of the local Conservative office.

In his speech he gave the famous V for Victory sign and then promised lower taxes, fewer controls and more homes. He said he would de-nationalise the iron and steel industry but not the health service.

There are several Kentish personalities and MP's in Churchill's first peacetime cabinet. Harold Macmillan of Bromley is Minister of Housing, Patrick Buchan-Hepburn of Beckenham is Parliamentary Secretary to the Treasury, Lord De'Lisle of Penshurst Place and MP for Chelsea is Minister of Air and Sir Walter Monckton, who lives in Ightham, is Minister of Labour.

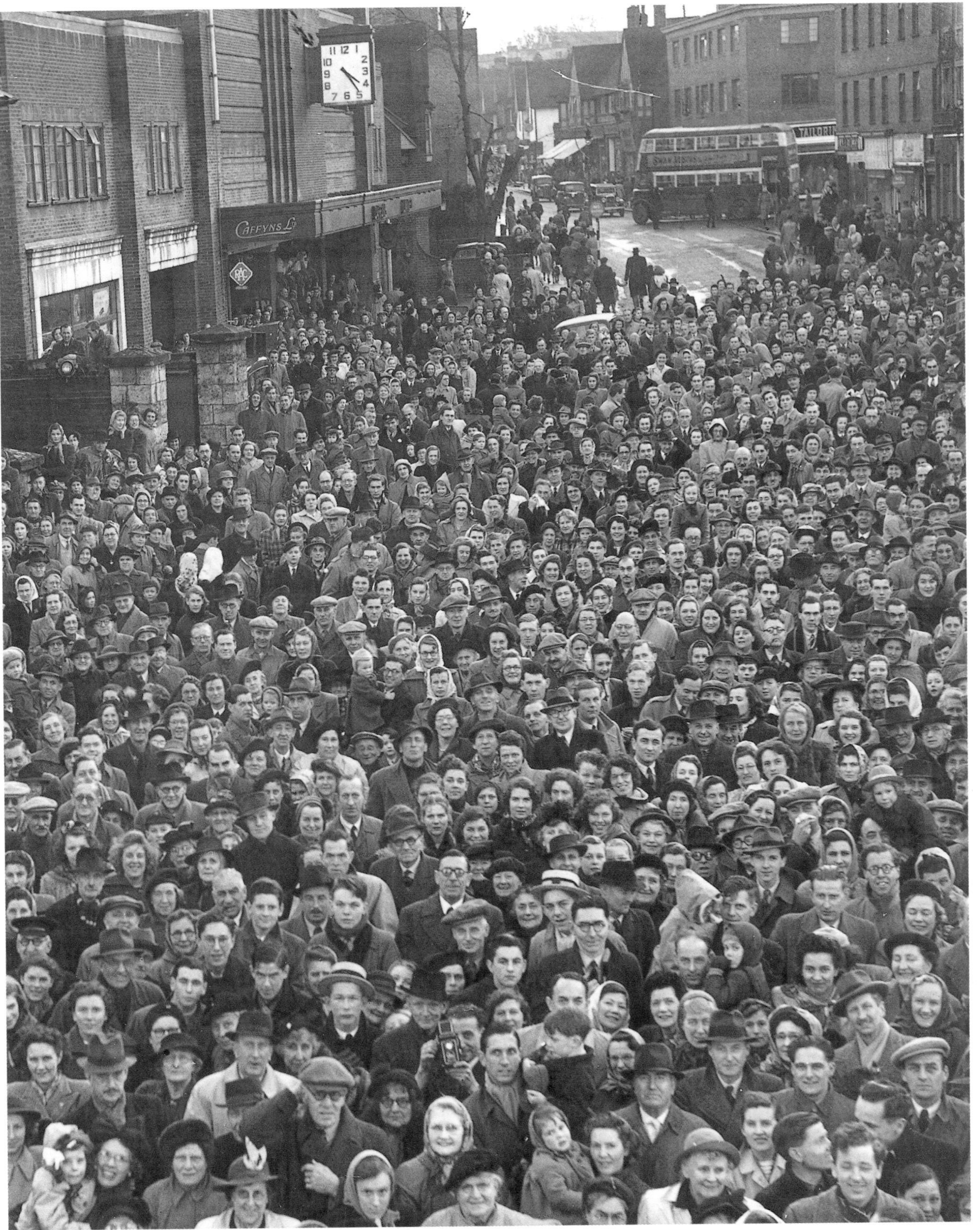
CAFFYNS Ltd
RAC

Double-decker bus ploughs into marching column: 23 cadets die

December 7th: Twenty-three Royal Marine cadets between the ages of eight and 15 were killed on Tuesday when a double-decker bus ploughed through their ranks in Dock Road, Gillingham. It is believed to be the worst road accident ever known in Britain. Eight are in hospital, some seriously injured.

The driver of the bus, Mr John Samson of Albany Road, Chatham, was on his customary early evening Medway Town run with conductress Mrs Dorothy Dunster. There was no red light to indicate the presence of a marching column in Dock Road. The driver simply did not see the cadets, who were on their way to attend a boxing tournament at the Royal Naval Barracks, Chatham.

Mrs Dunster said the bus had left the town hall with eight to ten passengers and went down the hill towards Dock Road.

"The next thing I knew was a series of bumps. 'Sammy' stopped the bus and I called out 'What's happened?' He replied: 'I don't know'. We walked up the road and saw youngsters lying on the road. Sammy said: 'What have I done?'"

Within minutes an emergency service had been put into operation. Doctors, sick berth attendants, nurses, police and sailors rushed to the scene. The injured boys were taken to St Bartholomews Hospital, Rochester, All Saints' Hospital, Chatham and the Royal Naval Hospital, Gillingham.

Throughout Tuesday night the police had the tragic task of sorting out the names of the dead and injured. There was a constant stream of inquiries from parents at Rochester, Chatham and Gillingham.

The bus, driven by John Samson, which ploughed into the marching column of cadets. He is to be charged with careless driving.

The dead and injured cadets

The casualty list is as follows. Dead: **James Edward Shepherd**, aged 11, of 137 Railway Street, Gillingham. **William Stone,** 12, of 11 Dale Street, Chatham. **James Scott,** 9, of 6 Palmerston Road, Chatham. **Albert Rose,** 11, of Grove Road, Luton. **Kenneth Walker,** 12, of 5 Christmas Street, Gillingham. **Garth William Mossop**, 11, of 18 Bramble Tree Cottages, Borstal. **Raymond Cross**, 10, of 33 Baden Road, Gillingham. **James Blomeley,** 9, of 17a Gadd's Hill, Gillingham. **Rodney McBride**, 10, of 111 Constitution Road, Chatham. **Allan John Evans**, 11, of 29 Singapore Drive, Brompton. **Richard C. Ongley,** 12, of 73 Constitution Road, Chatham. **James Robert Trigg**, 13, of 29 Danson Way, Rainham. **Colin Thomas Batty**, 12, of 87 St William's Way, Rochester. **David Tickner**, 11, of 100 Beatty Avenue, Gillingham. **James Cunningham**, 12, of 103 Corporation Road, Gillingham. **Brian Butler,** 11, of 115 Luton Road, Chatham. **Arthur John Calvert**, 11, of 7 Meeting House Lane, Chatham. **Peter Harry Eyre**, 11, of 32 Eden Avenue, Chatham. **John Edwin Lee**, 9, of 27 Bridge Road, Gillingham. **David Alexander Charles,** 13, of 13 Otway Street, Chatham. **Anthony Edward Aindow,** 13, of 86 Dale Street, Chatham. **Laurence Peter Murphy**, 12, of 7 Prospect Road, Brompton.

The following boys are injured: **Peter John Warneck, Michael John Steer, Brian John Allard, Peter Burke, John Henry Burdett, Howard Alistair Perris, John Frederick Lee, Ronald Thomas Miller, Norman Robert Swindell, Peter Griffiths, Bruce Campbell, Robert Campbell, Ian McArthur, Michael William Wilson, Paul Robert Hambrook, Robert Lyall, Alan John Morgan, Terence Aitkin, Denis Webb.**

* The tragedy is the largest single accident in which radio-controlled ambulances have been tested.

A Kent County Council official said: "The radio was used to call out more ambulances and to warn hospitals of the size and seriousness of the disaster. Contact was also kept with other areas in case they were needed."

Policemen stand by each lamppost along a deserted stretch of Dock Road waiting for the funeral cortege to pass. Among them will be the body of John Burdett who has since died.

Inquest hears stories of lucky escapes

December 14th: Mr John William Samson, the bus driver, was present at the inquest today as parent after parent came forward to identify their sons. He wept quietly but, after the hearing, collapsed and had to be assisted from the room by a nurse. It is understood he will be charged with careless driving.

The inquest heard many stories of lucky escapes. Ronald Beckett, aged 12, said he was near the rear of the squad and heard the bus hit the boys behind him. "I grabbed the boy next to me as the bus hit my arm and threw me onto the pavement. Then I saw it plough its way through the column. They didn't have a chance."

Three copper coins saved the life of Billy Walsh, also 12. Late home from school because of detention he was also late for the parade. "I saw them marching off", he said, "but couldn't join them because I had not paid my 3d subscription".

Messages have been pouring in from all over the world including those from the King and Queen, the Prime Minister, Queen Mary and Princess Elizabeth.

The funeral will be held next Tuesday with a memorial service at Rochester Cathedral. 18 of the boys will be interred in the Naval Reservation in Gillingham Cemetery. Others will be buried in family graves.

No arrangements have yet been made for a distress fund but the mayor of Gillingham said if one is organised it will be used to help children incapacitated in the disaster. "Cheques are already pouring in," he said.

Flags are flying at half-mast from all public buildings in the Medway Towns.

It's been another busy year for Kent Fire Brigade with more than 5,000 blazes to deal with —some very serious. It has also been a year of progress and Kent is the first county to introduce alloy extension ladders to replace the wheeled fire escapes which have been in use for more than 100 years. New appliances have also been issued all over the county. Here are the retained crew at Ashford Fire Station in the High Street with their faithful old Leyland appliance.

Hadlow Castle pulled down but the great tower remains

November: Hadlow Court Castle, built in the early part of the 19th century, has been demolished leaving behind the extravagant folly which towers 170 feet over the surrounding countryside.

Locals are not too depressed by the demise of their castle which had fallen into considerable disrepair.

It was built by Walter May with many "costly appendages" added by his son, also Walter. The main addition was the great tower built, it is said, by May when his wife left him so as to remind her of what she left behind.

It is far more elegant than the castellated mansion and was designed by May himself with help from George Ledwell Taylor, a distinguished naval architect. It became a convenient watch-tower for the Observer Corps during the second world war.

Another great landmark to disappear this year is Eastwell Church, Ashford, which was damaged in the war and subsequently abandoned.

The church collapsed in February leaving only the tower and chancel standing. They are to be demolished.

'The Dean is no atheist nor an official member of the Communist party, nor yet a danger to public safety...but he causes indignation and sorrow'— Geoffrey Fisher, Archbishop of Canterbury.

January 18th: A French freighter, *Agen,* foundered on the southern end of the Goodwin Sands and the 17,596-ton tanker *Sovac Radial* went hard aground at the foot of the cliffs below South Foreland lighthouse in a furious gale last night. The French ship broke in two and the crew took refuge in the bow half before being rescued by the Walmer lifeboat. The crew took five hours to find the men.

January 22nd: The driver of the bus which killed 23 cadets last December has been fined £20 and his licence endorsed for 3 years.

February 4th: Farmers have been offered £5 an acre by the Government to plough up grassland for crops.

February 6th: The King died peacefully in his sleep at Sandringham today.

February 13th: The Duke of Windsor has arrived in London to attend his brother's funeral at Westminster.

February 22nd: Cranbrook-born Elizabeth Taylor, who moved with her family to America at the start of the second world war and starred in such films as *Lassie Come Home* and *National Velvet,* was married to the film star Michael Wilding today.

February 26th: Churchill told the Commons that Britain has developed the atomic bomb. It will be tested this year in Australia.

March 9th: Miss Valda Osborn of Hoo is Britain's new Queen of the Ice in succession to Jeanette Altwegg who has retired. By the narrow margin of two points, 17-year-old Valda won the Ladies Figure Skating championship today defeating her friend and rival Barbara Wyatt of Brighton. Her mother and father have a smallholding at Mill Lane, Hoo.

March 17th: The Government-sponsored utility scheme has ended.

Cobtree Zoo, Maidstone, has lost one of its greatest friends. Daisy, the elephant, frightened by a low jet plane, ran amok and became so traumatised that eventually she had to be destroyed

The novelist, Victor Canning, now one of the country's finest story-tellers, has recently moved from his home in Stansted to Marle Place, Brenchley — a seventeenth century house surrounded by magnificent gardens. Canning became popular through his trilogy of books about the ebullient Mr Finchley but made his name as a master of his craft with such books as The Golden Salamander *and* Venetian Bird. *He writes with a marvellous entertaining style of love and hate, morality and evil, adds mystery to mystery and twist to cunning twist. His thrillers are impossible to put down.*

March 27th: America is in raptures over a new film in which one sequence shows Gene Kelly tap dancing his way through a thunderstorm. The film is called *Singing in the Rain.*

April 9th: The Queen says that she and her family will retain the surname Windsor.

May 2nd: The first scheduled Comet airliner left London airport today for Johannesburg with 35 passengers.

May 3rd: St James's Church, Dover, disused after the pounding it received from enemy shelling, collapsed yesterday leaving only the Norman tower.

May 10th: A commemorative east window in Warriors' Chapel, Canterbury Cathedral has been dedicated to the fallen of The Buffs in the presence of King Frederik of Denmark, Colonel-in-Chief.

May 16th: All-party support has been given to the principle of equal pay for women doing the same jobs as men.

June 4th: Faversham today celebrated the 700th anniversary of the granting of its charter by Henry 111 in 1252.

June 15th: A diary written by Anne Frank, a young Jewish refugee in Amsterdam, has been published.

Maureen Connolly, a 17-year-old American tennis player, today won the Wimbledon singles title.

July 16th: A former Kent College, Canterbury pupil, Lt Kenneth Macdonald RN, is missing, presumed killed, in an operational flight from *HMS Ocian* over Korea. His Sea Fury aircraft was hit by AA fire.

July 26: Eva Peron, the First Lady and "spiritual leader" of Argentina, died today aged 33.

August 3rd: Emil Zatopek, a 29-year-old Czech, dominated the Olympic Games by winning the 10,000 metres, 5,000 metres and the marathon. Britain won one gold medal thanks to the popular *Foxhunter* and his rider, Colonel Harry Llewellyn.

September 19th: Charlie Chaplin, born in South London, has been investigated in America as a suspected "subversive". His film *Limelight* is soon to be released.

Whitstable oyster yawl *Favourite,* now beyond restoration, has been hauled off the beach and used as part of the new sea wall to protect nearby cottages from flooding.

November 1st: 600 Squadron and 615 Squadron RAF were inspected today by the Hon Air Commodores, Queen Elizabeth, the Queen Mother and Mr Winston Churchill.

December 7th: On the first anniversary of the Dock Road tragedy, legal action is being persued against the bus company and two Royal Marine officers.

December 11th: Derek Bentley, a 19-year-old youth, is to be hanged for the murder of a policeman in Croydon. His accomplice, Christopher Craig, who fired the shots, gets life imprisonment.

OBITUARY

Well-known Bromley resident, David Grieg, who came to national prominence through his chain of grocery shops, died this year aged 87. He was buried at St Luke's Church, Bromley Common.

GREAT HIT OF 1952

Singing In The Rain

Kent mourns the death of George VI

February 6th: As the bells of Kent's two cathedrals tolled in salute today for a beloved sovereign, people find it hard to believe that King George V1 is dead. His recent illness had prepared everyone for the blow but the announcement this morning that he had died in his sleep at Sandringham still came as a great shock to the nation.

In the central tower of Canterbury Cathedral, Bell Harry — rung only at the death of a sovereign or primate — broke the city's silence. At Rochester, the bells tolled 56 times.

Throughout Kent, people are recalling the King's unselfish devotion to many varied tasks. He shouldered a burden as heavy as any in the land and carried it unflinchingly, even to his death.

One of his most intimate assocations with the county was his patronage of the Duke of York's holiday camp for boys at St. Mary's Bay, Dymchurch, which he founded. For many years he attended the annual camp and joined in the fun.

With the Duchess of York he has inspected a contingent of 2,000 Scouts and Guides, made a tour of Preston Hall, the British Legion Village, opened the miniature railway line at New Romney, laid the foundation stone at Ashford Hospital and visited the world-famous horticultural research station at East Malling. On one occasion he travelled in the royal train to Grove Ferry Station, enjoyed duck shooting at Stodmarsh Court and slept in the train in a siding before returning to London.

As King he came to Kent often but the most stirring were his frequent visits during the war to see the garrisons, gun emplacements and airfields and to cheer up the men and women of this front line county.

One of the best-remembered visits was to Dover in October 1944 when the King and Queen walked up to the warden's post at Archcliffe and gazed across the Channel towards the big guns at Calais. This followed an inspection of the badly-scarred town.

George V1 was the first reigning monarch to visit Canterbury since Charles II. On July 11th, 1946, attired in the uniform of Admiral of the Fleet, he attended a thanksgiving service for the preservation of the ancient Cathedral throughout the blitz. Later he visited King's School, the oldest public school in the country.

King George V1 will lie in state at Westminster Hall while the nation pays their last respects to a man who never aspired to be King but lived with his people through the darkest years of the century. He will then be laid to rest in the vault of his ancestors at St George's Chapel, Windsor.

Cliftonville evacuation

March 4th: Occupants of the former Cliftonville Hotel, now converted into flats, were evacuated today as one of the biggest fires since the war swept through the building.

So severe was the blaze that appliances from Folkestone, Canterbury and Maidstone came to the aid of the Margate firefighters.

It took 70 firemen with turntable ladders and all the modern equipment and expertise to quell the massive blaze. Many of the apartments were severely damaged.

The 63 men, women and children evacuated found temporary accommodation in Greylands Hotel.

Petition to the Queen: "Red Dean" must go

July 25th: The people of Canterbury, led by the *Kentish Gazette,* are to ask the Queen to remove Dr Hewlett Johnson from his position as Dean of Canterbury.

This quite unprecedented action follows the Dean's insistence that UN forces are using germ warfare in the Korean War — and that he has evidence to prove it.

In an extraordinary outburst from the pulpit of Canterbury Cathedral on Sunday the Dean devoted the whole of his sermon to a reaffirmation of the Chinese Government's "fraudulent" charges against the United Nations and America in particular.

His comments have provoked a public outcry and people of all shades of public opinion have combined solidly to denounce the Dean's allegations.

A few months ago, in a leading article the *Gazette* said: "As a serious and earnest Communist the Dean will want to devote his remaining years to plead the cause of the Russian way of life. In order for him to do so with complete liberty he should resign his position as Dean."

Archbishop Geoffrey Fisher said this week: "The Dean is no atheist, nor an official member of the Communist party, nor yet a danger to public safety. He may be a public nuisance and certainly a thorn in the flesh of us all. He causes indignation and sorrow."

The *Gazette* is inviting readers to sign a petition which asks "Your Majesty to revoke the Letters Patent granted to Dr Hewlett Johnson appointing him Dean of Canterbury on the grounds that he is guilty of action contrary to his calling as a clergyman of the Christian Church..."

Jeannette wins gold and quits

February 22nd: Miss Jeannette Altwegg, British, European and world figure-skating champion has added the Olympic title to her sensational list of achievements — and retired.

Jeannette's decision to give up competitive skating and refuse an offer of £2,000 a week to turn professional, follows her success in the Oslo Winter Olympics.

Certainly her friends in Downe, near Bromley, are astounded. Jeannette lives with her aunt at Greenways and local residents have watched her progress with proud and personal interest.

She intends to live in Switzerland with her boyfriend and to devote her life to caring for disadvantaged children.

Scotney Castle, a mile past the village of Lamberhurst, has a new owner — the well-known landscape architect Christopher Hussey, whose family have been ironmasters in the Weald for generations. He has succeeded to Scotney, a remarkably successful Gothic building of 1837 designed by Anthony Salvin, and has ambitious plans to look a generation ahead in planting out the gardens there. The house stands on high ground and a terrace of paths leads down to a lake and the ruins of a fortified 14th century manor house.

Down House at Downe, the home of Charles Darwin for more than 40 years, has become the property of the Royal College of Surgeons who have research laboratories on the estate. Darwin and his wife Emma moved to Down House in 1842 some six years after his famous scientific expedition to South America on HMS Beagle. The surrounding woodland abounded in botanical specimens and that pleased him as much as the rusticity of the place.

Hall Place, Bexley, has been opened as a pleasure park by Princess Marina, Duchess of Kent. The house, a Tudor building, was used by troops during the war.

Dangerous thief killed by booby-trap in trunk

November 27th: A Chatham motor mechanic, plagued by a persistent burglar, rigged up a double-barrelled spring gun in a large brown trunk knowing it would cause serious harm if the lock was forced and the lid lifted. He then went off to work.

At about 11am on July 10th Noah Eastwood, aged 34 — a professional housebreaker — smashed a window in the back of the house at 42 Baker's Row, Capstone Road, Luton and gained entry. He had a list of convictions for larceny, theft and receiving and his intention was to steal again.

Eastwood, of Ash Tree Lane, Chatham, saw the trunk, forced the lock open and lifted the lid. The twin set of cartridges exploded and he reeled backwards with terrible injuries to his abdomen. He died within hours.

This story was told to the Kent Assizes at Maidstone yesterday where Sidney Taylor, a mechanic, was charged with manslaughter. The jury heard that his cottage had twice been broken into so he rigged up a contrivance consisting of two connecting steel tubes working on a spring and into these tubes he inserted two 12-bore cartridges.

The police in evidence said that Taylor admitted that his trap had worked and during the investigation was frank and helpful at all times. He said his plan was to hit the would-be burglar below the knees, overlooking the fact that anyone forcing a lock of this type would actually kneel down to do it — and this is what had happened.

The jury was also told that Eastwood was a persistent and dangerous criminal and the police "were not overcome with grief by his departure".

After hearing the evidence, the jury returned a verdict of guilty but with a plea for leniency. Mr Justice Finnemore agreed and gave Taylor an absolute discharge.

Lancaster and Thunderjets crash in Kent

May 23rd: With crashed aircraft lying in various tangled shapes across Kent it's just like the Battle of Britain all over again — except there is no battle!

Yesterday a four-engined Lancaster bomber came down in an orchard at Mereworth with the loss of four of the crew. Two days ago an American Thunderjet exploded in mid-air over Manston, killing the pilot and a few weeks ago another Thunderjet crashed onto Lloyds Bank Broadstairs and three people died. There have been at least two other accidents at Manston involving American F-84s.

The Mereworth crash occurred when the Lancaster pilot overshot the perimeter of West Malling aerodrome and travelled about 150 yards on the ground before the final impact with fruit trees at Latter's Farm. About an acre of young apple trees and gooseberry bushes were devastated.

Four of the crew of 11 were killed and seven badly injured. They were taken to West Kent Hospital, Maidstone and the RAF Hospital at West Malling. The crash occurred at one o'clock in the morning and help only arrived after the pilot crawled out of the wreckage and fired Verey lights.

Just 48 hours after a flying ban had been lifted on the orders of the US Third Air Force a Thunderjet bomber exploded in mid-air over Manston. It was witnessed by hundreds of American ground and flying personnel who were watching a display of aerobatics. Captain John O'Brien was diving through a formation of four when his aircraft blew up over the airfield and crashed onto the runway.

Since the Korean War began Manston has been the home of the 123rd Fighter Bomber Wing. It is manned by some 3,000 USAAF personnel and is one of the most strategic bases in England.

In the last few months the people of Thanet have become accustomed to seeing F-84E Thunderjets, SA-16 Albatross and SB-29 Fortress aircraft.

Kent family survives the Lynmouth flood

***August 19th:* Several holidaymakers from Kent narrowly escaped death this week when the Devon resort of Lynmouth was hit by a disastrous flood. 36 people died**

Among those to survive were three from Sevenoaks — Mr and Mrs Thomas Anderson and their daughter Alfreda — who said flood water swept down from the hills and swamped the area so quickly that people had no time to flee. Homes were buried beneath a flow of mud, rocks and debris.

The floods followed nine inches of rain and swamped 250 square miles of Devon but Lynmouth suffered the worst.

Alfreda said: "All night we heard the sound of boulders crashing into our hotel. These served as a dam, diverting the water, which had reached the second floor."

Other Kent people to escape were Bernard Stone of Gillingham and two Maidstone girls, Miss Aileen Poole and Miss Joyce Coates.

July 1st: Princess Margaret, wearing a gossamer grey organza dress, today unveiled a plaque at the Bruce Porter Home for invalid children at Folkestone before visiting the Queen Victoria Hospital.

American claims that Marlowe wrote all Shakespeare's plays

September 22nd: A well-known theatre critic from New York claimed this week that William Shakespeare did not write all of the works attributed to him. Many were written, he said, by the Kentish poet and playwright, Christopher Marlowe.

Mr Calvin Hoffman, of Long Island, called a press conference in London to put forward his theory that Marlowe may, in fact, be the author of the whole Shakespearan canon.

"It is well known", he said, "that Shakespeare used any sources that were open to him, sometimes improving plots from other works. He was considerably influenced by Marlowe, whose plays immediately preceded his".

Hoffman also claimed the Elizabethan dramatist did not die at Deptford in 1593. "An unknown body was placed before the coroner while Marlowe was secretly spirited away to live in hiding at Scadbury, a manor house in Chislehurst. The flags of all nations at Stratford should be hauled down at once and hoisted instead across Chislehurst Common", he said.

Journalists from all over the world, who attended the conference, quickly realised that Hoffman was serious. He said the works of Shakespeare in the handwriting of Marlowe are almost certainly emtombed with the latter's patron, Sir Thomas Walsingham, who died at Chislehurst in 1630.

Hoffman is anxious that the Walsingham tomb in St Nicholas Church, Chislehurst, be opened and claims to have the support of the Bishop of Rochester, David Chavasse. The Rector, apparently, has refused.

The son of a shoemaker, Marlowe attended King's School, Canterbury and in 1581 matriculated at Cambridge. He was murdered in 1593.

see page 58

Mystery blaze in haunted village

October 10th: Surrenden Manor, Pluckley, once the home of the famous Dering family — who ruled the village for hundreds of years — and more recently a school, has been destroyed by fire. Only the stables remain.

Some locals say the blaze is the work of ghosts because the village is well-known for supernatural visitations; in fact it is believed to be the most haunted village in England.

Sir Edward Dering was a great supporter of the Crown during the Civil War and was well-rewarded for his loyalty. He built the manor house in the early years of the seventeenth century.

There are three "Dering ghosts" in Pluckley. A Lady Dering who lies in an oaken coffin in the family vault is said to walk in the churchyard of St Nicholas on certain unspecified nights with a red rose at her breast, the last gift of her lord. The Red Lady wanders among the gravestones looking for her baby and a White Lady Dering haunts the old estate at Surrenden Park.

There have been other ghostly goings-on in Pluckley. Furniture has moved by itself in the 700-year-old Black Horse inn and at the house next door Margaret Williamson has twice seen a "translucent apparition with dark curly hair".

At Fright Corner there is a haunted tree where a highwayman made his last stand. Other ghosts includes a pipe-smoking gipsy, a miller, a man who fell down a claypit and the figure of a soldier who committed suicide.

The question is: which ghost burnt down Surrenden Manor?

***May 11th:** Sidcup-born Neville Shute, seen here with the ballerina Moira Shearer at Harrods where they are autographing books in aid of polio research, is leaving Kent to settle in Australia.*

Neville Shute, pen name of Neville Norway, was a designer in the aeronautic industry, notably on the successful airship, R-100.

He worked alongside Barnes Wallis and was quite a hero in Sidcup when the airship entered service safely in 1929 carrying 100 passengers. It was the disaster which befell its successor R-101 which put an end to the construction of airships in Britain.

The airship background prompted Shute to write a gripping novel about people confronting a technological or scientific disaster. No Highway, *published in 1948, told of a desperate engineer struggling to persuade his superiors that he has identified metal fatigue in an airliner.*

Both Neville Shute and Miss Shearer have ambitious plans. The engineer-turned-author is planning to write a book about nuclear fallout while the Sadler's Wells ballerina wants to begin a second career as an actress.

Atomic bomb cameraman tells his story

October 4th: A photographer from Eynsford yesterday saw Britain's first atomic weapon successfuly explode in the Monte Bello islands off Australia.

Mr Stanley Fulton, aged 33, Ministry of Supply official photographer, was the third person to leave shelter just seconds after the initial flash. He was allowed 15 seconds to take his pictures.

He said: "I saw the heavy pall of smoke beginning to rise. It had a ragged shape, unlike the mushroom form of the American explosions".

Mr Fulton had been married for just a week when he set off for the highly secret Monte Bello assignment. His wife, Susan, said she had a premonition that it might be concerned with the atom bomb.

Living accommodation for Mr Fulton and scientists before and after the "big bang" was on *HMS Campania,* moored off the Monte Bello islands. On the day he slept in a tent on a nearby island.

The bomb was attached to a tower and the explosion was seen by many servicemen on British and Australian warships and also from a hilltop on the mainland 100 miles away.

The A-bomb was developed at the Government's Research Establishment, Fort Halstead, near Sevenoaks.

'Families were awakened by the roar as the wall burst, by the swish of the water as it rushed past, by the clatter and crash of debris striking the house' — author Hilda Grieve describing the great tide.

January 27th: A petition from 200 MPs for Derek Bentley to be reprieved is rejected. He will be hanged at Wandsworth Prison tomnorrow.

February 1st: The film company Twentieth Century Fox are converting to a wide screen operation called Cinemascope. The first production with the new system will be a Biblical epic, *The Robe*.

February 3rd: More than 1,000 people have died in Holland after the dykes burst following widespread flooding.

March 5th: Joseph Stalin, the man who ruled Russia for nearly 30 years, died today of a brain haemorrhage. He was 73.

March 25th: Queen Mary, the widow of George V has died in her sleep at Marlborough House.

April 15th: A big manhunt is under way for John Halliday Christie who is charged with the murders of six women.

April 24th: To the delight of his friends and staff at Chartwell, Winston Churchill is invested as a Knight Companion of the Order of the Garter.

May1st: Arsenal have won the League Championship for a record seventh time.

May 2nd: Described as the most exciting Cup Final yet known, Blackpool beat Bolton Wanderers today 4-3. The hero was Blackpool's 38-year-old right wing, Stanley Matthews.

June 1st: Edmund Hillary and Tensing, the Sherpa who accompanied him on the final assault, have reached the summit of Everest — at 29,002 feet, the world's highest mountain.

June 25th: John Halliday Christie has been captured and sentenced to death for the murder of four women at 10 Rillington Place, Notting Hill, London.

July 1st: The Freedom of Gillingham has been conferred on the Corps of Royal Engineers.

Ightham Mote, near Sevenoaks — one of Kent's finest gems — has been bought by an American businessman, Charles Henry Robinson, who intends to continue the restoration work begun by Sir Thomas Colyer-Ferguson many years earlier. The hall, chapel, kitchen and crypt of this charming building is 14th century. The banqueting hall is the finest of any moated house and the drawing room is Jacobean with an 18th century Palladian window and hand-painted Chinese wallpaper. Author Arthur Mee says: "Down lanes that never seem to end, away at what seems to be the bottom of the world lies Ightham Mote. There is nothing like it anywhere. It could be the home of Father Time. No secluded corner of our motherland holds a more delightful surprise for the traveller."

More than 20,000 people at the Kent County Show today gave the Duchess of Kent and Princess Alexandra a rapturous welcome as they drove around the arena in the open green Humber "Victory" car used by Lord Montgomery.

July 18th: St Mark's Church, Bromley, has been restored after war damage. It was consecrated today by the Bishop of Rochester.

July 19th: A parade of 10,000 Legionnaires were inspected today by Princess Marina at the British Legion Village at Preston Hall.

July 27th: After three years of bloody fighting and the loss of two million lives, the war in Korea is over.

The Goon Show, a wacky radio show that defies logic, is winning a cult following among young people.

August 19th: England have regained the Ashes. After four drawn Test matches they beat Australia at the Oval today by eight wickets.

October 9th: The Government announced plans today to establish a commercial television service.

October 20th: Ford Motor Company have produced a cut-price revival of the old Anglia. Renamed the Popular, it costs £390 and is the cheapest four cylinder car in the world.

October 28th: The Queen Mother was a guest today at the Marden Fruit Show, the largest of its kind in England.

November 14th: Anti-smog masks are being prescribed by doctors and can by worn by National Health patients who suffer from heart or lung disease and live in an industrial area.

An army corporal from St Margaret's-at-Cliffe has been arrested and charged with the brutal attack on a young girl, thanks to the vigilance of Kent County Constabulary's latest recruit — Nana the dog. Nana is a Dobermann Pinscher and his handler is Pc Lawrie.

November 18th: Thirty-three motor vehicles stored in Russell's Garage, next to Gammon's Wharf, Chatham, were destroyed yesterday in a massive fire that threatened a warehouse, pub and several homes.

December 10th: Sir Winston Churchill has won the Nobel Prize for Literature.

The last blacksmith in the village of Chalk, near Gravesend, has retired. Mr Arthur Mann's forge and cottage is believed to be Joe Gargery's Forge as immortalised by Charles Dickens in *Great Expectations*. They will be preserved.

GREAT HITS OF 1953

Diamonds Are A Girl's Best Friend

Rags to Riches

I Love Paris

January 1st: Forget Stanley Matthews, Denis Compton and Randolf Turpin. The hero of the moment, particularly among the boys of Judd School, Tonbridge, is 34-year-old Squadron Leader Neville Duke DSO, DFC (two bars), AFC and Czech Military Cross, who has been awarded the OBE in the Queen's first New Year's Honours list.

The former fighter ace — now chief Test Pilot of the Hawker Aircraft Company — was born in Tonbridge and lived with his parents on the Hadlow Road. After leaving Judd he became one of the first pilots to be trained in wartime and joined 92 Squadron at Biggin Hill. When Winston Churchill paid a visit to the station, Duke tipped a Spitfire on to its nose. The Prime Minister ignored the *faux pas* but must have wondered if there was a future for this "careless Kentish lad".

There was. Duke was constantly in action in Britain and the Middle East and took part in more than 60 sweeps over the English Channel. In the summer of 1944 he bagged his 28th victim — an ME 109.

The Tonbridge boy who

Joining the Hawker Aircraft Company as a Test Pilot he made an immediate impact. In 1948 he broke two point-to-point air records from London to Rome and to Karachi in a Hawker Fury.

Late last year he became one of the first British pilots to fly faster than the speed of sound — and win the kind of hero-worship enjoyed by the American Charles Yeager, who was the first to break the barrier in 1947.

His supersonic flight was achieved in the most harrowing circumstances on the clear sunny afternoon of September 6th last during the annual display of the Society of British Aircraft Constructors at Farnborough. First to fly was John Derry in a DH110. Test pilot with the De Havilland Aircraft Company, Derry was accompanied by Anthony Richards as observer.

Derry dived from a height of 40,000 feet towards Farnborough, causing sonic explosions like rumbling gunfire. As the DH110 swept low over the aerodrome, the crowd's admiration changed to horror.

can fly faster than the speed of sound

Without warning the aircraft broke up, its cockpit fell on to the runway and two engines hurtled through the air, hit the ground and leapt into a section of the crowd. Twenty-six were killed and 65 injured as burning debris continued to fall from the sky. Derry and Richards were killed immediately.

In these tragic circumstances, the show could have been cancelled but while the ruin of the DH110 was still being cleared from the runway, Neville Duke took off in his graceful Hawker Hunter. People could hardly believe their eyes as the test pilot went through the sound barrier with a series of sonic explosions and then produced a perfect exhibition of aerobatics. The atmosphere was tense. Duke had just seen an aircraft split to pieces, his friend killed yet he felt it necessary to attempt a "sonic bang".

Millions of people throughout the world admired Duke's cool nerve but one man wrote a quick note. "My dear Duke", he wrote. "It was characteristic of you and of 615 Squadron to go up yesterday after the shocking accident. Accept my salute" — Winston S.Churchill.

Neville Duke's fascination by flying stems from the days that Alan Cobham's flying circus visited Penshurst and, from a field next to the Old Barn at Hildenborough, he went up in an Airspeed Ferry and saw Tonbridge from the air. On another occasion he paid five shillings to stand in the cockpit next to the pilot. "There was no seat", he said. "I stood clutching the rim, practically blinded by the slipstream closing my eyelids, unable to see more than a blur of trees as we took off and landed. I was 10 years old and hooked".

Photograph shows Duke at Tangmere on September 7th, 1953, following another bid to beat the world airspeed record. His red Hawker Hunter had averaged 725 mph.

Neighbours queue for fresh water in the flooded streets of Sheerness.

Kent's sea defences breached by tidal surge: most catastrophic ever known

February 1st: The people of Kent are counting the damage caused by the most catastrophic floods ever known. A storm surge, driven by hurricane-force north-westerly winds, hit the north Kent coast in the darkness of early Sunday morning and generated a wave action so immense that whole beaches have been destroyed, sand dunes swept away and cliff faces eroded.

Every single community between Woolwich and Margate is under water and thousands have been evacuated from their homes. So far only one fatality has been reported — that of a sluice keeper near Belvedere.

Although the flood water hit Kent with hideous force it appears the county is lucky compared to Essex and East Anglia. More than 1,200 sites have been breached down the east coast and whole communities swept away. Worst still, it is believed that more than 300 people have lost their lives.

First indication of the disaster in Kent came when an official of the Anglo-Iranian Oil Company on the Isle of Grain noticed that water was pouring over the top of the sea wall into the new refinery.

Within minutes the sea wall collapsed and the water rushed inland, dislocating telephone systems and severing road and rail communications.

It was the same story right along the coast. The flood barriers at Dartford were carried away and workers at Littlebrook Power Station found they were cut off from the "mainland". At North Reach water poured into Joseph Wells' fireworks factory with such power that the contents exploded and windows in the town centre were blown out.

The Isle of Sheppey was quickly inundated. A submarine in dry dock at Sheerness was picked up by a wall of water, swept over the gates and deposited on the other side. Water streamed into homes and Kingsferry Bridge over the Swale was marooned in a vast expanse of swirling water.

The new wall at Whitstable was ineffective. The sea came over the top, destroyed boathouses and drove scores of vessels into basement homes. Oyster barrels were washed down the street and gardens were buried under a huge wall of shingle.

Here is the watery story across North Kent:

continued

All over North Kent lie carcasses of sheep, cows, pigs, chickens, horses and even dogs —drowned in the first onslaught of water. Some livestock stood around on knolls of land and what remained of sea walls. Many were rescued by farmers and firemen; others succumbed to the advancing waves. At Sheerness a horse stood for two days and two nights up to its neck in the freezing February water. It was eventually dragged on shore. A policeman rescued a piglet near Dartford and, in places, there was the bizarre sight of chickens and rats together in trees just feet above the swirling torrents.

Northfleet: 17 people evacuated from homes by army personnel. At the Deep Water Jetty scores of barrels of resin, used in the manufacture of paper, washed away and into gardens at Stonebridge Road.

Long Reach: Alfred Shrub, on night duty, returns to his bungalow home under the River Wall to find his greyhound on his floating bed. By the following day the roof was all that could be seen of the house.

Margate: Sea wall holds but gaps torn in the concrete facing to the promenade. Lighthouse at the entrance to harbour undermined and collapses into sea. Water is swept into the Classic Cinema. Streets leading to harbour choked with refuse and broken boats. Impossible to walk along Marine Drive. Margate blacked out but Dreamland, with its own generator, refuses to close and dancing continues until dawn with the waves roaring outside.

Herne Bay: Promenade is buried under thousands of tons of shingle and road is blocked by four-foot wall of smashed boats. Water swept into council offices.

Beltinge: Cliff face attacked furiously and sea advances more than 100 yards inland. Clifftop road tumbles into sea. Houses around Miramar Hotel are quickly evacuated.

Reculver to Birchington: Great northern sea wall is ruptured. Main London to Margate railway line is flooded and great lengths of rain are swept off the embankment.

February 6th: *From Chatham Dockyard to a point ten miles from the twisting River Medway stretches a lifeline along which the Royal Navy is maintaining a ceaseless flow of vital supplies to the 25,000 inhabitants of the Isle of Sheppey. They have been completely isolated since the flood waters cut the road and rail communications to the island at the Kingsferry Bridge. Along that lifeline a small fleet of Naval lighters, harbour craft and motor launches and also vessels of the Medway Ferry Service are operating non-stop to provide the only link between Sheppey and the mainland of Kent. Photograph shows postman Bradley in Clyde Street. All week he has been wading through the water at Sheerness, delivering mail by means of a basket. Here Mrs Clay and her family greet the heroic postman.*

***February 11th:** The task of reconstruction and of clearing debris from the flooded areas of the Kent coast is going ahead with great speed. Flood water is still prominent in most areas and more flooding is expected between Reculver and Birchington and the Isle of Sheppey during the next high tides, due to arrive tomorrow Thursday. This photograph, taken at Graveney, shows how the main railway line to Herne Bay, Margate and Ramsgate has subsided and the ballast under the sleepers carried away by the flood waters.*

Vital now to strengthen sea defences

February 8th: The people of Kent, insulated in the darkness of their homes and listening to the shrieking wind outside, had no idea of the horrors which unfolded across the water at Canvey Island last week. Between 12.30 and 2am the islanders were fighting for their lives and only those who had foreseen the danger and left, or taken refuge by climbing onto roofs, escaped.

Within 15 minutes of the sea wall being breached, a rushing torrent of water well above window-sill level was carrying all before it, including telephone boxes, front doors, dustbins — and bodies. Some people died in their beds, other grabbed floating furniture. The death toll at Canvey is now believed to be 58.

All this week gifts have been pouring into Kent and the East Coast communities as far as Lincolnshire. Offers of furniture, clothes, bedding, fuel, money, accommodation, sandbags, machinery and practical help have been freely given by thousands of people. Distribution and food centres have been set up. The gesture of sympathy and goodwill is unprecedented in English history.

There are plans also to reopen the famous Whitstable to Canterbury line until repairs to the coastline have been completed.

The inquest will follow. Already the Government has promised help for farmers and said that a committee will be established to investigate the cause and reinstate the defences.

They will need to act fast. Meteorologists are already suggesting that there could easily be an increase in the levels reached by the 1953 tidal surge and such occurences could be more frequent. The sea wall protecting industrial areas and towns must be heightened and strengthened. and storm surge barriers provided.

There is talk of building a giant flood barrier to protect London. This is vital. Another destructive surge and the city, with its vast underground system, could be a scene of total catastrophe.

A smiling Queen gives hope and encouragement to flood victims at Erith at she tours the stricken towns on the Thames Estuary. She supports the idea of a flood barrier in the area.

Secret Agent 007 is the man with a licence to kill!

June: An exciting book, written in just a few weeks by a former journalist who worked in naval intelligence during the war, has been hailed as one of the most remarkable first novels to be written in England for 30 years.

The author is Ian Fleming and the book is called *Casino Royale*. One critic, Kingsley Amis says it is apparent to many that a remarkable new writer has appeared on the scene.

Fleming, 45, is the brother of Captain Peter Fleming who formed Kent's "death or glory" squads — the would-be saboteurs waiting for the German invasion.

The hero of the plot is a secret agent called James Bond, or 007, who has "a licence to kill" and plays baccarat for enormous stakes to outwit a shadowy character who uses his gains for sinister projects.

Ian Fleming lives at St Margaret's Bay where he used to be a neighbour of Noel Coward. He enjoys golf at "the best course in the world" — the Royal St George's, Sandwich.

The success of *Casino Royale* means more James Bond thrillers. The author promises to write a second this winter at his holiday home, Golden Eye, on the Jamaican coast.

Who remembers Pip, Squeak and Wilfred?

Daily Mirror readers, young and old, who recall the weekly adventures of *Pip, Squeak and Wilfred,* will be sorry to hear the illustrator of the cartoon series, Austin B. Payne has died at 65.

Austin lived at Herne Bay and close to Chestfield, the home of Bertie Lamb, better known as 'Uncle Dick' of the Daily Mirror and creator of the intrepid threesome in 1919.

The cartoon was so popular that, in 1921, 26 instalments were animated for the cinema.

Another artist in the news is John Piper whose book, *Romney Marsh,* has been published by Penguin. Piper adores the "music of the Marsh" and has enjoyed a 20-year love affair with this corner of Kent.

Vivat Regina — Queen Elizabeth II is crowned at Westminster

A happy association with Kent

June 2nd: Queen Elizabeth, who has visited Kent so often as Princess, took the Coronation Oath at Westminster Abbey today in a ceremony attended by princes, peers and prime ministers from all over the world.

The service was conducted by the Archbishop of Canterbury, Dr Geoffrey Fisher and the Duke of Edinburgh was by his wife's side.

Thousands of people from Kent journeyed to London on a cold wet day to see the Queen travel to the Abbey in a golden coach pulled by eight grey horses.

Many more thousands watched the Coronation ceremony on their television sets, some of which were purchased just days before this wonderful occasion. They were able to see and hear the Queen, in a light clear voice, bind herself to the service of her people in Britain and the Commonwealth.

Her subjects in Kent know the young Queen Elizabeth well. On official occasions she has visited Canterbury, Gillingham and Margate. On unofficial visits she has been to many towns and villages including Maidstone and, of course, Mersham where her second cousin Lady Patricia Brabourne lives.

On July 11th, 1946, Princess Elizabeth attended the great thanksgiving service at Canterbury Cathedral with her parents. The following summer, on her own, she came to a Church of England youth conference in King's School. Four years ago, in July 1949, she and Prince Philip attended a service in celebration of the silver jubilee of the Kent Playing Fields Association.

In 1950 she unveiled the Chatham Port war memorial windows in the barracks and last year she was at Margate to present the prizes at the Royal School for Deaf and Dumb Children.

The Bishops pay homage to the new Queen

Her visit to Maidstone was the most informal. As a lover of horses she desperately wanted to see, in Sir Garrard Tyrwhitt-Drake's zoo at Cobtree Manor, the descendants of the cream ponies used by Queen Victoria.

Accompanied by her lady-in-waiting, the Princess met the ponies, visited the carriage museum at the Old Tithe Barn and looked round the parish church of All Saints to see the colours of the Royal West Kent Regiment.

Members of Mersham-le-Hatch Cricket Club this week recalled the occasion when Princess Elizabeth sat among the spectators to see her husband take three wickets for 27 runs against Aldington in July 1949.

The local side were one short and, as Elizabeth and Philip were spending a weekend at Mersham, Lord Brabourne invited Philip to make up the eleven.

Hatless and in a simple frock the Princess accompanied by Lady Brabourne climbed a stile and mingled informally with the locals.

Delighted to see her husband take three wickets she was also keen to see him bat. Sadly, he was lbw — first ball!

Churchill suffers severe stroke

June 27th: Prime Minister Winston Churchill today suffered a severe stroke at his country home, Chartwell. His left side is partially paralysed, he can hardly speak and his physician Lord Moran has taken up residence.

Few details have been given — only a medical bulletin to say that the 79-year-old premier needs complete rest and will be easing off on his duties for several weeks.

Although his cabinet colleagues have been told the truth about his illness the facts were suppressed on the initiative of Lord Beaverbrook, owner of the Daily Express and a friend of Churchill's.

One newspaperman man who knows the full story is the reporter in charge of the Westerham edition of the *Sevenoaks Chronicle,* Mr Percy Reid. He said today that the Chartwell staff had told him of Mr Churchill's stroke and he had noticed that two male nurses were caring for the invalid. Anxious that the story should not be traced to him, Mr Reid decided only to tell the American newsagency, Associated Press, who have now circulated it to the British newspapers.

Grain oil refinery the largest in Europe

March: The massive Anglo-Iranian Oil Company's refinery on the Isle of Grain is nearing completion. The project which began in 1950 covers 2,400 acres, cost £30 million and raises the refining capacity of Great Britain from 2.5 million to 20 million tons.

The Grain refinery, now the largest in Europe, will be operated by a new subsidiary company, Kent Oil Refinery Ltd.

The first refinery, opened in 1923, was a small enterprise run by the American Charles Ganahl who tried out a pioneer system of "cracking" petroleum liquids.

This closed in 1932 but the barge jetty and storage continued to be used and were eventually part of the famous "Pluto" pipeline, pumping petrol under the Channel to the Allies.

This and the now defunct Port Victoria has been swallowed up. Dutch engineers prepared the site and 800 men, mainly from the Medway Towns, have been engaged on the construction.

When the refinery is in full throttle with a staff of 1,500, supertankers will deliver thousands of tons of crude oil from the Middle East.

Alfred Reader and his winning cricket balls

August 19th: For the first time since winning the notorious "bodyline tour" of 1932-33 England have regained the Ashes — using cricket balls made by Alfred Reader of Teston near Maidstone. After four drawn matches, England won the fifth Test by eight wickets with Compton making the winning hit.

The 22 craftsmen who work for Readers at the Invicta works are delighted with the victory. After economic difficulties the cricket ball craft is flourishing again.

Kent cricketers in revolt over 'unsuitable' captain

August 10th: These are sad days for Kent Cricket Club and especially for the amateur captain, Bill Murray-Wood, who has been sacked by the committee — with several championship matches remaining.

This extreme step, unprecedented in the club's history, follows a revolt by the whole team who indicated this week that they would not play again for Kent if Murray-Wood captained another match.

Colin Cowdrey, the young Oxford undergraduate, who is making quite a name for himself will be skipper for the next match. Doug Wright will then take over as the first professional captain of Kent.

Murray-Wood has had a difficult time since he took over from David Clark in 1952. Kent ended last season in 15th place and this year they seem to be on course for the wooden spoon. The defeat by Middlesex at Canterbury was the club's 13th of the season.

Loyal supporters cannot understand why Kent should perform so badly with such players as Cowdrey, who scored a maiden century against India last year, Arthur Fagg (259 against Notts), Arthur Phebey, a new sound opening batsman, Doug Wright and Fred Ridgway who lead the way in the bowling department and the wonderfully agile England wicket-keeper Godfrey Evans.

'It's a remarkable example of modern art. It certainly combines force and candour' — Winston Churchill on receiving a portrait from his fellows MPs, painted by Graham Sutherland.

January 1st: Indicator lights which flash must be fitted on all new motor vehicles in Britain, replacing flip-up indicators.

January 31st: Last year it was devastating floods. This year Kent is in the grip of a severe winter in which 23 people have died across Britain.

February 12th: A Ministry of Health advisory committee has discovered a relationship between smoking and lung cancer. Tobacco manufacturers claim such a link cannot be proved.

February 15th: The BBC radio series *The Archers* has a record audience of ten million listeners.

February 24th: Billy Graham, the American evangelist, has arrived for a three-month tour of Britain.

March 1st: A Bill has been passed creating an Atomic Energy Authority.

March 5th: A television bill setting up an Independent Television Authority has been introduced by the Government.

March 21st: There are rumours in Fleet Street that the missing diplomats Guy Burgess and Donald MacLean were warned of their impending arrests by a "third man". The First Secretary of the British Embassy in Washington, Kim Philby has been recalled to London for questioning.

April 24th: British and African troops supported by armed police and Home Guards plan to arrest 40,000 men in Nairobi suspected of being Mau Mau terrorists.

May 1st: America is going wild over a new song released last month by a rhythm group, Bill Haley and the Comets. The song is called *Rock Around the Clock.*

May 6th: Edwardian clothes are becoming rather popular among many new men in Kent's town centres.They call themselves Teddy Boys and have been known to cause some trouble, although this is not widespread.

England leg-spinner Doug Wright has taken over as Kent's first professional cricket captain with a promise that he will do his best to improve the county's fortunes.

May 7th: Roger Bannister, 25-year-old medical student, has become the first man to run a mile in under four minutes. He achieved this yesterday at the Oxford University track and was paced by two fellow-graduates, Chris Chataway and Chris Brasher.

Welshman Dylan Thomas's radio play *Under Milk Wood* has been voted an instant success. It went out on the air with the voice of Richard Burton narrating it.

May 8th: Dien Bien Phu, the French fortress in Indo-China, has fallen to the Viet Minh today after a bloody 55-day siege.

May 18th: The Queen Mother attended a service at Rochester Cathedral today to mark the 1,350th anniversary of the founding of the diocese.

May 26th: Mau Mau terrorists have burned down the famous Treetops Hotel in Kenya. It was here that the Queen, as Princess Elizabeth, first learned of the death of her father.

June 2nd: Lester Piggott, aged 18, became the youngest jockey ever to win the Derby when he rode *Never Say Die* to victory at Epsom.

July 21st: A Geneva treaty calling for the division of Vietnam along the 17th Parallel, with the Communist Viet Minh controlling the north, should now bring peace to Indo China.

July 27th: More than 65,000 British troops and airmen are to be pulled out of the Suez Canal base under an agreement reached with the Egyptian leader Colonel Nasser.

August 8th: Jim Peters, 35-year-old marathon runner, collapsed exhausted close to the finishing line in the Empire Games at Vancouver and was beaten. Roger Bannister won the mile.

October 5th: The American "sex symbol" Marilyn Monroe has sued Joe DiMaggio for divorce.

October 13th: Chris Chataway, 23-year-old Oxford blue, has beaten the 5,000 metres world record by five seconds. He also defeated the European champion Vladimir Kuts in one of the greatest distance races ever seen.

October 20th: Chatham dockworkers today voted to join their brothers at Southampton, London and Hull and come out on strike. Sir Walter Monkton, Minister of Labour, is to try and end the deadlock.

December 1st: Old age pensions have been increased to £2 a week.

The ancient church at Paddlesworth, long used as a barn, has been purchased by Dr Chavasse on behalf of the Diocese of Rochester and converted to religious use.

The Calais branch of the British Legion has presented Dover with a piece of armour plating from the German long-range guns at Sangatte. It records that 2,226 shells were fired at Dover between 1940 and 1945. The plate has been erected on the sea front.

Street fire alarms in Kent have been scrapped resulting in a sharp decrease of malicious false alarms.

Ernest Hemingway has won this year's Nobel Prize for Literature with his allegory *The Old Man of The Sea.*

GREAT HITS OF 1954

Rock Around The Clock
Fly Me to The Moon

This is all that remains of Maidstone's much-loved Ritz cinema. The other factory buildings survived, thanks to the vigilance of firefighters.

Ritz destroyed as Pudding Lane fire threatens Maidstone

January 12th: The Ritz Cinema in Pudding Lane, Maidstone — which has enjoyed packed houses since the ABC takeover a few years ago — is no longer. The building was destroyed last night in a disastrous fire which woke up most of the town.

As forty firemen tackled the conflagration it was feared the fire would get out of control, leap the narrow streets and engulf the rest of the town. And here lay an historic irony, for it was a blaze in another Pudding Lane which led to the Great Fire of London, 300 years earlier.

The Maidstone Fire Brigade requested reinforcements from other towns. When they arrived they found the auditorium burning and the asbestos roof exploding violently, showering red-hot material over a wide area and on to nearby roofs. Part of a garage owned by Fremlins Brewery caught alight and some firemen had to be diverted to attack the fire-spread in the area. It took many hours, eight pumps, a turntable ladder, a hose-laying lorry and nine jets to bring everything under control.

The people of Maidstone will be devastated by the loss of The Ritz which could seat 1,421. Earlier in the century it was known as The Pavilion and was completely refurbished following the ABC acquisition.

There is little hope of the Ritz being rebuilt. ABC's other cinema, The Central, will take over bookings and the custom divided between the Central, the Palace Theatre and the Regal.

Myxomatosis may wipe rabbits off the map

KILLER VIRUS FIRST REPORTED ON A FARM NEAR TONBRIDGE

March: Kent's massive rabbit population is in danger of being wiped out by a virus called myxomatosis, previously unknown in this country.

More than 90 per cent of the burrows in the county are now affected and the Ministry of Agriculture says it was intentionally introduced by Kent farmers to stop rabbits damaging crops. It has now spread right across the Home Counties.

The disease was first reported on the Bough Beech estate near Tonbridge towards the end of last year. A gamekeeper noticed hundreds of rabbits lying dead or dying in woods and fields.

The Ministry identified the disease, fenced off 200 acres of land and introduced methods of gassing the rabbits in the area to prevent the spread of the infection.

It was all to little avail for the virus is now out of control. Environmentalists fear the rabbit may become a rare sight and ecologists say the balance of nature will be disturbed badly.

The Kent branch of the National Farmers Union admitted at a recent meeting that myxomatosis was introduced as guns were "a useless method of control of this insidious pest". Members complained of the "stupid law" of making the spreading of myxomatosis illegal but Mr E. Ledger opposed them for humane reasons. "Myxomatosis", he said, "causes a slow and disgusting death and it is a blot on the farmers who should think of spreading it".

The farming correspondent of the *Kent and Sussex Courier* newspaper wrote recently that the disease does not appear to affect any other kind of animal, not even the hare. "Wouldn't it be better", he asks, "to allow the disease to kill off millions of rabbits and let the tame ones take their chance? I think the country's overall food production would gain rather than lose".

The blitzed centre of Canterbury in 1942.

March: The furore which has accompanied the ambitious plans to rebuild the blitzed central area of Canterbury continues to rage as furiously as the city burned.

For years civic leaders have argued that historic styles should be the basis of new buildings but a recent letter in the *Kentish Gazette* echoes the feelings of many in this New Elizabethan Age.

"Any rebuilding in Tudor style", writes Mr T.E.Carling, "would be mere hypocrisy as no Tudor materials are available and the whole result would be that of a fake. The charm of Canterbury of the past has been the mixture of styles cheek by jowl. Each age built according to its ideals and the materials available and we should add our quota by building in contemporary style".

These views are shared by the newly-formed Canterbury Preservation Society but the City Architect (Hugh Wilson's) plan for St George's Street is controversial because all the buildings are flat-topped — and that is a compromise to the modern style.

Some citizens have said this "New Jerusalem" looks strangely akin to Bexleyheath High Street. Others believe that planning permission will come more quickly with a clean-limbed modern style.

Ration books burned as food crisis finally ends

July 3rd: Kent members of the National Federation of Housewives threatened this week to hold demonstrations across the county if they find that meat prices are failing to fall.

Their protests came as the Government announced the end to all rationing after 14 years. Meat was the last item to go and many butchers immediately predicted price rises.

Across the county ration books have been ceremonially burned as relics of the dark days. It was in 1947 that the economic crisis forced rationing back to wartime levels and the meat ration was reduced to a shilling a week.

One butcher from Ashford said today that Smithfield Market was open at midnight instead of 6am for the delivery of meat. "I saw porters handling huge sides of beef, some weighing 400 pounds and the quality looked superb."

Silver City has carried some distinguished passengers and this is one of them. Genevieve *is the veteran car which featured in the comedy film released this year. Driving the car from aircraft to airfield is Kenneth Moore, one of the stars of the film.*

Suicide pact fails so boyfriend must hang

December 2nd: **A 23-year-old machinist of Carnation Road, Strood, who took part in a bizarre suicide pact with a young woman, has been sentenced to death by hanging.**

Brian David Cass, 23, was yesterday found guilty of the murder of Mrs Evelyn Joan Imison at Maidstone in June.

Kent Assize Court was told that Cass, a married man, became romantically involved with Mrs Imison, also married with three young children.

So deep was their infatuation that they mutually decided to commit suicide by turning on gas taps and sealing all doors and windows.

Things went terribly wrong. A landlady found them next morning lying on a kitchen floor. She called the police and artificial respiration was effective only in the case of the accused.

Many MPs believe in the abolition of the death penalty and there is talk of a bill being prepared for Parliament. Too late for David Cass.

Ferryfield airfield opens near Lydd

July 13th: The famous Lympne aerodrome — badly mauled by the Luftwaffe during the Battle of Britain and later used as a crucial forward base — has closed and a new airport opened a few miles away between New Romney and Lydd.

Following the flooding last year it became clear that Lympne could no longer cope with the volume of traffic. Since Silver City Airways launched its inaugural flight in 1948, more than 208,000 passengers and 54,000 cars have been carried across the Channel to Le Touquet.

The new airport is called Ferryfield and the first commercial flight will take place today. It is clear that it will soon become one of the world's busiest airports.

Mau Mau terrorists mauled by the Buffs

December 1st: One of the greatest military campaigns ever encountered in "peacetime" ended yesterday when the last of the Buffs' 700 officers and men arrived at Dover Marine Station — having spent 21 months hunting down Mau Mau terrorists in the remote highlands of Kenya.

Only 12 officers and 171 soldiers saw the African adventure through from start to finish. For them it began in April 1953 with the news that a secret society, mysteriously named the Mau Mau, was dedicated to the expulsion of Europeans from the Kikuyu zone by murder and lawlessness.

An officer leads soldiers on a patrol through the Kenya forest.

For the men of Kent, led by Lt-Col J.F. Connolly — who a few months earlier had been dealing with gangsters and thieves in the desert wastes of Egypt — the battleground was now a vast jungle in which the enemy prowled with an animal's instinct for concealment and surprise. As their patrols made deeper penetration into the forest the Buffs also encountered wild animals.

There were many terrifying operations as the Buffs set out to locate Mau Mau hides. Six terrorists were killed in June 1953 with a subaltern, G.J.B. Edgecombe, leading the charge. Ten more died in August with a National Service officer, 2nd Lt K.J.Cross, distinguishing himself. Fifteen armed Mau Mau were killed in a banana grove in November.

As the numbers of "kills" increased almost daily to more than 100 by the end of 1953, an order arrived from the highest level placing a ban on "battalion score-keeping".

As Connolly gave way to Lt-Col M.A. Grace early this year operations continued in earnest. Eight men were killed by D Company in mid-February and, on the 28th, C Company Headquarters were in the thick of a fierce battle by the Nairobi-Nyeri road in which five terrorists died.

One of the most hair-raising moments came when a platoon was ambushed. As the men of Kent returned the fire, Sergeant P.A. Newman saw two gangsters advancing on him with rifles raised. He charged with fixed bayonet and plunged it into the nearer of the two men. With an instinct born of instructing recruits he yanked his bayonet out and drove it into the other man who turned out to be a Mau Mau general.

Newman's act was one of the bravest. By the time the sweeps ended a few weeks ago the Buffs had recorded 290 kills, captured 194 hardcore gangsters and arrested 3,100 suspects. More important they had left the region in such a settled condition that the Rifle Brigade, who replaced the Buffs, found themselves underemployed.

In return the men of Kent enjoyed remarkable immunity from harm. The only soldier to lose his life was Corporal M.A.Warrener who died after having a leg amputated. All the men will receive the African General Service Medal.

Four killed as submarine is swept into the Medway

December 16th: Four civilian workmen died yesterday when a submarine was swept from its moorings at Chatham Dockyard onto mud banks in the River Medway. After a long and dramatic rescue operation 31 survivors were picked up but many are seriously injured.

Onlookers say the submarine *Talent* was being refitted when a huge wall of water knocked down the dock gate, swept into No 3 basin, picked up the submarine and carried it at speed into the river.

Tugs and motor launches were immediately called into action but rescue attempts were hampered by the high tide. No-one knew for certain at the time how many men were missing.

When the tide eventually receded and the boat stabilised, a night-long rescue operation got under way. Hampered by thick fog the Medway tug and a ship from Dover picked up 31 survivors from the water while firemen from Chatham brought in pumping equipment to clear excess water.

The *Talent*, a 1,571-ton boat built by the Royal Navy during the war, was a sister ship of the *Truculent* which sank off Sheerness four years ago.

Sutherland's portrait of Churchill nears completion

September: The well-known Kent artist, Graham Sutherland, who won critical acclaim for his paintings of air-raid devastation in London, flying bomb sites in Normandy and other evocative work, has been commissioned to paint a portrait of Winston Churchill as a birthday present for the great man.

It was in 1949 that Sutherland painted a startling, full-length portrait of Somerset Maugham which is now hanging in the Tate Gallery. He followed that with an equally brilliant portrait of Lord Beaverbrook which led to a request by the all-party committee of both Houses of Parliament for a portrait of the Prime Minister.

Graham Sutherland began his career by etching landscapes in a style influenced by Samuel Palmer, the Victorian landscape impressionist painter who lived at Shoreham. Sutherland's inspiration was the scenery in Pembrokeshire.

He and his wife Kathleen have spent most of their married life in Kent, first at Farningham, from 1927, then Eynsford (1931), Sutton-at-Hone (1933) and now at the weatherboarded White House near the green at Trottiscliffe, which the couple purchased in 1937.

Churchill is proving to be a rather difficult "sitter" but the artist hopes to complete the portrait in time for his 80th birthday in November. Sutherland will then turn to an even more challenging commission — a tapestry of *Christ in Glory* above the altar of the new Cathedral at Coventry.

October 1955: *The Churchill portrait completed, Graham Sutherland and his wife prepare to leave Ferryfield Airfield, Lydd for Le Touquet. They will travel by car to the South of France where they will spend a few months. "The first week will be holiday", said Mr Sutherland "and after that I have a great deal of work to do".*

'I am mindful of the Church's teaching that a Christian marriage is indissoluble and conscious of my duty to the Commonwealth'— Princess Margaret on her decision not to marry Peter Townsend.

January 1st: The RAF's new *Vickers Valiant,* the only aircraft able to carry atomic bombs, entered service today.

February 2nd: More than £2 million will be spent on new motorways in Britain in a four-year plan to modernise Britain's outdated road system.

March 3rd: It was announced today that London is to become a smokeless zone.

March 25th: Because of its dangerous state, Sheerness Pier at Blue Town has closed. Repairs would cost approximately £90,000.

April 5th: Winston Churchill today resigned as Prime Minister. He hands over to his great friend and long-time colleague Anthony Eden with the comment: "No two men will ever change guard more smoothly."

April 5th: The Queen and the Duke of Edinburgh yesterday visited the Grain Oil Refinery. Special stands were built to accommodate the tens of thousands who came to see them.

April 7th: Harold Macmillan, MP for Bromley, has been appointed Foreign Secretary by Anthony Eden.

April 15th: Roads throughout Kent were jammed on Monday as thousands took advantage of perfect Whitsun weather to visit the sea and countryside. There was a seven-mile queue of motionless motor cars between Sellindge and the Maidstone side of Ashford and an even longer queue at Charing. By passes for Maidstone, the Medway Towns and Ashford are imperative.

April 21st: National newspapers were printed today at the end of a month-long strike by electricians and maintenance engineers.

April 28th: Ruth Ellis, a 28-year-old blonde model, has been sent for trial accused of the murder of her lover, David Blakely, outside a London pub.

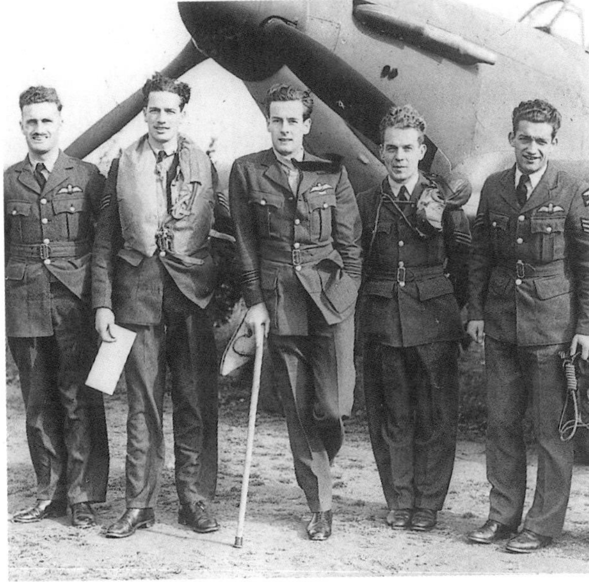

Group Captain Peter Townsend (centre), who has been romantically linked with Princess Margaret for a number of years. This picture was taken in 1940. See page 51.

April 30th: Many Kent cinemas are introducing 3-D films. Customers have to wear red and green glasses.

May 16th: *The Dambusters*, a film about the bombing of the Ruhr dams, has opened in London, starring Richard Todd.

May 14th: The Warsaw Pact forming a military alliance between all Europe's Eastern block countries was signed today.

June 27th: Another fire has destroyed a Maidstone cinema. This time *The Central* was destroyed and firemen had a narrow escape when the blazing balcony collapsed near them. A £10,000 new screen had just been installed.

July 13th: Ruth Ellis was hanged today at Holloway Prison.

July 23rd: Donald Campbell, 34-year-old son of the late Sir Malcolm Campbell, broke the world water speed record on Ullswater today. *Bluebird* averaged a speed of 202.32 mph.

August Bank Holiday: The biggest influx of visitors in living memory crammed into Thanet for the Bank Holiday. Every guest house, boarding house, hotel and caravan within miles of Ramsgate and Margate was booked. Thousands of disappointed people swarmed into information bureaux clamouring for accommodation. They were disappointed.

The 73 extras conceded by Kent in the Northampton innings of 374 was the highest ever recorded in a first-class match.

August: Blue jeans which have been popular with men for many years are now being worn by women. The craze which swept America has now arrived in Britain.

September 18th: After a four-year silence the Foreign Office admitted today that Guy Burgess and Donald MacLean, the diplomats who left Britain in 1951, were spies.

September 22nd: The BBC has a rival at last. Commercial television, complete with advertisements, opened in London tonight. The first advertisement was for SR toothpaste.

September 30th: James Dean, the American actor who earned worldwide fame with his films, *Giant, East of Eden* and *Rebel Without a Cause,* has been killed in a road accident.

October 21st: For the 150th anniversary of the Battle of Trafalgar, three mayors and thousands of people will pay homage to Nelson's ship *Victory* built at Chatham at a cost of £50,000. Her keel was laid when Nelson was a baby.

November 10th: The BBC is given exclusive rights to televise Test Match cricket.

November : Peter Broadbent and James Murray from Elvington, Dover were both in the Wolves side against Moscow Dynamo. Dover is proving to be a nursery for England's brightest soccer stars.

November 28th: Following the shooting of two more British soldiers, a state of emergency has been declared in Cyprus.

December 2nd: Rootes Motors have taken over Singer Motors.

December 9th: Seventeen policemen from Kent have been instructed to go to troubled Cyprus to help British bobbies strengthen the police force there.

GREAT HITS OF 1955

Give Me Your Word

Rosemarie

Rehearsal time for Noel Coward and Marlene Dietrich.

Tories home with a big majority

May 27th: For the first time since 1865 a party in office has applied for a fresh mandate and obtained it with a substantially increased majority. In yesterday's General Election the Tories, led by Anthony Eden, gained an overall majority of 58 to break the political deadlocks of 1950 and 1951.

There were no surprises in Kent except, in most cases, there was increased support for dominant Conservative candidates while the Labour members managed to hang on with the slimmest of majorities — 2,447 for Bottomley at Rochester and Chatham, 4,198 for Irving at Dartford and just 59 for Wells at Faversham.

At the age of 80, Sir Winston Churchill fought and successfully defended his Woodford constituency. The party scoreboard now reads: Tories 344, Labour 277, Liberals 6, Others 3.

Noel Coward leaves England "for tax reasons"

February: Noel Coward, the 56-year-old English playwright, actor and master technician of the theatre, has decided to leave England and his home, Goldenhurst in Aldington and move to Bermuda for what he calls "tax reasons".

He insists it is nothing to do with a lack of patriotism but "a perfectly legal method of defeating the monstrously unfair tax situation in England".

Coward has written more than 50 plays, many of them sentimental and patriotic pieces which are distinguished for their craftmanship and versatility. He is currently working on a new play which dramatises a deceased artist's frauds. The working title is *Nude With a Violin.*

The playwright is being described as a "tax exile" but Coward predicts he will soon be followed by other well-known "disillusioned" celebrities.

Another Kent personality in the news this month is Jocelyn Brooke, novelist, poet and former professional soldier, who has completed his long-awaited third novel which he describes as *The Orchid Trilogy.*

Brooke was born in Folkestone in 1908 on the undercliff just below Spade House, the home of H.G.Wells.

The Romney Marsh, Hythe, Sandgate and Folkestone areas feature strongly in all his novels, which have great character and charm.

April 5th: *Crowds of people lined the route to the Anglo-Iranian Oil Company's new refinery on the Isle of Grain today for the long-awaited visit by the Queen and Prince Philip. The royal couple toured the refinery, now the biggest in Europe, and saw a supertanker unloading thousands of tons of crude oil from the Middle East. After the visit Prince Philip went on by helicopter to open the new Medway College of Technology at Chatham.*

Memorial at Eastchurch to pioneer airmen

July 25th: Lord Brabazon of Tara, the first Briton to make a powered flight in England, was among the distinguished aviators who watched Lord Tedder, Marshal of the RAF, unveil a memorial at Eastchurch today to Britain's pioneer airmen.

Also present were Lord Cornwallis, Lord Lieutenant of Kent and Oswald Short, the only survivor of the three famous Short Brothers who established their aerodrome on the Isle of Sheppey almost 50 years ago.

Lt Col Claud Moore-Brabazon (or Moore-Brabs as he was better known), won the Daily Mail prize of £1,000 for the first flight of one mile in a closed circuit. That historic event took place at Leysdown in 1909 and it was a year later that Oswald and his brothers Horace and Eustace transferred their works to Eastchurch. In four years they built scores of experimental aeroplanes before moving to a bigger site at Rochester.

March: The seven eponymous oak trees, ceremoniously planted in 1727 next to the White Hart public house at the southern entrance to Sevenoaks, have been felled — unnecessarily.

Sevenoaks Urban Council held that they were diseased but when Peter Smith of the Invicta Company took them down they proved to be as sound as other oak trees in nearby Knole Park.

The embarrassed councillors will now plant seven saplings in their place . According to legend seven oak trees have stood on Sevenoaks Common since time immemorial and it was from one such group that the town took its name. Distinction by seniority passes to the seven oaks around the northern perimeter of the Vine Cricket Ground, planted in 1902. *Photograph shows the new saplings.*

Three killed in Thanet gun battle as American airman goes berserk

August 25th: A 22-year-old coloured American airman turned gunman yesterday, shot dead three people, wounded nine others and then killed himself near Broadstairs.

Napoleon Green, a 2nd class airman from Chicago, started his reign of terror at the USAAF base at Manston. It spread to the beach near Stone Gap, North Foreland and ended when Green shot himself twice in the chest.

The drama began at 9.30. Green, armed with a .30 carbine and a .45 service revolver walked into the accounts office and killed Master Sgt Lawrence Valesquez, aged 33, who lived with his wife and four children at Cliftonville.

Green then killed Airman 2nd class Nelson Gresham and Corporal Peter Grayer, 22, of the RAF police.

He held up a car belonging to the American Express Bank and shot Ian Yeomans, a 24-year-old cashier from Ramsgate, who is now critically ill in hospital. He kept on firing. A bullet pierced the leg of Miss Wendy Welton of Birchington. Miss Anne Cockburn of Broadstairs, Mr Aubrey Easto of Ramsgate, the camp tailor, Mr Peter Hewitt and Mr Kemp an Air Ministry driver were all wounded as bullets whistled around them.

The gunman ordered a sergeant to drive him to the coast and the shooting continued at Stone Bay where bullets ricocheted among the boulders. By now American Air Force police, armed with Tommy guns had been called and holiday makers told to clear the beach.

A Chicago-type gun battle ensued until Green, riddled with bullet wounds, turned a gun on himself.

Dover harbour has witnessed some stirring sights in its long history as the gateway to England but this is among them. It shows an air cushion vehicle or ACV which can travel by hovering over any relatively flat surface such as water, marsh or desert. Designed by Christopher Cockerell the unusual machine uses jets of air within a protective skirt to provide the necessary cushion. Mr Cockerell, 45, has been working on his invention since 1953. With his original working model he used a hair dryer and two tins. Eventually he hopes it will carry vehicles and passengers across the Channel but sceptics say it will never catch on. Those who rushed to the harbour yesterday were certainly impressed with the ACV. A suggested name is a hovercraft.

See page 76

Chatham's haunted theatre closes: TV is blamed

September: The Theatre Royal, Chatham, which has welcomed such famous artists as Charlie Chaplin, Stan Laurel, Gracie Fields, George Formby and Max Miller is to close.

Audiences, in the last few years, have been woefully low and part of the blame lies with the popularity of television broadcasting and the introduction this year of a commercial channel to compete with the BBC.

The Theatre Royal opened in 1899 and was built of concrete and steel — at the time relatively new construction techniques. It quickly won a reputation as a theatre specialising in the very best of the performing arts.

One of the best-known regular performers is a ghost called Humphrey. Many believe he was an artist who hanged himself in the theatre. Others say he was a member of staff responsible for counting the takings at the Theatre Royal and the Barnard's Theatre of Varieties which once stood opposite. He is mischievous, friendly and has appeared so often that the theatre has earned the reputation as one of the most haunted in Britain.

'Godders' hits out —and England keep the Ashes

February 2nd: The exuberant and brilliant Kent wicket-keeper, Godfrey Evans, today hit the winning run to ensure England retains the Ashes. Australia, beaten by five wickets at Adelaide, have already lost the series and Evans, along with captain Len Hutton and fast bowler Frank Tyson is one of the heroes.

Born at Finchley in 1920, Evans lived at Sheldwich, near Faversham, for most of his boyhood life in a house called Lords — which had no connection with cricket. He later moved to Bearsted with his wife Jean and then to Aylesford.

Godfrey made his debut for England in 1946, toured Australia with Freddie Brown's team and was part of the great Ashes-winning side of 1953. With Fred Huish, Les Ames and Hopper Levett, Kent has provided England with some of their best wicket-keepers but many believe the agile Evans to be the best.

He has that miraculous ability to score runs quickly for county and country, stand up to fast bowlers like Alec Bedser and zoom down the leg side to take breathtaking catches. One critic says that Evans reminds him of a sea lion taking a mouthful of herring in mid-air.

This wonderful acrobatic sportsman has already played 54 Tests. And at 35 he has plenty of cricket left in him.

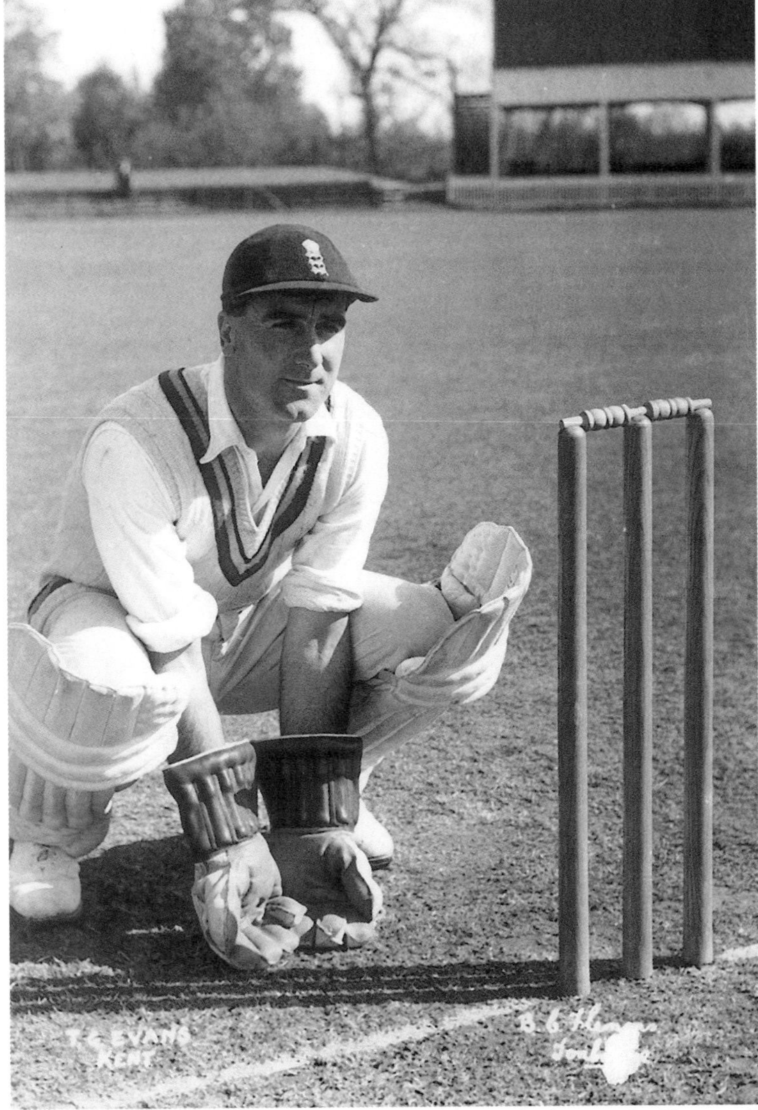

Godfrey Evans was educated at Kent College and taken on the Kent staff when he was only 16. For a few years he was also a professional boxer but after three fights and a broken nose he received an ultimatum from the Kent committee —cricket or boxing.

***April:** Thanet's seaside resorts are bracing themselves for a bumper season following the busiest Easter ever known. Requests for the Margate Guide from all over the country has already exceeded last year's figure by 6,000 and many hotels and boarding houses are fully booked. The four hotels owned by Butlins said that 25,000 enquiries had been received —and that is an extraordinary number. The Ramsgate beach entertainers will be especially busy as our photograph clearly indicates.*

New channel record on 80th anniversary

October 12th: An American girl, Florence Chadwick, today set a new record by swimming the Channel from England to France in 13 hours 55 minutes. It was the third time she has achieved the feat and, in favourable conditions, she knocked 47 minutes off her previous best.

The courageous swim came on the 80th anniversary of Captain Matthew Webb's trail blazing performance in 1875. Since then scores of intrepid men and women have emulated the gallant Captain's feat.

Miss Chadwick does not hold the overall record. That belongs to an Egyptian Abd el Rehim who took the easier route from France to England in 10 hours 50 minutes in 1950.

England to France (top ten)

1. Florence Chadwick (U.S.)	1955	13 hrs 55 mins
2. William Pickering (G.B.)	1955	14 " 6 "
3 Florence Chadwick (U.S.)	1953	14 " 42 "
4 Florence Chadwick (U.S.)	1951	16 " 19 "
5 Philip Rising (G.B.)	1952	18 " 38 "
6 Thomas Blower (G.B.)	1951	18 " 42 "
7. Philip Mickman (G.B.)	1952	18 " 44 "
8. Matthew Webb (G.B.)	1875	21 " 45 "
9. Thomas Burgess (G.B.)	1911	22 " 35 "
10.Henry Sullivan (U.S.)	1923	26 " 50 "

France to England (top five)

1. Abd el Rehim (Egypt)	1950	10 hrs 50 mins
2. Arnst Vierkotter (Germany)	1926	12 " 40 "
3. Brenda Fisher (G.B.)	1954	12 " 42 "
4. Thomas Blower (G.B.)	1937	13 " 31 "
5. Jenny E. James (G.B.)	1951	13 " 55 "

Princess says no: Peter Townsend is devastated

October 31st: After two weeks of intense press speculation Princess Margaret has decided not to marry Captain Peter Townsend. The couple have been romantically linked for a number of years and the former aviation hero is devastated by the Princess's brave decision to put the royal family and the Commonwealth first.

In a statement last night she said: "I have been aware that subject to renouncing my rights of succession it might have been possible for me to contract a civil marriage but mindful of the Church's teaching that Christian marriage is indissoluble and conscious of my duty to the Commonwealth, I have resolved to put these considerations above all others."

Captain Townsend, a divorcee and former equerry to the Princess's late father lives at Uckfield House, Sussex. According to his butler he is "very distressed" by the news. He was well aware that, should the marriage have gone ahead, the Princess would lose her payments from the Civil List and her place as third in line to the throne.

Townsend, 41, is well known in Kent. Before the war he completed a course at the School of Navigation, Manston and went on to become a fearless fighter pilot with the distinction of destroying the first enemy aircraft to fall on English soil, on February 3rd, 1940.

In August of that year Townsend was shot down over Tunbridge Wells, baled out and landed, injured, at Cranbrook Road, Hawkhurst. His Hurricane crashed at Goudhurst and the young pilot was admitted to Hawkhurst Cottage Hospital with a broken foot.

After the Battle of Britain he completed several station commands, including that of RAF West Malling. It was in 1944 that he was appointed Equerry to the King and first met the young Princess Margaret, then only 14.

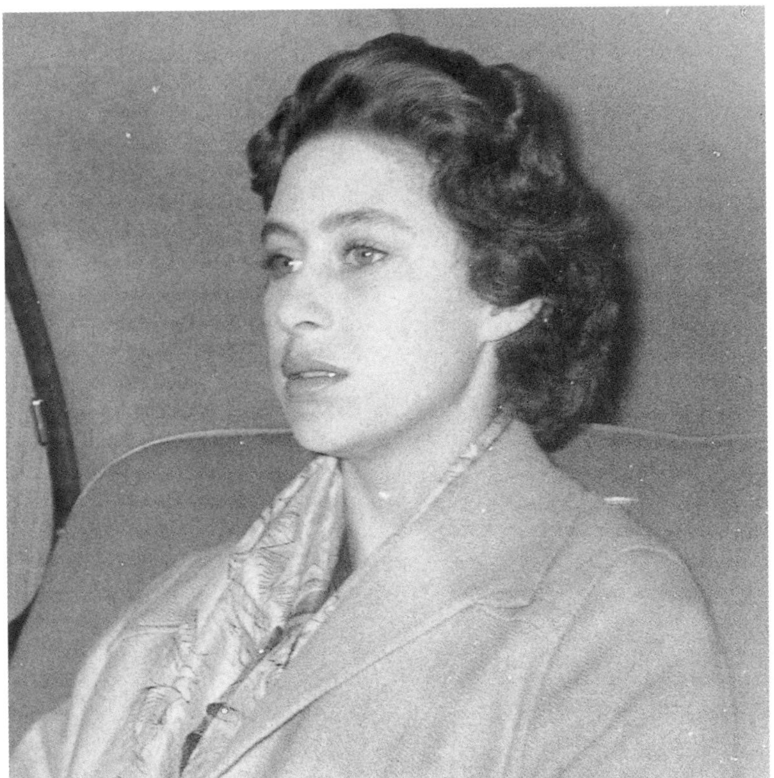

A distressed Princess Margaret arriving at Clarence House. She has finally decided not to marry Captain Peter Townsend.

Goodbye Westminster — a village of happy memories

November: The tiny village of Westminster, midway between Queenborough and Sheerness, has finally been abandoned by the inhabitants. Bulldozers will soon move in and all that will remain of this once-thriving community will be memories.

Westminster has never recovered from the devastating floods of two years ago. On that unforgettable night every home was inundated to a depth of five feet and the village became marooned, cut off from the rest of the island, surrounded by the fast-flowing, icy waters of the North Sea.

There were no human casualties. Apart from one young man sleeping downstairs on what became a floating mattress, all the inhabitants were in the upper storeys. The unfortunate man was rescued.

It took weeks for the water to subside but it left behind a deposit of slimy mud that was almost impossible to clean. Gradually the residents moved away to be rehoused in other areas of Sheppey but everywhere on the island they still talk about the village that "was washed away".

Westminster comprised of two main streets, Montague Road and Cromwell Road. There were two pubs, The Globe Inn and Medway Tavern, a post office and general store and a small hall known as the Bethel Chapel which doubled for Sunday School. The gas works, still prominent, dominated the village. Most of the men worked at the dockyard.

Enid Blyton at Highbury Studios where the first two episodes of her Noddy books are being filmed. With her and Noddy are Chris and Tiny Lawrence, sons of the director, plus the policeman and Big Ears.

Britain's first light railway has closed

December 4th: The Kent and East Sussex railway, opened early in the century to great acclaim — and much relief among villagers who suddenly found they could travel by train to both London and Hastings — has closed. For Tenterden it is a bitter blow; the town now has no railway and the nearest station is at Headcorn. The Kent and East Sussex was Britain's first light railway. The section from Robertsbridge to Tenterden opened in 1900 and the extension to Headcorn followed five years later. Railway enthusiasts loved the journey along the Rother Valley through miles of unspoilt countryside.

Noddy, a racist! — Enid Blyton ignores her critics

November: Her many friends in Bromley and Beckenham where she lived for more than 30 years are delighted that Enid Blyton, the well-known children's writer, is enjoying world wide acclaim with her latest series about a little fellow called Noddy.

Although this is a harmless story about a wooden puppet who goes to live in toyland, some people are suggesting the books are racist. One story shows Noddy set upon by three golliwogs and another is about a little black doll whose blackness is washed off by magic rain.

Enid is taking no notice of her critics. The Noddy stories, she says, are full of simple humour, with troubles, adventures and happy endings — and like her other series, they are phenomenally successful.

The writer, aged 57, spent all her childhood in Beckenham and the first four years of married life in Shortlands, Bromley. She now lives at Beaconsfield and is enjoying her most prolific writing years.

In fact so prodigious is her output that rumours abound of a team of ghost writers. It is far from the truth. On an average day she can write 10,000 words and has been known to produce an entire book in a week. Currently she has almost 40 British publishers and her total output is in excess of 300 titles.

Among the books which appear to be most popular are *Sunny Stories, The Secret Island* (published in 1938) and the adventures of *The Famous Five* (1942).

'They came towards the hotel like a strange regiment in knee-length jackets, velvet collars and drainpipe trousers. They wore sideburns and black string ties' — pub landlord on Teddy Boys in Dartford.

January 4th: Dr Arthur Michael Ramsay is named as the new Archbishop of Canterbury.

January 12th: Soldiers from Kent are among the new wave of British troops sent to Cyprus. It follows the murder of a Turkish Cypriot by EOKA terrorists.

February 6th: Most Britons still favour the death penalty, according to an opinion poll published today.

February 29th: The American State of Alabama is in turmoil today as black civil rights activists attempt to ride on buses and enter segregated colleges.

March 9th: Archbishop Makarios, leader of the Greek Cypriot community, has been deported by the British. He is believed to be in exile in the Seychelles.

March 22nd: Civil rights leader Dr Martin Luther King said today he will use passive resistance and the weapon of love in continuing the fight for black rights.

April 20th: American actress Grace Kelly has married Prince Rainier II, ruler of the tiny principality of Monaco. The wedding took place yesterday in a glamorous, fairytale setting.

May 21st: The US today dropped a hydrogen bomb from an aircraft over Bikini Atoll.

May 10th: A new play by a young writer, John Osborne, has upset many conventions of middle-class England. Called *Look Back in Anger*, some critics have said it is "rotten with self pity".

June 19th: South London Harrier Gordon Pirie ran 5,000 metres in a record time of 13 minutes 36.8 seconds to beat European champion Vladimir Kuts.

June 29th: Arthur Miller, the playwright and Marilyn Monroe, the actress, were married today.

July 10th: The House of Lords today voted overwhelmingly against the abolition of capital punishment. The Bishop of Rochester, David Chavasse, voted against the Bill and was alone among the distinguished clerics who sit in the Lords to do so. "I am not an abolitionist but I do believe the law of murder should be changed", he said. "My fellow bishops have been too woolly".

***March 5th:** Dame Edith Evans, the milliner who became one of England's best-loved thespians, yesterday presented prizes at Kent Young Farmer's annual speaking contest at Maidstone. Dame Edith, who lives at Kilndown, has set great store by her clear diction which has an extraordinary effect on her audiences. She is often critical of the slovenly standards of speech in the theatre. Here, Barbara Dowsey, 13, receives the junior cup on behalf of the Northfleet team.* See page 185.

July 12th: The British colony of Cyprus is to be given a new liberal constitution and will be guided towards independence, Sir Anthony Eden said today.

July 26th: The Egyptian president, Colonel Nasser has seized control of the Suez Canal.

July 27th: Jim Laker, the Surrey off-spinner, has taken a record 19 wickets for 90 runs to rout the Australians in the fourth Test match at Manchester.

October 25th: The London to Folkestone Road (A20) has been chosen for a double white line experiment. Any motorist crossing the lines may face prosecution for careless driving.

September 30th: The 415 (Thames and Medway) Coast Regiment Royal Artillery has been disbanded. It was founded in 1794.

October 28th: The unit which manned the guns at "Hellfire Corner" — the 410 (Kent) Coast Regiment Royal Artillery, T.A., has been disbanded.

October 31st: British and French jet bombers took off from Cyprus this afternoon to begin bombing military airfields near Cairo.

November 1st: Premium bonds were on sale today.

November 5th: The Hungarian revolution has been crushed by the Red Army. More than 1,000 tanks attacked key positions and then Soviet forces entered Budapest.

November 6th: Royal Marine commandos were involved in heavy fighting today as they attempted to reach the centre of Port Said.

November 8th: A ceasefire in the Suez Canal zone has been imposed by the UN and accepted by British and French forces.

November 22nd: The Duke of Edinburgh opened the Olympic Games at Melbourne today.

November 23rd: Following pressure from the United States the Government agrees to begin military withdrawl from Egypt.

November 30th: Refugees from the Hungarian uprising are pouring across the Austrian border. An estimated 100,000 have already escaped.

December 6th: Judy Grinham, 17-year-old swimmer and Chris Brasher, 3,000 metres steeplechaser, have won gold medals for England at Melbourne

An enterprising Dane, Ole Lauritzen, has started an international freight and transport shipping business between Vlissingen, Holland and Ramsgate. It is called Olau Line.

GREAT HITS OF 1956

Heartbreak Hotel

Que Sera Sera

I'll Be Home

March 24th: *To the great dismay of the Royal family and racegoers all over the country the Queen Mother's great steeplechaser* Devon Loch *unexplicably "sat down" just 50 yards from the winning post in today's Grand National. Trainer Peter Cazalet of Fairlawne, Shipbourne and jockey Dick Francis are completely puzzled. They think this strong Irish-bred gelding was startled by the great wall of cheering for the Queen Mother as he entered the home straight. His legs suddenly splayed out, Francis was unseated and ESB went on to win the race. The vets have confirmed that the horse is not injured. The photograph above was taken from a film sequence of* Devon Loch's *dramatic fall.*

Chatham policeman shot dead in Cyprus

March 16th: A former Chatham police constable, Gerald Thomas Rooney, was shot dead in Nicosia, Cyprus today as EOKA terrorists continue to demonstrate against British rule.

Pc Rooney was one of three Medway policemen flown to Cyprus last December to help strengthen the local force. He was actually on duty in the Greek sector of Nicosia when a sten gun opened fire from just three yards. He died immediately.

The Chatham policeman, 24, was engaged to Miss Rita Sykes who works on the Isle of Grain.

Hundreds of young men from Kent are with the British troops helping local police to try and bring law and order to this troubled island.

The British Government has invited Greece and Turkey to discuss the crisis. Turkey welcomes the initiative but Greek leader Archbishop Makarios says formal recognition by the British of the principle of self-determination is an essential pre-requisite. EOKA is fighting for union with Greece

New town of 25,000 at Allhallows

June 1st: A new town, accommodating 25,000 people, will be built on an 800-acre site at Allhallows-on-Sea if Kent County Council gives planning permission.

The scheme has been announced by Dolphin Development and will take 10 years to complete. It has been welcomed by the British Petroleum Company whose oil refinery at Grain creates an ever-increasing housing problem for their employees.

The site proposed for the development is on the estuary of the Thames opposite Southend-on-Sea.

August 7th: *As most of Kent basked in fine Bank Holiday weather, Tunbridge Wells and its surrounding villages yesterday experienced one of the most dramatic summer storms ever recorded. Thunder and lightning was followed by rain and then hailstones, as big as cherries. Shop ceilings collapsed, skylights were smashed and blinds torn to shreds under the weight of the hail. Here is the astonishing scene in the centre of Tunbridge Wells.*

Lonnie Donnegan, the 25-year-old singer and guitarist, who played with the Ken Colyer and Chris Barber jazz bands, has now gone solo and released his own record called Rock Island Line. *Well known in Kent as a skiffle singer he is planning concerts in most towns including Dartford, Margate and Maidstone.*

Rioting Teddy Boys rock around the clock

September 11th: Kent police have been called to several cinemas in the county this week to eject youths who have been 'jiving' in the aisles, clapping and chanting to the music of the film *Rock Around the Clock,* which features Bill Hayley and the Comets. Some teenagers dressed in Teddy Boy clothing have let off fireworks in cinemas and ripped the seats with their flick knives. Police plan to stop this anti-social behaviour; they are being extra vigilant.

It is not only in cinemas that Teddy Boys are causing problems. In July, a group of these modern day "Edwardians" stormed the Princes Hotel in Dartford. Landlord Mr Charles Stow refused to serve them and called the police.

"I have never seen such an extraordinary sight in my life", said Mr Stow. "They piled off a bus and came towards the hotel like some strange regiment in knee-length jackets, velvet collars and drainpipe trousers. They wore sideburns and black string ties. I called the police, a car load arrived and the youths began to run in all directions".

There has been more trouble in Maidstone. In August one Teddy Boy from the tent encampment at Vinters Park kicked and butted Police Inspector George Harwood after a fight on Gabriel's Hill. It was the worst outbreak of Teddy Boy violence in the town for weeks. Several appeared in court and were fined up to £10 each.

Local magistrates deplore these youths and refuse to accept their dandy nickname, associated with Edward VII. They also refuse to believe police claims that American singers like Bill Haley and Elvis Presley are inciting trouble — but it is a fact that songs such as *Hound Dog* and *Heartbreak Hotel* are sending the youngsters wild — particularly girls. Presley is 21 and already a millionaire. Three years ago he was a truck driver.

Tunbridge Wells has had more than its fair share of Teddy Boy trouble. On Saturday afternoons they can be seen standing in the town, as if exiled from home, wearing stove-pipe trousers, longish coats and preening laminated heads. In the evening they are usually found at The Roxy, formerly known as The Great Hall.

One youth was told by the chairman of the bench: "Discipline is imminent. Your call-up papers have arrived."

***July 5th:** A mechanical digger being used on road widening operations at Polhill, near Sevenoaks, has unearthed five male skeletons in a good state of preservation. The site is directly in line with the Pilgrims Way which crosses the London to Hastings road at this point. Archaeologists believe they are the remains of Danish warriors who fought a battle with the English under Edmund Ironside in 1016.*

Hungarian refugees pour into Kent

November 30th: Hundreds of refugees from the Hungarian uprising and the brutal Soviet repression are pouring into Kent with stories of the atrocities which followed last month's revolution.

Some are arriving by aeroplane and others by sea. All of them had managed to cross the Hungarian border into Austria. There, some stayed in refugee camps while others continued to make their way across Europe to the French sea ports.

The revolution began on October 23rd when demonstrators throughout Hungary called for independence and the withdrawal of the USSR. The fighting followed. For three days the Hungarian people rose in revolt against Soviet domination.

But all hopes of freedom died under the weight of the heavy Red Army tanks which even flattened houses in an irresistible assault. Thousands were killed and the last words heard from the Prime Minister, Mr Imre Nagy, came over Radio Budapest when he told the world of the Russian attack. "Help Hungary", he said. "Help...help...help".

Kent responded quickly to the crisis. Accommodation was immediately made available at Detling Airfield for 400 refugees with a further 1,000 at Old Park Barracks, Dover. Cross-Channel steamers were laid on to pick up the beleaguered people from France and Belgium. Relief funds and clothing stores were opened in every town and village in the county and ordinary people offered their homes to those who had lost everything.

Many stories are reaching astonished ears. A Bromley woman, Mrs Julia Owen, whose relatives were trapped in Budapest when the iron curtain came down, tried to reach them and actually got into the country. "I saw Russian soldiers dancing on a pile of dead bodies", she said. "I saw young women and children with home-made bombs fighting to the death".

Service clubs, led by Lions, Rotary and Round Table are organising money-raising events while the WRVS, Red Cross and St Johns are providing food at all reception centres.

December 10th: Yesterday the cross-Channel steamer Prince Phillipe arrived at Dover Marine with a further 300 refugees who had been near to the bitterest fighting. Wounded men and women were among the party and they told how their relatives had been murdered in cold blood.

Polio closes a primary school

October 19th: Despite the availability of a new vaccine, there has been an new outbreak of poliomyelitis in Kent. Yesterday it was confirmed that a primary school has closed, a 10-year-old girl has died and children from other schools are in hospital.

The medical officer of health said 79 cases have been notified during the year but "there has been an outbreak of a somewhat unusual character in the area of Capel, Tudeley and Five Oak Green — east of Tonbridge."

Capel School was closed immediately and, if the disease spreads, Skinners School, High Brooms Infants at Tunbridge Wells and Judd, Tonbridge may follow.

In May, thousands of Kent children were accepted for anti-polio vaccination and among those were more than 2,000 children in Tonbridge and Tunbridge Wells.

The new outbreak is a big blow, for the introduction of the vaccination was considered to be the first step towards elimination of the disease.

Poliomyelitis, or infantile paralysis, is an acute viral infection which enters the body through the mouth and invades the bloodstream, attacking the nervous system.

Tomb reveals Christopher Marlowe was not William Shakespeare

May 1st: With the dramatic opening today of the Walsingham tomb at St Nicholas, Chislehurst, it has finally been proved that Kent is not the true "home" of the great works attributed to the pen of William Shakespeare.

With Mr Calvin Hoffman and representatives of the world's press looking on, the tomb revealed only a quantity of sand. No bodies were found and certainly no manuscript.

This finally kills Mr Hoffman's well-publicised theory that Christopher Marlowe, born in Canterbury, in 1564, was the real genius and creator of the plays.

The decision to open the tomb was preceded by a long meeting of St Nicholas church council. Eventually they gave permission for masons to enter Scadbury Manor chapel.

As the coffin was lifted out Mr Hoffman said: "This is the moment I have been waiting 20 years for. I am convinced the manuscript will be discovered."

His disappointment was clear to see as he calmly announced the result. "It does nothing to disprove my theory. It simply eliminates another clue."

Calvin Hoffman and his wife watch the opening of the Walsingham tomb. It soon revealed its secrets —pure sand!.

Kent men in fierce fighting as Eden wins back control of Suez

November 16th: As petrol prices increase by a massive 1s 5d per gallon, the people of Kent are firmly behind the decision of Prime Minister Anthony Eden to take back, by force, full control of the Suez Canal.

It was in July that the Egyptian president Col Nasser nationalised the Anglo-French Suez Canal Company to lay his hands on the vital lifeline for oil supplies to Europe.

Within a month British forces, including a unit of the Royal West Kents, were sailing for the Eastern Mediterranean.

As RAF Vickers Valiants and Canberra jet bombers, led by Sqd Ldr John Garstin of Marine Parade, Tankerton, began bombing raids over military airfields near Cairo, United States officials — convinced that Britain and France were in collusion with Israel — were furious.

Also taking part in the Suez operation were Cpl Peter Simmons of Penlee Close, Edenbridge, Senior Aircraftsman John Sears of Glanbrydan, Leybourne and Lt-Col T.J.Wilson of Deal who was wounded at Port Said.

After fierce fighting Royal Marine commandos forced the governor of Port Said to surrender but within two days the United Nations had imposed a ceasefire and taken control.

Conservatives throughout Kent are strongly behind Anthony Eden and the only protest meetings — all poorly attended — have been organised by the Labour Party.

Kent's motorists are suffering badly with Mr Macmillan's announcement that the price of petrol is increased.

Most garages are out of supplies and the only happy dealers are those who sell Italian scooters. Hundreds of Kent motorists are switching to the inexpensive and very popular two-wheelers.

'Let's be frank about it. Most of our people have never had it so good' — Harold Macmillan, Prime Minister and MP for Bromley at a Conservative rally in July.

January 10th: Harold Macmillan, Conservative Member for Bromley, has been appointed Prime Minister following the resignation of Sir Anthony Eden.

January 14th: Screen tough guy Humphrey Bogart died from lung cancer yesterday aged 56. "Bogey", married to Lauren Bacall, starred in more than 50 films.

January 23rd: Princess Grace of Monaco has given birth to her first child, Caroline.

February 7th: American "rock" star, Bill Haley and his Comets were given a rapturous reception at the Dominion Theatre, London, where an audience of 3,000 sang in time to the beat *Rock Around the Clock.* Haley's record sales have now reached 22 million.

March 25th: Six European countries today created the Common Market and the European Atomic Pool (Eurotom).

March 30th: The Queen and the Duke of Edinburgh yesterday took their children Charles and Anne for a ride on the miniature railway at Hythe.

April 11th: Britain has granted self-government to the island of Singapore.

April 30th: Prince Philip today visited Aylesford Paper Mills and East Malling Research station

May 14th: Emergency petrol rationing ended today.

May 15th: Britain's first hydrogen bomb was dropped yesterday on Christmas Island in the Pacific.

June 1st: ERNIE (Electronic Random Number Indicator) today will pick the first premium bond winners.

June 26th: "A relationship between lung cancer and smoking exists", according to a special Medical Research Council report published today.

May 4th: Manchester United narrowly failed to become the first team this century to achieve a league and cup double. When their goalkeeper was carried off injured, Aston Villa scored twice to win the cup.

June 26th: Princess Alexandra, the beautiful 21-year-old daughter of Marina, Duchess of Kent and the late Duke today reviewed the Centenary Parade of the Kent County Constabulary *See page 61*

Charlton Athletic have been relegated from Division One of the Football League.

July 5th: Lew Hoad has beaten Ashley Cooper to win the men's singles title at Wimbledon. Althea Gibson is the women's champion.

June 12th: The Queen Mother has opened a new Great Hall for Kings School, Canterbury.

July 19th: Harold Watkinson, Minister of Transport has opened the Ashford bypass (A20).

July 20th: Stirling Moss has become the first Briton to win the British Grand Prix since 1923.

August 7th: Oliver Hardy, the 20-stone partner of Stan Laurel, died today aged 65. Together the couple made 200 pictures.

August 11th: Myxomatosis has now spread from Kent to 11 English counties.

August 13th: Figures just released show radio audiences have decreased to 3.5 million a year on average. Eight years ago, when television was in its infancy, the average was eight million.

August 30th: 170 years of British rule came to an end yesterday as Malaya became the last Asian colony to gain independence.

September 23rd: An outbreak of influenza, currently sweeping Britain, has been diagnosed as "Asian Flu". Children are particularly affected.

Tommy Steele, Britain's teenage rock 'n roll idol, is a guest performer at the Ritz, Chatham, Kent's largest cinema.

October 3rd: A petition signed by 1,000 parish councils, has been presented to the government requesting that branch railway lines should not be closed.

October 4th: The Russians launched a satellite into space today. *Sputnik-1* will soon be orbiting the earth at 18,000 mph.

October 22nd: 13 US servicemen have been injured by terrorist bombs in Saigon.

October 24th: Christian Dior, the fashion designer who made history with his New Look, died today in Italy aged 52.

C Ross-Parker, the well-known songwriter is now living at The Denes, Pollyhaugh, Eynsford. His most famous song *There'll Always be an England* has taken a lasting place in the heritage of English songs.

November 19th: A new pier has been built at Deal.

December 25th: The Queen today made a Christmas broadcast on television.

OBITUARY

The first Baron Leslie Hore-Belisha, formerly of Eynsford, died at Sholden, near Deal. In 1934 he gave his name to the Belisha beacon, drafted a new highway code and inaugurated driving tests for motorists. He was Secretary of State for War between 1937 and 40 and awarded a peerage in 1954.

The prolific Irish poet/playwright, Lord Edward Dunsany, who lived at Dunstall Priory, Shoreham for many years died on October 25th, aged 79. At six foot four inches tall this conspicuous, charismatic figure was renowned as the creator of fantasy. Formerly Professor of English Literature at Athens, he was there when the Nazis captured the city. Among his best-known work was *The Glittering Gate,* written on Yeats' suggestion.

GREAT HITS OF 1957

Love Letters in The Sand

All Shook Up

January: Following her divorce from Sir Oliver, Lady Zoe Hart Dyke is leaving Lullingstone Castle near Eynsford and taking her famous silk farm to Hertfordshire. The scooter and sidecar is proving useful during the move.

Foot-and-mouth tragedy

***August:* Almost 1,000 animals have been destroyed in a devastating outbreak of foot-and-mouth disease around the farming communities of Tonbridge and Tunbridge Wells. Ministry of Agriculture officials insist that wholesale slaughtering must continue**

Farms particularly affected are The Beeches, Lower Stonehurst and Woodlands Farms, Cowden; Greybury, Clatfield and Ockham Farms, Marsh Green; Speed's Farm, Langton and Brook's Farm, Plaxtol. Among the victims are hundreds of pedigree Ayrshire and Jersey cattle.

Local markets have been closed, Drag Hounds and Hunter Trials postponed, horses and ponies excluded from village fetes and even anglers told to respect foot-and-mouth notices.

In some cases the carcases of the dead animals have been burnt but generally excavators have been used to dig giant graves.

'Dirty Half Hundred' celebrates 200 years

October: Various ceremonial events to commemorate the 200th anniversary of the founding of the Queeen's Own Royal West Kent ('Dirty Half Hundred') Regiment have been held in the county during the year.

In July, Princess Marina as Colonel-in-Chief and Lord Cornwallis, Lord Lieutenant joined the Battalion's bi-centenary celebrations at a church service at All Saints, Maidstone.

This was followed by the presentation of silver trumpets and silver-mounted flutes by civic heads of 19 West and North Kent towns.

A few weeks later at the Angel Ground, Tonbridge, the Duchess of Kent inspected the now combined 4/5th Battalions and presented it with new colours which bear distinguished battle honours. Among them is the now legendary defence of Kohima — the West Kent are the only British unit entitled to this honour.

This month ceremonial belts have been presented to the Regiment by the County Society.

June 26th: Princess Alexandra today reviewed the Centenary Parade of the Kent County Constabulary at Maidstone headquarters. With her, inspecting those who have been decorated for long service and bravery, is the Chief Constable, Major Sir John Ferguson.

When 'Pc Whiskers' was compulsory

June 30th: Kent County Constabulary this week celebrated 100 years of service with a centenary parade, a modest dinner and the publication of a fascinating book which looks at the early years of policing in Kent and ahead to the problems likely to face tomorrow's busy copper.

The Constabulary was established in 1857 with Captain John Ruxton as Chief Constable and a force of 222 officers and men. The chief's salary on appointment was £400 per annum. He could read and write and that was one of the qualifications necessary for the appointment of a senior police officer. There were no such criteria for a constable whose wage was 18 shillings a week.

In the villages these largely illiterate and ill-equipped policemen were responsible for law and order but had to interpret the law according to the ideas of the local squire — almost invariably the magistrate — and administration and penalties varied from parish to parish.

Many people objected to the creation of "this unnecessary county force". We have managed very well for a number of centuries, they said, and the "village constables" and "watchmen" have achieved everything asked of them from collecting taxes, administering harsh vagrancy laws, arresting wrongdoers and even rounding up miscreants who fail to attend church. They have protected the common lands and dealt with anyone who undermined the authority of the landowners.

Now, they argued, affairs would eventually be taken away from the parish to a distant authority. This was the beginning of the creation of a "police state".

In those early days all policemen were encouraged to grow beards and it was not until 1873 that the Chief Constable issued a memorable instruction by granting "a relief of the order not to shave" — so ending the era of compulsory whiskers.

Looking ahead, writes the editor of the centenary book, the police will have problems associated with the small family aeroplane or helicopter in a congested lower air space. He will deal with aliens making unauthorised entries and, who knows, he may even have to control the Kent terminal of a Channel Tunnel. Television will play a big part in traffic control and there will almost certainly be a "magic eye" checking car speeds and property.

We've never had it so good, says Macmillan

July 20th: Harold Macmillan — whose elevation to Prime Minister ahead of Anthony Eden's deputy, Rab Butler, surprised many politicians — has made a good start in repairing Anglo-US relations after the Suez fiasco.

The MP for Bromley has also made a series of speeches aimed at raising morale. This week he told a Conservative rally at Bradford: "Let us be frank about it. Most of our people have never had it so good."

Mr Macmillan was referring to the difference in the living standard compared with six years ago. Instead of austerity there is now an abundance of goods and freedom of choice.

It was in January that Mr Macmillan, at 62, became Britain's new premier — just a few hours after Sir Anthony had resigned from the post because his health was causing anxiety.

There was high drama before the decision was announced. Chief Whip Edward Heath, MP for Bexley, reported that party ranks would have split if Mr Butler had won the power struggle.

In fact the only minister who voted for Rab Butler was Patrick Buchan-Hepburn, MP for Beckenham.

One of England's greatest wartime fighter aces, Catford-born Robert Stanford Tuck, has retired from the RAF and taken up an occupation far removed from shooting down enemy aircraft. He is a mushroom farmer at The Lynch, Eastling, near Sandwich. Tuck had a remarkable war which ended when he was shot down in France and locked away in Stalag Luft III. He escaped to fight alongside the Russians. His autobiography Fly For Your Life *was published last year.*

Mrs Churchill orders portrait to be destroyed

October: It is now known that the portrait of Sir Winston Churchill — given by his fellow MPs as an 80th birthday present two years ago — was taken to Chartwell and destroyed on the orders of Churchill's wife, Clementine.

The painting, by Graham Sutherland, was presented by Mr Attlee. It showed Churchill seated, gripping the arms of his chair. As he accepted the gift with an obvious lack of enthusiasm, Sir Winston said it was a remarkable example of modern art and added: "It certainly combines force and candour."

It is now known that Lady Churchill ordered her gardener to burn the portrait, although she did not witness the act of destruction.

Mr Sutherland, who is noted for being unflattering towards his sitters such as Somerset Maugham and Helena Rubinstein, is currently engaged on a tapestry for the new Coventry Cathedral.

October 6th: *Thanks to the BBC receiving and measurement station at Tatsfield, high on the North Downs above Westerham, radio listeners all over England were able to hear the "cheep....cheep....cheep" of Russia's Sputnik 1 as it orbited the earth today. This is the start of the "space age" which everyone has been waiting for since both super-powers, America and Russia, said it might be possible to put a man in space within the next ten years and possibly even on the moon before the turn of the century. The engineer in charge, Mr H. Griffiths (standing) is pointing out on a globe the exact position of the satellite as it orbits the earth 500 miles high at a speed of 1,800 mph. Listening to the signal, which can be heard every 90 minutes, is senior operational engineer Mr G. Pearson.*

Six killed, many injured as tower collapses after fire

November 29th: Six people were killed and at least 20 seriously injured today when a 120-foot ventilating shaft collapsed following a fire at Oakwood Hospital, Maidstone. Three of those who died were firemen.

It was 6.30 am when the night superintendent at the mental hospital saw flames in the upper part of the building. Maidstone firefighters were quickly on the scene but, because of the severity of the fire, extra pumps were required.

They had the fire under control within an hour with no harm to the 350 patients who had been evacuated when the blaze first broke out.

Relief crews from West Malling and Loose had just arrived to continue the clearing-up work when the ventilation tower collapsed and buried scores of firemen and hospital staff under tons of brick and rubble. It was not clear how many people were trapped.

Disaster procedures were immediately put into operation. Firemen with special rescue equipment were joined by Civil Defence squads from six Kent towns. Twelve ambulances stood by and took the injured in relays to hospital. The casualty department at West Kent Hospital was cleared of patients to receive the injured.

While rescue workers were digging furiously to reach those trapped, doctors gave morphine injections for the badly injured. It took more than 100 men several hours before the first casualties were reached and it was two days later when the last body was recovered.

The 10th anniversary year of Kent Fire Brigade has not been a happy one. On June 3rd Dreamland's "haunted house" at Margate was destroyed. At the end of July a fire at Bowaters Lloyds Paper Mills, Sittingbourne needed 10 units and 23 jets to bring a paper fire under control.

During the weekend of June 29/30th 250 calls were received to control fires caused by the sparks of passing trains. The total for the year was an unprecedented 1,100 calls.

Firemen take a breather after many hours of exhausting work at Oakwood Hospital.

New diesel trains for Kent: the great age of steam is fading fast

Summer: Two years ago the Transport Act introduced plans for a massive modernisation and investment programme. With the war-damaged Cannon Street station rebuilt, coastal defence work completed at The Warren, Folkestone and diesel-electric locomotives coming out of Ashford's great railway works, that ambitious programme is under way — and it is certain to change the face of Kent's railway network.

A major Kent Coast third-rail electrification scheme has already been given the go-ahead and next week the first diesel trains will be introduced on the Hastings line, via Tunbridge Wells.

To the dismay of enthusiasts all over the county, the decision has been made to progressively withdraw steam traction from Southern Region. In the next few years many stations will be extended or rebuilt.

Some politicians suggest this multi-million pound project will lead to financial crisis, particularly if there is an economic decline, as many in the City are predicting.

Summer: Although Margate and Folkestone continue to be popular, many holidaymakers are deserting the Kent coast and heading for a stretch of coastline in southern Spain called Costa del Sol. They are being lured there by the sun and cheap prices. In one village, called Benidorm, hotels are going up everywhere.

While a crane lifts a carriage in the background, work continues in extracting bodies from the wreckage at St Johns.

92 killed as two trains collide in the fog

December 8th: Ninety-two rail passengers from Kent died on Wednesday (December 4th) when two trains crashed at Lewisham in thick fog under a bridge. On impact one of the coaches reared up smashing the supports of the bridge which then collapsed onto the wrecked coaches. Moments later a third train approached the scene of the disaster. Peering through the fog the motorman saw a girder at an angle and stopped the train just a few feet short of the crumbling edge.

All three trains had been packed with City and West End workers and many Christmas shoppers. Most of the two hundred injured were pinned down in the tangle of concrete and twisted metal.

Ambulancemen, stationed only 200 yards away, were quickly on the scene followed by police, firemen and Royal Engineers. Their task was immense. Scores of the dead and injured were trapped under 500 tons of concrete which acted like the lid of a tomb. This had to be lifted away before help could get through.

The accident occurred at 6.20 pm. Despite the weather a fog service was not in force and trains were running late and out of turn.

The 4.56 fast steam train from Cannon Street to Ramsgate via Folkestone, carrying about 700 passengers, ran into the back of the 5.18 electric from Charing Cross to Hayes which was standing on the up gradient with brakes full on just south of St John's station. The impact was about 30 mph, sufficient to destroy several coaches.

The tender and the front coach of the Ramsgate train were crushed together and thrown left bringing down one of the steel stanchions supporting the overhead bridge carrying the Nunhead-Lewisham loop. The bridge collapsed immediately.

The tragedy immediately threw the whole of the network into total chaos. Hundreds of services were cancelled and commuters either had to stay in London or find alternative ways home. As the dreadful news of the 92 fatalities was broadcast relatives across Kent waited anxiously for news.

Most of the dead and injured came from Tonbridge (first stop) Folkestone, Ashford and Ramsgate.

A spokesman for the Ministry of Transport, who plan to hold an inquiry into the accident, said today that the four lines from New Cross to St John's represent one of the busiest railway sections in the world, with 990 passenger trains in the 24 hours of a normal weekday.

Speculation as to the cause of the tragedy is rife but many believe the driver of the Ramsgate train is responsible. He passed two caution signals after New Cross and made no attempt to stop. Even so experts believe the accident could have been avoided by the use of automatic warning control.

December 6th: *The scene at St John's yesterday as a man in the foreground uses an acetylene cutter on the remains of a carriage as others strive to clear the railway lines of debris. The twisted remains of the fallen viaduct, with supports to prevent it slipping any further, can be seen in the background. At least three more bodies are trapped in the wreckage underneath the girders.*

'The very worst the bomb could do would be to sweep a vast number of people from this world into the other, more vital world, into which anyhow they must all pass at one time' — Geoffrey Fisher on CND.

Put new motorway across downs say angry farmers

The new 25-mile motorway through Kent to the Channel Ports has been welcomed by everyone except the farmers whose land it has to cross.

That land must be lost from farming is inevitable "but", say some of the farmers involved, "why didn't the planners take more trouble in finding out where our boundaries lay and then, where possible, route the new road where it hurts the least"?

The road will run from the Rochester Way — linking with the new Dartford to Purfleet tunnel — across the River Medway, over the Stockbury Valley, through to Bredgar, Milsted and finally join up with the Faversham coast road.

It has been scheduled as a special road and that means there will be no access to it except at roundabouts and flyovers. Farms which have been cut in half will have connecting tunnels or bridges across.

Some farmers have held a protest meeting to suggest the road should be routed over the downs and away from the best low-lying farmland. ***See Page 103***

January 8th: The *Daily Worker,* Britain's last communist newspaper, closed down today.

January 14th: BOAC has awarded Vickers a contract to build the VC-10.

January 29th: Smoking cigarettes is the chief cause of lung cancer, according to a BMA report published today.

February 1st: America today put a satellite called *Explorer* into space. It was developed by a team led by Werner von Braun, the German scientist who masterminded the V2 rocket.

February 6th: Seven members of Manchester United Football Club were killed today in a plane crash on the runway at Munich. The "Busby Babes" as they were known had just qualified for the European Cup semi-finals. Manager Matt Busby is critically ill.

February 8th: The British film *The Bridge Over The River Kwai* has won three film academy awards.

February 17th: "The Campaign For Nuclear Disarmament" was formed in London tonight. They intend to organise protest meetings and regular marches.

February 21st: Manchester United and England star Duncan Edwards died today from injuries received in the plane crash.

March 2nd: West Indian all-rounder, Garfield Sobers today hit a record Test score of 365 not out against Pakistan to beat Len Hutton's 1938 record.

March 12th: The Bishop of Woolwich said that mothers who work are enemies of family life.

March 24th: American Rock 'n Roll star Elvis Presley, who has sold over 40 million records in the last two years, has been drafted into the armed services.

March 27th: Nikita Khrushchev is now Prime Minister of the Soviet Union and secretary of the Communist Party. Yesterday he toppled Marshal Bulganin.

March 28th: The Queen and Prince Philip disembarked at Dover from the Royal Yacht *Britannia.* They visited the castle, town hall and drove to Folkestone.

April 7th: More than 3,000 marchers reached Aldermaston for a CND rally at the gates of the Atomic Weapons Research Establishment.

April 30th: After two years on Broadway, Alan J.Lerner's musical *My Fair Lady*, starring Julie Andrews and Rex Harrison, has opened at Drury Lane.

May 3rd: Manchester United lost the Cup Final today to Bolton, three months after losing eight of their top players at Munich.

May 29th: The Central Electricity Generating Board has selected a site at Dungeness for its next nuclear power station.

June 29th: Brazil has won the World Cup in Stockholm by beating Sweden 5-2.

July 6th: There was a service in Canterbury Cathedral today to mark the Golden Jubilee of the Territorial Army in Kent.

The Dean and Chapter of Canterbury has purchased the remains of the Greyfriars for preservation.

July 26th: Prince Charles has been created Prince of Wales.

August 27th: A new stereophonic recording has been introduced at this year's Radio Show. New words among record enthusiasts include "stereo" and "hi-fi" — high fidelity.

September 18th: Kent Archaeological Society today held its centenary lunch in Maidstone.

October 19th: Mike Hawthorn became the first British motor racing driver to hold the title of world champion. He came second to Stirling Moss in the final Grand Prix at Morocco but wins the championship by a single point.

October 26th: A new airliner, the Boeing 707, flew across the Atlantic just 22 days after the British Comet started its transatlantic service.

November 10th: Donald Campbell, son of the late Sir Malcolm Campbell of Chislehurst, today achieved a new water speed record of 248 mph.

November 23rd: After five years as captain of the Southern League side, Gravesend and Northfleet, the great Jimmy Logie — former Arsenal and Scotland inside forward — plans to retire and spent more time running his local pub, The Greyhound.

December 5th: The eight-mile Preston bypass in Lancashire — Britain's first motorway — was opened today by Harold Macmillan.

Obituary:

Marie Stopes, who lived for a number of years at the Mansion House, Swanscombe, died on October 2nd aged 78. An advocate of birth control, she founded the Mothers' Clinic in London and published in 1918 *Married Love,* a discussion of sexual relations, unusually frank and greeted with uproar. It was a great success.

GREAT HITS OF 1958

Magic Moments

All I HaveTo Do Is Dream

The Gravesend bus ploughs its way through the lake in Crayford caused by the surprise deluge.

North Kent hit by 'storm of the century'

September 6th: In a two-hour thunderstorm which broke over North Kent yesterday, a staggering 5.14 inches of rain fell with such tropical intensity that thousands of pounds worth of damage was caused. It is being described by hydrologists as the "storm of the century".

It started as a tornado in West Sussex where the largest hailstones ever known fell. Guided by upper winds and accompanied by continuous thunder and lightning, it headed into Kent and cut a huge swathe of destruction.

Floods and landslides disrupted trains. The Sevenoaks tunnel was blocked, services between Mottingham and Dartford were suspended and it will be many days before the branch line to Westerham can be reopened.

At Horton Kirby, five acres of hops were ruined and waves of mud 18 inches deep still cover roads at Southfleet.

It was at Southfleet that the one-time River Fleet was brought back to life. Mrs Elsie Cripps of Red Street said: "The electricity went off and I was sitting alone in the dark when I heard a noise like a train coming. The river went straight through the bungalow carrying with it scores of boxes of potatoes from the field."

The rain, amounting to more than 300 tons per acre, was responsible for massive subsidences across North Kent. In Betsham, a crater 50 feet deep and 60 feet wide opened up. At Swanscombe, a man fell 20 feet when a footpath caved in near a disused chalkpit. At Singleton Road, Gravesend, a dene hole was uncovered, under a sun lounge.

In many communities people had to fight for their lives as water poured into ground floor flats. At Farningham, the world-famous giant horse chestnut tree was hit by a swirling torrent from the River Darent and felled.

So severe was this storm that Kent Fire Brigade received 1,345 calls in less than five hours. All personnel were recalled from leave and all AFS units with Green Goddesses mobilised.

At Gravesend, 45 foot ladders had to be used to build a bridge across flood waters to reached trapped people.

At the BP refinery on the Isle of Grain two tanks, each containing crude oil, were struck by lightning. It took 12 appliances and eight water and foam jets to control the ensuing fire.

Restoring the churches of bomb alley

SOME of Kent's finest churches which were so badly damaged during the war are nearing the final stages of restoration. Many others, particularly those in range of the German shells, have been demolished.

One church — at **Little Chart** — victim of a doodlebug has been deliberately left and shored up to remain a symbol of Kent's ordeal between 1940 and 1945. Like all ruined buildings buddleia, willowherb and ivy have taken over. A new church for the people of Little Chart, St Mary of the Holy Rood, has been built in the grounds of Surrenden Dering near the village centre. It was consecrated by the Archbishop of Canterbury in 1956.

Throughout the county, parishes have undertaken the task of raising thousands of pounds; builders have worked many hours.

The most astonishing story concerns the new church at Biggin Hill, half a mile away from the former Battle of Britain station.

Known throughout the area as "the moving church" **St Mark's** was built brick by brick, timber by timber from materials salvaged from the ruins of the church of All Saints in North-East Peckham.

The vicar, the Rev Vivian Symons, is the inspiration behind this remarkable feat. He organised the lorries and and spent many months instructing volunteers on what to take from the derelict site. He then worked closely with the architect, Sir Gilbert Scott and himself made the sacred vessels and ornaments.

Rev Vivian Symonds and the moving church of St Mark's, Biggin Hill

The church is now complete and a dedication service will be held soon.

The Bishop of Rochester, Dr David Chavasse, said this week that the renewed churches will bring fresh hope and courage to all in these days of anxiety. "God must have had a purpose for England in bringing the country through two world wars and now it is up to the people to rise to the challenge of the times and renew their faith."

There was a packed congregation to see the Bishop consecrate the church of **St Peter and St Paul, Bromley.** It was destroyed in 1941, except for the tower which has been restored and married to a new functional body designed by J. Harold Gibbons.

Dr Chavasse said Bromley now had a parish church worthy of the town; it was the very best that had ever stood on the site.

Among Kent's other churches now restored after war damage are **St. Andrew's, Paddock Wood, St Mary's, Shortlands** and **St Nicholas, Deptford.**

The latter, rededicated by the Bishop of Southwark, contains a stone tablet to Christopher Marlowe erected by the county society.

The Archbiship of Canterbury re-dedicated **Hawkhurst Parish Church** in February this year and, in another ceremony, dedicated a new Kent Corner in the church of **St Mary Woolnoth** in the City of London.

Burham Old Church has been restored and **Challock Church,** once little more than a ruin, nears completion. It now contains the chancel screen salvaged from the former church at Eastwell.

One of the biggest projects concerns the rebuilding of **All Saints, Lydd —** the cathedral of Romney Marsh. It was hit by a German bomb in 1940 which destroyed the chancel and damaged the chapels and roofs.

Much of the original Caen stone was saved for reuse but other stone was recovered from the precincts of Canterbury Cathedral and other damaged buildings in the town.

St Laurence, Hawkhurst, another victim of the doodlebug and out of use until February last year. Part of the flying bomb that caused the damage can be seen at the back of the church and a new window to the Glory of God has been dedicated by Archbishop Geoffrey Fisher.

Many of Kent's churches, damaged in the doodlebug attacks of 1944, have now been repaired and one — St Mary of the Holy Rood at Little Chart — entirely rebuilt and placed nearer to the centre of the village (above left). It was consecrated by the Archbishop two years ago. Meanwhile, there are no plans to demolish the ruins of the bombed church one mile away. It will remain as a symbol of Kent's ordeal in the summer of 1944.

Burham Church (above left) stands on its own close to the industrial Medway with the downs magnificent above. A Gothic-revival church, it has now been repaired after bomb damage. Challock Church (above right) in Eastwell Park is also some way from the village and was restored in 1950. The complete east end of the 15th-century church of All Saints, Lydd (right) has been beautifully restored and now includes colourful lancets to the new choir by Leonard Walker. The original tower, commissioned by Cardinal Wolsey, stands proud, 132 feet high.

1958

September 22nd: An Invicta monument, commemorating the famous confrontation between William, Duke of Normandy and the Kentish men, was unveiled today by Lord Cornwallis.

The monument has been erected at Park Corner, Watling Street, Swanscombe on the very spot where, 890 years earlier, the Normans

When Duke William met a forest on the march

encountered what looked like a forest on the march.

The forest turned out to be the Kentish army holding green boughs but heavily armed.

They told William they would offer him their allegiance if he would, in turn, allow them to keep their ancient Saxon laws and privileges granted by Edward the Confessor. Otherwise, they said, he could expect "war most deadly". William, shrewd tactician, chose not to fight, Kent negotiated an honourable partnership and proudly adopted the word Invicta — *Unconquered* — as its motto.

For our lovely debs, the party is over

March 18th: *For many years hundreds of young ladies have been presented at Court and curtsied to the Queen. The debutantes, as they are called — daughters of the aristocracy and those prominent in the community — today travelled to Buckingham Palace for the last time. Prince Philip believes this traditional practice to be archaic and certainly not in keeping with the new Elizabethan age. Here we see (right) Gilly Herapath from Rochester with two friends Camilla Johnson (left) and Caroline Donald-Smith on the way to their presentation in 1956. Gilly is descended from the Woodgates of Somerhill . Henry Woodgate was a director of the Tonbridge bank when it collapsed in the last century.*

Gravesend welcomes Princess Pocahontas

October 5th: A bronze statue of Princess Pocahontas, presented by the people of Virginia in the United States, was unveiled in Gravesend today by the Governor of that American state.

Everyone knows the story of the Princess, daughter of a Red Indian chief, Powhattan, whose courage saved the life of the English captain John Smith when her father had planned to kill him.

John Smith returned to England and Pocahontas was falsely told he had died. She married John Rolfe, came to England and, by chance, met John Smith in London. The shock and grief broke her heart. She died on the eve of leaving Gravesend for home in May 1616 and was buried beneath the chancel of St George's Church. Americans often come to Gravesend to see the stained glass windows presented by the Colonial Dames of Virginia in 1914.

'There came out of the shop a remarkable family: father a perky, sprightly character with sideburns, Ma a handsome woman of enormous girth, shaking with laughter like a jelly' — Kent author H.E.Bates.

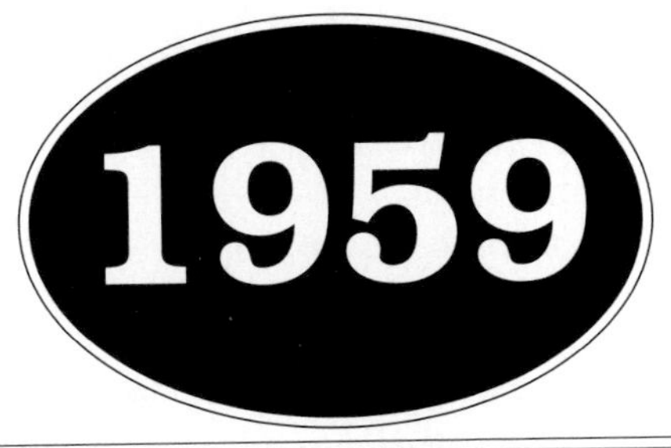

January 2nd: Cuba's rebel leader Fidel Castro has set up a new Government after his two-year-old struggle against the dictator General Fulgencio Batista.

January 22nd: Two-thirds of the adult population of Britain now own a television set, according to a BBC report issued today. ITV continues to be more popular.

January 23rd: Mike Hawthorn, 29-year-old British racing driver and current world champion was killed yesterday in his own car on the Guildford bypass near his home.

January 29th: Road and rail communications throughout Kent have been crippled by winter fog.

February 3rd: The American rock singer Buddy Holly died today in a plane crash in Iowa. Holly, 22, toured Britain last year with his backing group *The Crickets.*

February 5th: England, captained by Peter May, have lost the fourth Test at Adelaide. This means the Ashes change hands.

February 23rd: The fighting has ended in Cyprus with the signing of a peace deal between Greek and Turkish Cypriots. It ends 80 years of British rule.

February 28th: Mr Harold Macmillan, or "Supermac" as he is now nicknamed, arrived today in Moscow for arms talks with Mr Khrushchev.

April 20th: Winston Churchill, now 85, said today that he will stand again for Parliament.

May 2nd: Roy Dwight of Chievely Parade, Belvedere, was one of the heroes of the Cup Final today, scoring for Nottingham Forest in the 2-1 win over Luton Town.

Chevening House, the home of Lord Stanhope, has been vested in the State, with all its contents, following an Act of Parliament.

***August:** The British Motor Corporation's revolutionary new mini-car is on sale in Kent. Designed by Alec Issigonis there will be a Morris and an Austin version costing about £500. Here is an advertisement for the 4-cylinder, 848cc Austin Seven.*

June 17th: The *Daily Mirror* was successfully sued today by Liberace. It follows an article in the Cassandra column implying the American entertainer was homosexual.

Lord Cornwallis, Lord Lieutenant of Kent, has joined the board of Southern Television. The company has a satellite transmitter at Church Hougham, near Dover.

June 26th: World heavyweight champion Floyd Patterson was knocked out yesterday by Swede Ingemar Johansson.

Bexleyheath is celebrating the 100th anniversary of William Morris, the designer and poet who lived at the Red House near Danson Park from 1859, when he married Jane Burden.

August 8th: British Rail were today given the go-ahead to raise railway fares by up to 50 per cent.

August 26th: Manufacturers of radios who use transistors instead of valves and batteries that can run for a year, presented their new portable models to the Earl's Court Radio Show today.

October 4th: Following one of the most glorious summers of the century, temperatures at Dartford reached 82F today.

October 9th: The Tory Government was re-elected today with a majority of more than 100 seats over Labour. Mr Macmillan told his Bromley consituents that it had all gone rather well. Margaret Thatcher, who was unsuccesful at Dartford a few years ago, has eventually secured the seat for Finchley.

October 14th: Hollywood's swashbuckling actor, Errol Flynn, who began his acting career at Northampton Rep, died in Jamaica today at the age of 50.

November 11th: The film *Ben Hur,* starring Charlton Heston, which has won 11 Oscars, opens in Britain today.

GREAT HITS OF 1959

What Do You Want To Make Those Eyes At Me For

Living Doll

Sheriff dies as he takes office

May 29th: A few minutes after he had been elected Sheriff of Canterbury on Saturday, Cllr Gilbert H.G. Kennett collapsed and died.

Sheriff Kennett, aged 66, a former pupil of the Simon Langton Boys' School and an authority on antique clocks, had been seriously ill but felt well enough to take the office of Sheriff.

Chiefly associated with such "outlaws" as Robin Hood and the city of Nottingham, the office of Sheriff is ancient and of Saxon origin. He was once the chief law enforcement officer of the Crown but today the Sheriff has little power and the holder is considered very much a municipal odd job man.

From a junk yard to a best seller: 'perfick', says Pop

March: A short story written last year by the Kent novelist Herbert Ernest Bates, "H.E.", as he is better known, has become such a phenomenal success that it is in demand all over the world and may soon become a stage play.

The book is called *The Darling Buds of May*, in which the unconventional natures of Pop and Ma Larkin and their children are unashamedly revealed.

H.E. said this week that he had long been fascinated by a rural junkyard he used to pass two or three times a week. Its crazy mess of old iron, rusting implements, pigs, horses, geese, turkeys and haystacks sat incongruously next to the most beautiful bluebell wood. "The junk mocked the beauty", he said, "and the bluebells mocked the junk". Later he came face to face with the inhabitants, the remarkable Larkin family who looked as if they had come out of Merrie England. The eldest and most beautiful girl, unmarried, is revealed as being pregnant, but exactly by whom she doesn't know. Does it matter? Not on your life — 'perfick', says Pop.

H.E. Bates and his wife Madge live at Little Chart Forstal, near Pluckley in a converted barn, The Granary, which was in desperate need of repair when they moved in 28 years ago. Today the house is a beauty and the garden rich in maturity.

During the war he worked in RAF public relations and helped to immortalise The Few in short stories under the pseudonym of *Flying Officer X* which sold two million copies.

Other Bates' classics include *Fair Stood the Wing for France*, a love story amid the terror of the resistance; *The Purple Plain* and *The Jacaranda Tree*, both set in Burma and *Love for Lydia* which is partly autobiographical.

See page 179

H.E. Bates writes most of his books in a garden chalet at his home in Little Chart Forstal, near Pluckley. He has lived there since 1931.

Our 'Enery is champion of Europe

January 13th: **Thousands of his supporters from Lewisham and Catford were at Earl's Court last night to see the popular, likeable lad from South London, Henry Cooper, become British and Empire heavyweight champion.**

"Our 'Enery", as he is called along the Old Kent Road, scored a well-deserved points victory over Brian London from Blackpool after 15 punishing rounds. His eye was badly cut and his trainer fears that it might become a hallmark.

With a first title under his belt, Cooper has ambitions to fight for the world title currently held by Floyd Patterson. The American, however, has a tough date with Swedish heavyweight Ingemar Johansson in June — so Henry will have to wait.

Frank Muir with his wife, Polly — a photograph taken in 1954.

Where will Frank take it from here?

The popular show *Take It From Here,* which epitomised a golden period of radio comedy, has now ended its long run stretching back to 1947 when two young writers, Frank Muir and Denis Norden, introduced The Glum family and a number of other topical sketches.

The success of the show has given Ramsgate-born Frank Muir an opportunity to write more witty entertainment in collaboration with his partner and branch into other areas of radio and television.

Muir, now 39, was born in the Derby Arms Hotel which was then kept by his grandmother. His mother and father, Charles and Margaret, later moved to Thanet Lodge and young Frank went to Stone House School, Broadstairs.

He was drawn into show business following a fascination with the regular Ramsgate beach entertainers, many of whom he liked to imitate. On one occasion he entered a talent contest and sang *White Cargo* accompanied by Uncle Mac on his banjo. Frank modestly disclaims a victory but locals remember differently.

Frank was a photographer with the RAF during the war but after demob he joined the Windmill Theatre, that remarkable breeding ground for talent, where comedians such as Jimmy Edwards and Alfred Marks vied with nude girls for the attention of the audience. His now-legendary creative partnership with Denis Norden followed — almost springing out of postwar austerity.

Lewisham disaster: train driver acquitted

The driver of the Cannon Street to Ramsgate train which ran into the back of an electric train in December, 1957— killing 92 people and injuring more than 200 — has been formally acquitted of manslaughter in view of his mental and physical state.

Mr Bill Trew, of 20 St David's Road, Ramsgate, first appeared at the Central Criminal Court last year when the jury was told that he was a driver of vast experience with 45 years' service on the railways. He had been driving Battle of Britain class engines for 13 years and was described by his supervisors at the Ramsgate Motive Power Depot as loyal, conscientious, reliable and sober.

Among those to give evidence at the original hearing was the fireman Mr Cyril Hoare, of Highfield Road, Ramsgate — well known as a keen local footballer. The jury heard that the stunned crew worked for over an hour carrying bucketfuls of damp earth from the embankment and pouring them onto the fire box, fearing that the engine might explode.

At the resumed hearing the prosecution offered no evidence. Mr Trew was acquitted.

At last: electric trains to the Kent coast

April 3rd: Canterbury's first electric train pulled out of the East Station this morning cheered by a group of children on a trial run to Selling. It was the first to be made in preparation for the full electric service beginning in June.

During the trip to test the current-carrying third rail a stop was made at Chartham Hatch crossroads where there were more cheering children. As it sped through Selling tunnel the walls were lit up by brilliant blue flashes caused as the pick-up shoes met dust and rust on the live rail.

The great electrification scheme, approved by the British Transport Commission in 1956 is almost complete. It has cost millions of pounds.

First phase was the lines from Gillingham to Ramsgate, Sittingbourne to Sheerness and Faversham to Dover Marine — a total of 178 miles. Phase two comprised the lines from Sevenoaks to Tonbridge, Ashford, Dover, Deal and Ramsgate, Paddock Wood to Maidstone West, Maidstone East to Ashford and Ashford to Canterbury West — 132 miles.

With new footbridges, sidings and platform extensions it will be three years before this massive programme is fully completed.

Hovering across the Channel on just a cushion of air

July 25th: Fifty years to the day after Louis Bleriot's great pioneering flight from Calais to Dover, a new hero has crossed the great watery divide — and this one is an Englishman!

Mr Christopher Cockerell, the 49-year-old inventor of the hovercraft, was with the crew on board his Mark 1 prototype as it crossed from Dover on its initial passenger journey.

His revolutionary new concept of a vehicle that will travel on a cushion of air moved quickly from drawing board into realistic development.

The first two-ton Hovercraft was constructed by Saunders Roe on the Isle of Wight. Trials carried out in June were so successful that the government-backed National Research and Development Corporation gave its backing.

Mr Cockerell, a Suffolk boat builder by trade, has ambitious plans. They include the design of a 100-ton hovercraft capable of carrying passengers and, after that a 1,000-ton version which could be used for carrying freight. *See P 130*

Here is a list of the Channel pioneers up to date:

Jean Blanchard in a hydrogen balloon, Jan 1785.
Matthew Webb by swimming, August 1875.
S.F.Cody in a "kite boat", November 1903.
Louis Bleriot in a monoplane, July 1909.
Charles Rolls, first to fly both ways, June 1910.
Harriet Quimby, first female aviator, April 1912.

'Death Hill' claims another five lives

November 5th: Deaths on the roads in Kent have reached an appallingly high level. Every town now has its black spots and pressure on the highways authority to build more bypasses grows with every fatality reported.

One of the worst areas is the A20 at Gorse Hill, Farningham, known locally as "murder mile" or "death hill". This week alone three died in separate accidents which means the hill has now claimed the lives of five people in nine days. Two years ago four were killed when a car collided with a coach.

Swanley is another notorious black spot and here villagers are planning a protest march in favour of a bypass. In just a few years eight people have been killed on the A20 just trying to cross the road.

Kent's regiments return with more battle honours

February: There has been no respite from front-line duty for soldiers of the two Kent regiments. With the return of The Buffs from Aden and the Queen's Own Royal West Kents from Cyprus the stage is now set for their amalgamation which was first announced two years ago.

A family spirit animates the two regiments and it is entirely fitting that two long and illustrious histories should end with successful campaigns in the Middle East.

The Queen's Own 1st Battalion has been on anti-terrorist duties in Cyprus since 1957 and how well they succeeded is summed up by the island's Governor, Sir Hugh Foot who said "the West Kents have been in the thick of the troubles and answered every call made upon them magnificently".

The 1st Battalion of The Buffs returned from Aden this month. Since they moved to the Protectorate a year ago they have been involved in the much-publicised swoop on the town of Lahej for the arrest of Nasser's agents, taken part in the Battle of Jihaf and ended with anti-riot duties.

A photograph taken a few years ago of the Queen Mother (then the Queen) at Biggin Hill when she was Honorary Air Commodore of 600 Auxiliary Squadron. The old airfield is still operational but only for one day each year when a spectacular "At Home" display is held close to September 15th. It was on this day in 1940 that Hitler sent over massive formations of bombers and fighters in a bid to "wipe the RAF from the map".

Biggin Hill's farewell to the fighters

October: An eerie silence has fallen across two of the most famous wartime airfields in the south-east with the news that the RAF will no longer fly from Biggin Hill and Detling has completely closed

For Detling the decision was not a surprise. The old aerodrome in heavily wooded country on top of the North Downs has long been the headquarters of Kent Gliding Club — and ceased to be operational as long ago as December 1944. It will now become a permanent site for the annual Kent County Agricultural Show.

For Biggin Hill, perhaps the best-known fighter station in the world, the news was at first received with almost disbelief. This was a senior sector station — one of the ramparts from which The Few launched their attack against the Luftwaffe and guarded the southern approaches to London. More than 1,600 enemy aircraft were shot down by the pilots of the Biggin Hill wing.

The decision to turn the airfield into the headquarters of the Ground Officer Selection Centre was made some time after the Auxiliary squadrons of 600 and 615 left and 41 Squadron flew on alone. It quickly became clear that this crowded air space was not the ideal location for manned fighters. 41 Squadron amalgamated with 141 and, in April, the selection centre staff moved from Uxbridge.

With their departure a significant era in Kentish history ends. Changes, too, are affecting the other stations. For many years Hawkinge has been a depot for the Womens Royal Air Force and houses a gliding centre, West Malling is the home of 29 Squadron flying Javelins — but the future is uncertain — and Gravesend is a large private housing estate with two schools and a sports centre.

Manston alone flies the flag, although the United States Air Force has left. In March it was announced that the aerodrome would again become part of No 11 Group Fighter Command with the civilian side expanding rapidly.

1959

Teenagers! The name that was born in the fifties

On one of the many rubble-strewn bomb sites which still exist all over north Kent, four girls in jackets and trousers, pointed shoes and neck scarves, prove that the new teenage fashion culture is not the exclusive domain of the boys. Market research has shown that girls now have money to spend and they spend it on records, cosmetics, clothes and going to the cinema.

They adore not only Elvis Presley and Bill Hayley but home-grown talent such as Tommy Steele, Vince Eager, Billy Fury and Marty Wilde. Another one is Cliff Richard, whose real name is Harry Webb, and who made his name in the musical satire *Expresso Bongo.*

The girls hang out with the boys in Italian-style coffee bars all over Kent. Each town has its steaming, frothy, Gaggia machine-dispensing coffee shop where the juke boxes play the latest chart-toppers. For several months now High Streets have resounding to the distinctive strains of Guy Mitchell *Singing The Blues,* Lonnie Donnegan *Puttin' On The Style* and Adam Faith asking *What D'ya Want Make Those Eyes At Me For.*

When the fifties began there were no teenagers, just children and students. Now teenagers have a name and an identity and they are often at odds with their parents who find that pre-war values are clashing badly with these casual attitudes.

There is hardly a town in Kent without a "teenage problem". The era of the Teddy Boys with their flick knives and bicycle chains is passing. Now it is the age of the motorbike which proclaims a kind of individual mastery, group solidarity, noise, speed, risks. It's also the age of racial tension and youthful cynicism.

Parents, wishing to impose a wartime discipline, are failing badly. They yearn for the social cohesion of the Blitz. But those days are gone.

'An army of ghouls who pour out of the slums, stews and ghettos and drag their misshapen bodies along the byways of a countryside which does not want them' — author Jack London on hoppers.

February 3rd: Addressing the South African Parliament in Capetown, Prime Minister Harold Macmillan said that "a wind of change is blowing through the African continent". He urged the country to move towards policies of racial equality.

February 26th: 400 miners, who staged a stay-down strike at Betteshanger Colliery in protest at the NCB decision to sack 140 men and were underground for 160 hours, are now planning to march to the House of Commons to get the dismissal notices suspended. *See pages 135 & 178*

February 19th: The Queen gave birth to a son, Prince Andrew Albert Christian Edward.

February 22nd: Subscriber trunk dialling inaugurated in Kent as the mayor of Chatham dialled the mayor of Portsmouth from the Medway Telephone Exchange at Chatham.

March 1st: An earthquake, followed by a tidal wave, destroyed the Moroccan resort of Agadir today and killed at least 1,000 people.

March 14th: The Government announced that a barrier will be built across the Thames to protect the capital from tidal flooding. It will cost in the region of £17 million.

March 21st: 56 Africans died and 162 were injured as police opened fire in the black township of Sharpeville in the Transvaal.

April 1st: A state of emergency now exists in South Africa. Britain refused to condemn the country at a meeting of the U.N.

April 25th: Ten black people were shot dead in the worst ever race riots in Mississippi.

A statue to Lord Kitchener has been unveiled in Chatham.

May 7th: Lord Bossom of Maidstone is elected President of the Kent County Society.

May 16th: A Bill to curb the activities of Teddy Boys is given a second reading in the House of Commons

A book published last year by Richard Church , The Crab Apple Tree, *has earned him the description of the Laureate of the Weald. The story is centred around his home at Curtisden Green. A few years ago his biography of childhood* Over the Bridge *was critically acclaimed and shortly afterwards he was awarded the CBE.*

May 17th: Senator John F. Kennedy of Massachusetts has won the Democratic nomination for the Presidential elections. The fight against the Republicans' Richard Nixon can now begin.

May 17th: The Queen Mother started the hydro-electric turbines of the Kariba Dam and said it was a marvel of modern engineering.

May 25th: Charles II Walk on Dover seafront is opened.

June 18th: King Christian of Denmark presented new colours to the 4th and 5th Battalions of The Buffs at Shorncliffe.

June 20th: Floyd Patterson today beat Ingemar Johansson to regain the world heavyweight boxing title.

June 30th: Following years of bitterness and acrimony, the independence of the former Belgian Congo was announced today.

July 6th: Aneurin Bevan, the controversial politician and the Labour Party's finest orator, died of cancer aged 62.

A number of Punjabi families have arrived in Kent to pick strawberries. They say they do not want to return to India.

September 8th: Britain has won two gold medals in the Rome Olympics — Don Thompson in the 50 kilometre walk and Anita Lonsborough for the 200 metres breaststroke.

Work has commenced on the motorway bridge over the Medway at Borstal. The central span will measure 150 metres.

October 17th: The *News Chronicle* has closed and merged with the *Daily Mail.*

October 19th: The villagers of Swanley have marched up the A20 to demand a by-pass. In recent years eight people have died just trying to cross this road.

October 21st: Britain's first nuclear submarine, *Dreadnought,* launched by the Queen.

November 2nd: Penguin Books, prosecuted over the publication of Lady Chatterley's Lover, has won this test case at the Old Bailey. The judge has ruled that the D.H.Lawrence novel, banned for 30 years, is not obscene.

November 9th: John F. Kennedy, aged 43, today became the youngest President of the United States, securing a narrow victory over Richard Nixon.

The 97th (Kent) Yeomanry has combined with the County of London Yeomanry.

December 2nd: Vivien Leigh and Sir Laurence Olivier have been divorced.

December 15th: The Edward Harris Gold Medal for service to Kent was presented to Lord Cornwallis.

There has been an alarming outbreak of vandalism on Kent's electric trains with upholstery slashed and fittings broken or removed. There have also been 178 cases of schoolboys throwing stones at passing trains.

GREAT HITS OF 1960

Cathy's Clown

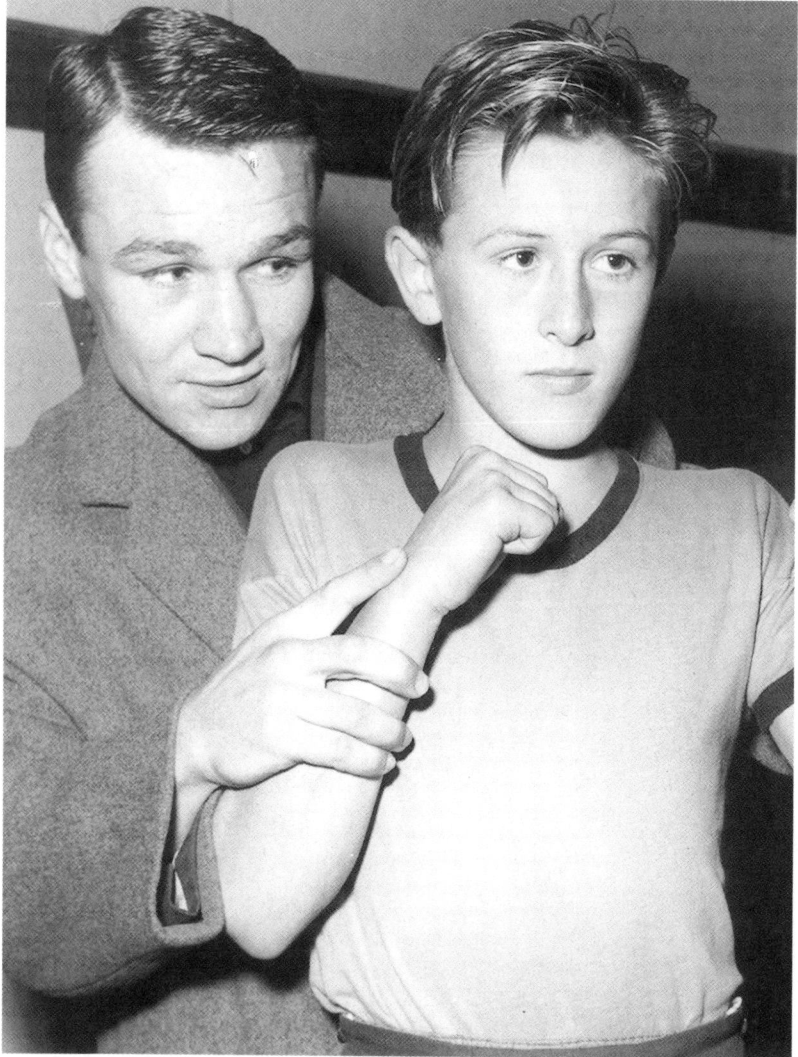

Dave Charnley gives a little advice to Brian Pattison, 15, of Northfleet, who was the national schoolboy champion of Great Britain when this picture was taken just over a year ago.

Dartford salutes the 'destroyer'

March 15th: The man they call the "Dartford Destroyer" yesterday added the European lightweight crown to his growing list of boxing triumphs.

Dave Charnley defeated Earl Hubble at Wembley and is now British and European champion. Only a few months ago he annexed the Empire title by knocking out Willie Toweel in the tenth round.

Charnley, son of Mr and Mrs W. Charnley of Attlee Drive, Dartford, is a southpaw with an aggressive all-action style. He lives in Bexleyheath with his wife Ruth and is enjoying both his heroic status and new-found wealth. Newspapers call him the "Pocket Hercules".

Born in 1935, he was a schoolboy champion in 1954, ABA featherweight holder in 1954 and won a gold in the Empire Games in the same year.

He worked for J. and E. Hall until turning professional in 1956.

Hop-picking machines may soon replace the Cockneys

September: It seems impossible to believe that sights like the one on the right may soon be seen only in picture books of bygone Kent — but it's true. The advent of mechanical hop-picking means the annual East End invaders will no longer be required.

It will be sad to see the end of this great Kentish tradition. The Cockneys bring with them great skills and a junketing as colourful as the wine harvests of the Continent.

Many Kentish hop farmers have already installed machines — both mobile and static — and they find the price of picking per bushel is much cheaper. Mr J.A.Worley of Court Lodge Farm, Yalding, installed a KEF Rotabank last year and says the throughput of the machine is from three to four thousand bushels an hour and it takes only 12 people to operate it.

"21 people and a machine can achieve the work of 200 hand pickers", he said. "The present price of a bushel is 1s 3d. With machines that is reduced to 4d."

Many hop villages have supplied their own local pickers but the most boisterous group have always been the Londoners, pouring into the areas where they were really needed — especially around Paddock Wood, Yalding, Marden, Hunton, Horsmonden, Goudhurst and the hop-growing belt between Faversham and Canterbury around Selling, Chilham and Molash.

The majority of locals seem delighted that machines are replacing the Londoners. One lady from Selling recalled: "They bring all their dirty,

continued

The two sisters, pictured here a couple of years ago, Mrs Mary Wright, 64, and Mrs Alice Smith, 68, come from Millwall and, like hundreds of their friends, they are regular visitors to Nettlestead Farm, Paddock Wood.

filthy, stinking bedding with them — and bugs and bed bugs.

"They are as lousy as cuckoos."

Another lady, from Laddingford, with unsavoury memories said: "We are in constant dread of being infected by fleas and I remember the council issuing free diarrhoea tablets to the locals to protect them from the side-effects of the habits of Londoners."

This year's annual hop festival at the Whitbread Hop Farm, Beltring, may be the last which means that "Beltring Bill" from Stepney will retire unconquered as the Yard of Ale drinking champion.

It will also mean the end of the popular songs, colourful language and high spirits which the Londoners have injected into the quiet rural society since the middle of the last century.

A photograph of the vertical-lift bridge under construction taken from one of the 200-foot towers that now span the River Swale. On the right is the old bridge, still in use.

Sheppey gives thanks for new Kingsferry Bridge

April 13th: The first rising-platform bridge to be built in 25 years was opened today by Princess Marina on the only road to the Isle of Sheppey.

The original bridge — the only link between the island and the mainland — was built 100 years ago and has been damaged many times. On each occasion the traffic was held up for days, sometimes weeks, and a ferry was the only form of contact.

The old bridge was built under the guidance of Sir Benjamin Baker who was the consulting engineer for the Forth Bridge. The builders of the new bridge are also concerned with the new Forth Bridge.

The Kingsferry Bridge, as it is called, will link Sheppey with Sittingbourne over the River Swale. Costing £1,300,000 it has a roadway nearly 100 feet wide with a vertical lift on the central span which rises 95 feet above the water. Operation is by electricity.

Sheerness Dockyard closes — and so does a way of life

March 31st: After nearly 300 years as a naval base and a place of employment for thousands of men Sheerness Dockyard has closed. In a sad but moving ceremony, led by the band of the Royal Marines, the flag which has fluttered over some of England's greatest warships was lowered for the last time. A strange silence has settled over the town as a way of life comes to an end.

From sunset today the owners of the naval dockyard will be the Sheerness Harbour Company, whose chairman Mr David Finnie was presented with a wooden replica key.

The decision to close the dockyard, purely on the grounds of economy, is not a surprise; in fact it had been expected for many years.

The net result, however, is a disaster for the island and especially Sheerness, for the dockyard has been the sole livelihood of the town. Already there is acute unemployment, shops and cinemas have closed and the High Street — once a seething mass of people — is deserted.

Blue Town, the area of small wooden houses where the dockyard families have lived for so many years, is to be demolished and replaced by flats. The residents have been promised new houses but the majority are terrified. "We lived like one large happy family", said one former dockyard wife. "We knew poverty and illness and hard work. But we also knew neighbourliness, loyalty and warmth."

Built in 1665, the dockyard's greatest years were during the Napoleonic Wars when a new threat to the country's security arose, not only from France but from a serious mutiny in the Nore. In 1805 the body of Nelson returned home to Sheerness in a barrel of alcohol from HMS Victory. He was taken to Chatham and thence to Greenwich.

The dockyard developed as a naval base from 1813 and became full of the famous hulks which were such a familiar sight to Dickens off Upnor. The main anchorage was in Stangate Creek where they were used for hospitals, houseboats, quarantine, prisoners of war and convicts. For the last few years the Dockyard has been engaged in the repair of small warships.

May 23rd: The Kent team takes the field in the match against Yorkshire at the Bat and Ball ground, Gravesend, where the future of county cricket is under considerable threat. Left to right Halfyard, Cowdrey, Leary, Jones, Wilkinson, Catt, Dixon, Brown, Wilson, Richardson and Ridgway.

Kent wins by an innings on the first day

June 15th: Kent Cricket Club never fails to surprise. In the first season since the war without Godfrey Evans who has decided to pack away his gloves, with Fred Ridgway injured and with Colin Cowdrey — now England captain — completely out of touch, the county has stunned the cricketing world.

Yesterday at Tunbridge Wells they bowled Worcestershire out twice to win by an innings — in ONE day! The heroes were Dave Halfyard and Alan Brown who took 18 of the 20 wickets to fall. Replying to Kent's all-out 187 the Midlands side scored 25 and 61 and immediately complained about the state of the Neville Ground pitch.

Kent are climbing up the table but are certainly missing "Godders" who was awarded the CBE in the New Year's Honours. Since he made his debut in 1939 this great stumper has bagged more than 1,000 victims. They include 219 for England and he has played in 91 Tests.

There is now a keen contest for his place between Edenbridge's Tony Catt and the Charlton footballer, Derek Ufton, who is the better bat.

If the responsibility of captaining England is proving a burden for Cowdrey, then he is pleased with the form of his Test colleague, Peter Richardson, who has joined Kent from Worcestershire and is making lots of runs. So are the younger players, Alan Dixon — recently awarded his county cap — and Peter Jones. Bob Wilson and Arthur Phebey are as reliable as ever and Kent's second Charlton footballer, Stuart Leary, is making a solid contribution.

Ridgway has also said he will retire at the end of the season having obtained a permanent job in industry. Since his debut in 1946 he has been Kent's only bowler of real pace. He has taken more than 900 wickets and only Blythe, Fielder, Freeman, Hearne, Woolley and Wright have taken more.

Kent desperately needs more younger players. Derek Underwood (16) and Alan Knott (15), who have both been capped for Kent schools, are likely prospects and second eleven players like Mike Denness, Brian Luckhurst and David Nicholls may come through.

The old (nearest to the camera) and new Dungeness lighthouses can be clearly seen on the seaward side of the complex building works where Britain's great nuclear power station begins to take shape. Due to open in 1966, this massive development is a symbol of the modern age. It will be linked to the National Grid by more than 400,000 volt lines supplying the South Coast and London.

Trinity House opens new lighthouse at Dungeness

June 29th: Three Royal Navy frigates patrolled the sea off Dungeness today as the Duke of Gloucester, Master of Trinity House, opened the first lighthouse to be built in Britain for 50 years.

The lighthouse on the site of the old fog signal and the low light structure, rises to a height of 140 feet. The tower is of revolutionary design and fitted with a rotating AGA Gearless Pedestal light whose intensity is equivalent to four million candela and has a range of 27 miles.

The new lighthouse is necessary because of the rapidly receding sea and the fact that one navigation light will soon be partly obscured by the new power station.

The old lighthouse was built in 1904 to supersede the one built in 1702.

November 5th: Following a week of monsoon-type rain much of Kent is under water again. Yesterday the Medway burst its banks and shop workers and residents in vulnerable areas of Maidstone were evacuated. East Peckham and Yalding are under water and food supplies are being delivered by the vicar in an amphibious vehicle. It's the same story along the Rother and Stour valleys. Scores of Kent villages are badly flooded and parts of Canterbury are under water. Firemen are now faced with their largest pumping operation since February 1953. Many areas of the country are on a state of emergency and John Wells, MP for Maidstone, is to support a motion in the House to launch a national disaster fund.

Last civilian soldier falls in as conscription is abolished

December 31st: Conscription — the word that has struck terror into the lives of thousands of young men and is more associated with cold showers, square bashing, parade grounds and military discipline — is to end.

The last national servicemen received their call-up cards today bringing the total number of men enlisted since the scheme began in 1939 to more than five million.

A number of Kent's young men are among the last intake. They received their Ministry of Labour papers a few months ago requiring them to attend a medical examination at the Drill Hall, Boundary Road, Chatham.

Those joining the army will be based in Aldershot with Southern Command. The air force recruits will go through RAF Reception Centre at Cardington.

The compulsory enrolment of young men into military service has been the chief means of staffing European armies since the time of Napoleon. It was first introduced in Britain in 1916 and re-introduced on the day war broke out again — September 3rd, 1939.

The draft act continued to be applied after the war. Every young man in Kent, unless he was medically unfit or a conscientious objector, was enlisted for a two-year period of military training. There have been unsuccessful attempts at resisting the patrol ground regime and several cases of AWOL but most men have accepted the discipline and demands.

Several conscripts have joined the regular army in such hot-spots as Malaya, Korea, Cyprus, Aden, Egypt and Kenya. Other, more lucky ones, have found themselves in peaceful climes.

***August 1st:** The Bank Holiday scene today on Death Hill, Farningham, as motorists anxiously make their way to the new Grand Prix circuit at Brands Hatch.*

Roads jammed as thousands flock to Brands Hatch

August 1st: Kent police and the motoring organisations say they have never seen a traffic jam like it. Thousands of cars, two deep, stretched from Eltham to West Kingsdown as motorists inched their way towards the new circuit at Brands Hatch which has been upgraded to Grand Prix status with the track extended to 2.65 miles.

Many were unable to complete the journey but those who did saw Formula One motor racing given a glorious send-off on a track that was once used only by cyclists.

It was appropriate that the winner of the first Formula One race at Brands Hatch should be the Australian world champion Jack Brabham who took the Silver City trophy and £400 cash prize with an exhibition of immaculate driving in his Cooper Climax.

British driver, Graham Hill finished second to take the £200 prize and New Zealander, Bruce McLaren was third for £100.

Brabham did not have things all his own way. For 21 laps he was hotly pursued by 21-year-old Scot, Jimmy Clark, who is new to Grand Prix racing. Clark had to retire when his Lotus Climax developed gearbox trouble but he showed great promise.

Brabham's time for the 50 laps was one hour 25 minutes and 36 seconds but Clark had the honour of sharing with Brabham the fastest lap speed, an incredible 92.86 mph.

Among the 60,000 plus spectators at Brands Hatch was Stirling Moss, the runner-up in the world championship in four successive seasons between 1955 and 1958.

See page 117

'I want to manage those four boys. It wouldn't take more than two half days a week' — record shop owner and former RADA student Brian Epstein about a Liverpool pop group, *The Beatles.*

January 30th: An oral contraceptive pill is now available for women.

February 1st: The Right Rev Richard David Say has been enthroned as the 104th Bishop of Rochester. Born in 1914, educated at Cambridge and ordained in 1939, Bishop Say has enjoyed a distingished theological career. He was rector at Hatfield, Herts and for many years secretary of the Church of England Youth Council. Before coming to Rochester he was hon Canon at St Albans. He lives in Wye with his wife Irene.

February 6th: Spurs captain, Danny Blanchflower, today refused to appear on the BBC programme *This Is Your Life.*

February 8th: BBC radio is to drop the programme *Children's Hour* which has been a regular feature since 1922.

March 8th: Conductor Sir Thomas Beecham, who founded 4 orchestras including the Royal Philharmonic, has died aged 81.

March 31st: The Nore Command has been abolished, the last Commander-in-Chief being Admiral Sir Robin Durnford - Slater.

April 12th: Russian Major, Yuri Gagarin, aged 27, became the first man to fly in space. He orbited the earth in his Vostok spaceship and returned safely after a flight lasting 98 minutes.

April 19th: Armed Cuban exiles today attempted to overthrow the Marxist Government of Fidel Castro with an invasion at the Bay of Pigs. The incident sparked off a wave of international tension as US President John Kennedy and Soviet leader Nikita Krushchev exchanged serious personal messages.

Land at Bromley has been valued at £1 million an acre.

May 6th: Tottenham has become the first team this century to win the FA Cup and League double. Today they beat Leicester City 2-0 in the Cup Final.

Scenes like this have been common in Maidstone town centre since the early 1920s. With the completion of the bypass —seven miles long, three flyovers, 13 major bridges and a dual 24 foot carriageway —traffic (estimated to be 60,000 vehicles daily) will no longer plague the town centre and the pedestrianisation of Week Street can go ahead. The new road has cost £1.5m.

May 5th: Alan B.Shepard, a commander in the US Navy, completed a 15-minute sub-orbital flight which took him 115 miles above the earth.

May 18th: Princess Marina has been appointed the first Chancellor of the newly formed University of Kent at Canterbury.

June 4th: The price of cigarettes has increased to 1s 9d for ten.

July 2nd: Ernest Hemingway, who was stationed in Kent during the war, committed suicide early this morning. He was 62.

July 12th: The Government has granted £1 million towards the establishment of a National Theatre.

July 8th: Angela Mortimer beat Christine Truman 4-6, 6-4, 7-5 in an all-British women's final at Wimbledon today.

July 11th: Cockney Terry Downes won the world middleweight title by beating holder Paul Pender at Wembley.

July 31st: Mr Macmillan has announced that Britain had applied to join the Common Market.

August 31st: The Communists have built a wall across the western sectors of Berlin outraging Western powers. The Foreign Office say it is contrary to the four-power status of Berlin.

September 17th: More than 800 people have been arrested following the biggest "ban-the-bomb" demonstration ever seen. Among those held are John Osborne and Vanessa Redgrave.

September 18th: Dag Hammarskjoeld, the UN Secretary-General, has died. The DC6 airliner in which he was a passenger crashed in Northern Rhodesia.

September 27th: The ninth HMS Kent, a 6,200-tons guided missile destroyer, has been launched at Belfast by Princess Marina.

Builders have completed the rebuilding of the Longmarket at Canterbury.

October 3rd: Anthony Armstrong-Jones has been created the Earl of Snowdon.

December 8th: A converter station has been opened at Lydd for the transmission of electricity under the English Channel.

Hawkinge, one of the most famous and heavily bombed of Kent's forward fighter stations, closed today when the Officer Cadets Training Unit move to Jurby. *See page 146.*

December 15th: The former SS Colonel, Adolf Eichmann, has been sentenced to hang for the murder of millions of Jews during the Nazi occupation of Europe. The sentence comes 19 months after his capture in the Argentine.

Jezreel's great tower, a prominent landmark in Gillingham for almost 70 years, has been demolished. It was built at the top of Chatham Hill for the Jezreelites — a sect founded by Michael Keyfor Mills which at one time had more than 1,500 members. During the demolition a workman was killed.

OBITUARY

Charles Hamilton, 86, who created Billy Bunter, the greedy fat boy of Greyfriars School, has died at his home in Broadstairs. Under the non-de-plume Frank Richards he appeared in the *Guinness Book of Records* as one of the most prolific writers ever, his lifetime output totalling 72 million words.

GREAT HITS OF 1961

You Don't Know

Wooden Heart

Coronation was his finest hour

January 18th: Geoffrey Fisher (pictured right) 73, Archbishop of Canterbury since his predecessor William Temple died in 1944, has announced his resignation just weeks after his historic meeting with Pope John Paul XXIII in Rome. Downing Street received the news yesterday.

Archbishop Fisher has been involved in some of the greatest political and social issues of the century and has never failed to give advice or speak his mind. They include the Suez crisis, the law in relation to homosexuality, marriage and the introduction of premium bonds which he strongly opposed.

His finest hour came in June 1953 when he conducted the Coronation ceremony at Westminster Abbey with great dignity and an obvious concern for the welfare of the young Queen. She and other members of the Royal Family sought his advice freely and he once said: "I who am no courtier by nature at all found myself at ease with them."

During his archiepiscopate he became widely travelled and, because of the advent of television, the best known in Anglican history. He visited all five Continents and was particularly well-known in the United States.

Archbishop Fisher's relationship with the press was not good. He criticised them on several occasions for abusing their freedom. However, he fostered close person-to-person relationships with successive prime ministers, Sir Winston Churchill, Anthony Eden and Harold Macmillan.

Last year he became the first Archbishop of Canterbury to visit the Holy See since 1397. Fisher said: "We talked as two happy people who had seen a good deal of the world and of life, and of the churches."

Michael Ramsay, Archbishop of York, is the new primate

January 19th: Michael Ramsay, aged 56, Archbishop of York and a former Liberal candidate for Cambridgeshire, has been appointed the new Archbishop of Canterbury. He will be enthroned on June 27th.

Ramsay, born in Cambridge, took holy orders in 1925. He was ordained to the curacy of St Nicholas, Liverpool, became vicar of a parish in Cambridge and was chosen in 1940 to be professor of divinity at Durham University.

His rise to the top has been meteoric. Professor of divinity at Cambridge, canon and prebendary of Lincoln Cathedral, Bishop of Durham and then York. His colourful personality — and his bald dome — was introduced to the nation during the televised Coronation when he stood to the Queen's right.

See page 189

King's School gives three cheers for boy who stammered

September 21st: When Somerset Maugham was a pupil at King's School, Canterbury and lived with his uncle in the vicarage at Whitstable, he was an unhappy child. For a long time he spoke only French, was inflicted with a speech impediment, had no desire to enter the church, as his guardian wished, and left with few academic qualifications.

That same boy returned on Saturday to his old school to bequeath his private collection of books and present a library to keep them in. The whole school turned out to meet him.

The little boy who stammered left King's in 1890 at the age of 16. By the time he was 49 he had earned the description of "the most famous living Englishman". As a novelist and playwright his books had sold in excess of 64 million copies.

Maugham admitted on Saturday that he was unhappy at school and the vicarage but discovered that travel was his escape. That became a lifelong habit. As he travelled he read and wrote.

His first book, *Liza of Lambeth,* was followed by a number of witty comedies which were so appealing that, at one time, he had four plays running in the West End at the same time.

His most important book was *Of Human Bondage.* Then came such classics as *The Moon and Sixpence, The Painted Veil* and *Razor's Edge*. He wrote prolifically but prided himself on his lack of literary frills. In 1947 he founded the Somerset Maugham Award which gave young writers an opportunity to travel.

The whole of King's School was present on Saturday to hear the headmaster talk of Mr Maugham's long friendship. "Not content with providing us with a boathouse and physics lab, he is now giving his books and a library. Please give him three cheers!"

Somerset Maugham consults a British Railways breakfast menu as he leaves Victoria station en route for his home in the South of France. He was delighted with the reception he received from King's.

June 9th: *Thousands of cheering people yesterday lined the route from York Minster to the tiny North Riding village of Hovingham as the Duke of Kent, 25, and his charming bride, Miss Katharine Worsley, 28, led the procession of cars conveying royal wedding guests back to the reception at the bride's home, Hovingham Hall. The service was conducted by Dr Michael Ramsay, Archbishop of York, who was making his last major public appearance before his enthronement as Archbishop of Canterbury. Among the guests were the Queen and the Duke of Edinburgh, Queen Elizabeth, the Queen Mother, Princess Margaret and Mr Anthony Armstrong-Jones and the bridegroom's mother — now to be known as Princess Marina, Duchess of Kent.*

Teenage lovers strangled on Denton Marshes

September 10th: Edwin David Sims, a 28-year-old bachelor of Hampton Crescent, Gravesend has been charged with the murder of Lilian Edmeades of Peppercroft Street and her sweetheart Malcolm Johnson of Abbey Road, Gravesend. They were both aged 16 and had been strangled.

The naked body of Lilian was found in a dyke near the Ship and Lobster, Denton Marshes. Malcolm was discovered after a long search by police, soldiers and members of the Kent police frogmen's squad. His body was found some way off, also in a dyke.

Sims was arrested immediately and made a brief appearance before magistrates the following day with a crowd of more than 100 people waiting outside the town hall for a glimpse of the man. He was remanded in custody.

Lilian, a shop assistant and a member of the Baptist Church and Malcolm, a former pupil of Gravesend Technical School and a member of the Boys Brigade, had met at a youth club. They left Lilian's home together on Sunday morning at 10 am to go to church, taking the path across the marshes at Denton.

The Queens Own Buffs, The Royal Kent Regiment

BATTLE HONOURS

Blenheim
Vimiera
Ramillies
Corunna
Oudenarde
Almaraz
Malplaquet
Dettingen
Guadaloupe 1759
Belleisle
Douro
Talavera
Albuhera
Vittoria
Pyrenees
Nivelle
Nive
Orthes
Toulouse

Paardeburg
South Africa
1900-02
Aisne 1914
Mons
Ypres 1914-15-
17-18
Loos
Hill 60
Somme 1916-18
Arras 1917
Vimy 1917
Otaly 1917-18
Amiens
Gallipoli 1915
Gaza
Hindenburg Line

Defence of Kut Al
Amara
Struma
Sharqat
Jersusalem

Peninsula
Punniar
Moodkee
Ferozesha
Aliwal
Sobraon
Alma
Inkerman
Sevastopol
Taku Forts
Lucknow
South African 1879
New Zealand
Chitral
Egypt 1882
Relief of Kimberley
Nile 1884-5

Afghanistan
Bagdad
North West
Europe 1940
Alem Hamza
El Alamein
Madjes Plain
Robaa Valley
Centuripe
Sicily 1943
Sangro
Trigno
Cassino
Anzio
Trasimene Line
Argenta Gap
Leros Malta
1940-42 Shweli
Defence of
Kohima

New infantry regiment is born in Kent

March 2nd: A new regiment, long in germination and the result of many hours of heated debate at the highest level has, at last, been born. Yesterday, The 1st Battalion The Queen's Own Buffs, The Royal Kent Regiment was introduced to a large crowd during a short ceremonial parade at Ross Barracks, Shorncliffe.

The amalgamation of the two famous Kent regiments was first mooted during a major review of British defence policy four years ago when it was announced that greater reliance on the nuclear deterrent would mean a reduction in the infantry. It was recommended there would be 52 battalions of the Line instead of 67 — and that meant just one infantry regiment in Kent.

Historic Dover Castle, occupied by the army for centuries and strengthened considerably during the Napoleonic invasion scare of 1803, has been de-garrisoned. The military have gone and the castle is in the hands of the Ministry of Works who will organise guided tours. From the town it stands magnificently and proudly on the skyline and continues to represent a strategic English stronghold.

King Frederick of Denmark is Colonel-in-Chief of the new regiment and Princess Marina, Duchess of Kent, Colonel. Buff is the regimental colour and the Dragon has yielded to the White Horse of Kent for pride of place on the cap. The most difficult decision concerned the title and prolonged bargaining over the claims of respective regimental traditions ended in a narrow victory for East Kent.

Both the Buffs and the West Kents lost their depots at Maidstone and Canterbury but they went down bravely with all guns firing at the respective passing-out parades. A few days later the Buffs moved into Ross Barracks, Shorncliffe, adjacent to The Queen's Own in Moore Barracks.

Yesterday, accompanied by a trumpet fanfare the flag of the Queen's Own Buffs with its white horse on a background of blue and buff was raised.

Immigrants help to swell Kent's population

June 7th: Kent's new arrivals, first from the West Indies and then the Indian sub-continent, have contributed greatly towards the population increase, according to census figures just released.

There has also been a continuing shift in population from north to south and more births than deaths. The result is shown by sharp increases, particularly in the commuter belt of Sevenoaks and Tonbridge and the Medway Towns.

More people are living in the suburbs rather than town centres as they prefer to travel by rail to their workplace and to live nearer the country.

RURAL DISTRICTS

Bridge Blean	18,893	Malling	36,348
Cranbrook	13,786	Romney Marsh	4,540
Dartford Rural	37,476	Sevenoaks Rural	32,828
Dover Rural	10,504	Sheppey	9,451
East Ashford	10,214	Strood Rural	20,842
Eastry	22,822	Swale	19,685
Elham	9,124	Tenterden Rural	7,089
Hollingbourne	16,558	Tonbridge Rural	22,305
Maidstone Rural	18,062	West Ashford	10,045

BOROUGH AND URBAN

County Borough of Canterbury Pop 27,817

Ashford	24,783	Folkestone	45,203	Ramsgate	35,801
Beckenham	74,836	Gillingham	70,676	Rochester	43,936
Bexley	88,781	Gravesend	44,560	Royal Tunbridge Wells	38,400
Broadstairs	15,081	Herne Bay	18,348	Sandwich	4,140
Bromley	64,179	Hythe	9,220	Sevenoaks	14,866
Chatham	44,424	Lydd	2,774	Sheerness	15,796
Chislehurst & Sidcup	83,850	Maidstone	54,045	Sittingbourne	21,931
Crayford	27,950	Margate	42,512	Southborough	8,820
Dartford	40,870	New Romney	2,356	Swanscombe	8,433
Deal	24,309	Northfleet	18,821	Tenterden	4,247
Dover	35,215	Orpington	63,364	Tonbridge	19,237
Erith	46,270	Penge	15,012	Whitstable	17,459
Faversham	12,293	Queenborough	3,137		

Man hangs for the murder of his lover and her husband

September 8th: Hendryk Neimasz, a Polish national who speaks little English, was hanged at Wandsworth today for the murder of a young couple in the village of Aldington, near Ashford, earlier this year.

The bodies of Alice and Hubert Buxton were found in Pantiles Cottage on May 13th. Hubert had died of shotgun wounds and Alice was bludgeoned to death with a blunt instrument. They had lived in the village for two years in a bungalow belonging to Gladys de Pomeroy of Pantiles House, where Hubert was employed as a gardener.

Scotland Yard detectives, who conducted the murder inquiry, quickly discovered that Alice was having an affair with Neimasz. The couple, in fact, had been seen "enjoying each other's company" by a policeman who was investigating a "rocking car" parked in an isolated quarry near Hythe.

Neimasz had admitted the relationship but said Alice wanted him to get rid of his wife, Gypa, hoping they could start a new life together. Such talk had greatly worried him and he thought it likely that Alice herself would kill Gypa and his children.

He claimed a man called George, whom he met in a pub in Gillingham, agreed to solve Henryk's problems by killing both Alice and her husband. He paid him £60.

Detectives failed to come up with any evidence to support the existence of George but they found part of a double-barrelled shotgun at Neimasz's smallholding in Mersham. Forensic evidence showed traces of human blood.

Neimasz was charged, sent for trial at Lewes Assizes and sentenced to death.

'She shines with a candle-it radiance and stalks on legs like beech trees, pink glowing, grape clustered and pearl hung' — Virginia Woolf on Vita Sackville-West after a shopping expedition in Sevenoaks.

January 14th: A Pakistani woman has been taken to the Long Reach Isolation Hospital at Dartford following an outbreak of smallpox in the country which has already claimed five lives. MPs are demanding compulsory vaccination.

January 20th: Liverpool pop group *The Beatles* have been rejected by the recording company, Decca, whose experts say they will never make the music charts.

January 27th: Peter Snell, New Zealand's Olympic champion, broke the mile record today with a time of 3 mins 54.4 seconds.

February 17th: James Hanratty was sentenced to death today for the murder of Michael Gregsten in a lay-by near Bedford. Hanratty pleaded innocence throughout the trial.

February 20th: Lt-Col John Glenn today became the first American to orbit the earth. He travelled in a Mercury capsule called *Friendly.*

March 19th: Motor Vessel *Alignity* was ripped apart today by a huge explosion while being loaded with 300 tons of motor spirit at the BP Refinery, Isle of Grain. With the refinery severely threatened by the fire which followed, 12 appliances from Kent Fire Brigade had to be mobilised.

April 2nd: A push-button "Panda" crossing was introduced today in London.

April 30th: The Queen Mother was at Folkestone today to watch her two horses run in the Fremlins Elephant Chase. It was not her lucky day.

May 31st: The man who organised the transport of Jews to death camps, Adolf Eichmann, has been executed. It is believed he was responsible for the death of six million Jews.

June 17th: Brazil beat Czechoslovakia 3-1 in today's final of the World Cup.

Harold Nicolson, the diplomat and biographer who covered his wife's bed with flowers from Sissinghurst Garden shortly after she died in the Priest's Cottage.
See page 94

June 25th: Film star Sophia Loren and her husband, film producer Carlo Ponti, have been charged with bigamy in Rome.

July 1st: Immigrants from east and west have been pouring into Kent in a bid to beat the Commonwealth Immigration Act which became law today.

July 11th: An American frogman, Fred Baldasare became the first person to swim the English Channel under water.

July 13th: Prime Minister Harold Macmillan today sacked seven members of his cabinet including Selwyn Lloyd, Chancellor of the Exchequer. It has been described as "the night of the long knives".

July 18th: *HMS Worcester,* the floating school, moored off Greenhithe, welcomed the Queen and Duke of Edinburgh today. Hundreds of ship's officers from all over the world have been trained on *HMS Worcester.*

A large commercial Romano-British villa farm with bath houses and possibly a kiln and pottery has been found at Eccles near Maidstone. It belongs to a period not long after the famous Battle of Medway.

August 6th: Jamaica gained its independence today after 307 years of British rule.

August 5th: American actress Marilyn Monroe was found dead today, lying naked in her bed at home near Hollywood. There was an empty bottle of sleeping tablets by her side.

August 20th: An 18-year-old youth from East Berlin was shot dead today trying to climb over the wall to the west. The shooting has sparked off a massive protest.

September 25th: Sonny Liston today knocked out Floyd Patterson in the first round to become heavyweight champion of the world.

October 3rd: A tablet commemorating the Battle of Solefields during Jack Cade's rebellion in 1450 was unveiled today by Lord Cornwallis in Solefields Road, Sevenoaks.

October 28th: Mr Khrushchev promised today to dismantle Russian missiles based in Cuba. In return President Kennedy will lift the blockade on the island. The world's reaction has been one huge sigh of relief.

November 7th: Nelson Mandela, 44-year-old African nationalist leader, has been found guilty of incitement and leaving South Africa illegally. He has been jailed for five years.

December 17th: Objections are pouring in to the BBC over some of the sketches in a new satirical show called *That Was The Week That Was.*

Kent Fire Brigade tugs answered an SOS call from a Dutch motor vessel today and found a man trapped in the crew's quarters by a raging fire. After a dramatic rescue, with the ship in danger of capsizing, the man was saved and the ship towed to Sheerness.

December 18th: Severe frost, which last week accompanied the killer smog, shows no sign of abating causing more chaotic conditions on both road and rail. On the higher ground at Goudhurst there has now been several weeks of continuous frost.

The Nore Command, named after a sandbank in the Thames Estuary opposite the mouth of the River Medway, and applied to the anchorage between the sandbank and the north Kent coast used by naval fleets since the 17th century, has been abolished.

GREAT HITS OF 1962

Stranger On The Shore

Tory majority destroyed by Eric Lubbock

Eric Lubbock addresses his supporters in Orpington.

March 15th: In what has been described as the most sensational by-election result of the century, the Liberals took the Orpington seat today with a bombshell victory which left their own supporters breathless and shaken. A Tory majority of 14,760 in the 1959 general election was turned into a Liberal one of 7,855.

The victor is Mr Eric Lubbock of High Elms Farm, Downe — grandson of John Lubbock (later Lord Avebury) who instigated Bank Holidays. He said after the count: "This is beyond my wildest dream. It's fantastic. I can hardly believe it."

The count was watched by millions of people throughout the country on both television channels and the result was announced after two hours of mounting excitement. Such was the roar that greeted Mr Lubbock's victory that both his supporters inside the Civic Hall and viewers on television were unable to hear the exact tally of votes, which turned out to be 22,846.

The defeated candidates, Mr Peter Goldman (Conservative) with 14,991 and Mr Alan Jinkinson (Labour), 5,350 were stunned by the size of the majority. It is the first seat the Government has lost in a by-election since the general election.

Pundits now believe there will be a return to three-party politics in Britain after more than 30 years of a Tory-Labour duopoly of power. Mr Lubbock told his supporters: "This is an historic day. You are the vanguard of a great resurgence of Liberalism."

Orpington's new MP, who is cousin and heir presumptive to the present Lord Avebury, is 31 and married with two sons and a daughter.

After two years' National Service, Mr Lubbock served as an apprentice with Rolls Royce at Derby. He is now technical director to the Charterhouse Group and a member of Orpington Council, representing Downe.

From Knole to Sissinghurst via the Bloomsbury elite

June 3rd: Victoria Mary Sackville-West — Vita to her family and friends — who died at Sissinghurst today after a long battle with cancer, was a prolific and successful novelist who made her name among the Bloomsbury literary elite.

She came from a rich and romantic background, for her father was the 3rd Baron Sackville, and Knole, the great rambling mansion at Sevenoaks, was her home.

Her personal life was a reflection of her parents' own emotional and stormy relationship. From 1918 to 1921 she had a passionate love affair with a woman, Violet Trefusis, with whom she went off on several occasions but always returned to resume her marriage with the diplomat, Harold Nicholson.

Virginia Woolf, whose fantasy *Orlando* was an open love letter to Vita, was another close and unconventional friend and Vita was devastated by the novelist's suicide in 1941.

In 1930, the Nicolsons moved house from Long Barn in Weald to the derelict ruins of Sissinghurst Castle and set about turning several acres of wilderness into a magnificent garden.

This was a challenge that Vita relished. By 1955 it had reached a state of such colourful and romantic profusion that Vita was awarded a gold Veitch memorial medal by the Royal Horticultural Society. The garden was opened to the public and last year (1961) more than 13,000 people came to Sissinghurst.

As a writer her best-known books are *Knole and the Sackvilles* (1922), a history of her home and ancestors, *The Land* (1926) which won the Hawthornden prize and *The Edwardians,* a novel.

Other work after her move to Sissinghurst included *All Passion Spent, Family History* and *Pepita*, the life of her Spanish grandmother. She also wrote a biography of *Saint Joan of Arc.*

Vita never lost her love of Knole and always remembered fondly the great state rooms and magnificent park. As a female she could not inherit the estate and that distressed her for many years.

Vita died yesterday at the age of 72. She leaves a husband and two sons, Ben and Nigel.

Hell-raiser's mutiny wins new acclaim

June: The British actor Trevor Howard, who was born and spent much of his early life in Cliftonville, has given another powerful performance alongside Marlon Brando in a remake of *Mutiny on The Bounty.*

The film was released earlier this year. In it Howard provides the kind of performance that won him a 1958 Best Actor award from the British Film Academy and an Oscar nomination for his role in *Sons and Lovers* last year.

Howard, with his craggy face, gravelly voice and upper-class accent, embodies the traditional Englishman. He has starred in many classics but still remembers his former school chums and neighbours in Thanet. In the world of showbusiness he is known as "A Gentleman and a Player".

Among his best-known films is *Brief Encounter* in which his co-star was Celia Johnson. This won an award at the Cannes Film Festival. There followed *I See a Dark Stranger* and *Green For Danger.* His reputation, however, was secured in *The Third Man* alongside Orson Welles.

In 1947 he was invited by Sir Laurence Olivier to play Petrucchio in *Taming of the Shrew* and again won critical acclaim.

Howard has also achieved some celebrated off-stage performances, particularly when fuelled by alcohol and was once arrested in Vienna.

A photograph taken a few years ago of Trevor Howard with the young singer Petula Clark at the premier showing of the film, Vice Versa *at the Odeon, Leicester Square.*

Railway lines have closed, RAF stations been abandoned and hop-picking has been mechanised but one Kentish tradition continues — the craft of cricket ball making. Jacob Playfoot, now approaching his 86th birthday, is one of the best stitchers in the business. In fact the cricket ball maker from Tonbridge is so skilled that he has converted a garden workshop and continues to work after his retirement from the Hildenborough firm of Gray Nicholls.

With such reputable ballmakers as Dukes (at Chiddingstone Causeway), Readers (at Teston), Ives, Wisden, Lillywhite and Froud, Surridge and Kingswood, the Tonbridge area has always been the centre of the ballmaking industry.

Is it possible that the ball old Jacob is carefully stitching together will be in the formidable hands of Fred Trueman during this summer's Test series against Pakistan?

Sutherland's tapestry in new Coventry Cathedral

May 25th: Graham Sutherland, the great landscape and portrait painter of Trottiscliffe, was at Coventry today to see the new Cathedral consecrated — 22 years after it was demolished by German bombs.

Sutherland has taken some years to complete his giant tapestry of Christ enthroned among the four Beasts of the Revelation. It is more than 70 feet high and complements the baptistery window set with richly stained glass designed by John Piper.

The Cathedral was designed by Sir Basil Spence.

Lord Astor of Hever must leave the country he loves

September 21st: John Jacob Astor, 76, the first Baron Astor of Hever, owner of *The Times* and a former MP for Dover for 23 years has been forced to leave England and the home he loves, to live in the south of France. He and his wife Violet Mary announced their decision today in a dignified statement which has brought widespread sympathy from his family and friends.

Astor is the younger son of William Waldorf Astor who turned Hever into a magnificent home in the early years of the century. On his father's death he inherited the use of the great Astor Trust in New York and immediately donated money to good causes. Among them was the Middlesex Hospital who benefited by almost a million pounds. Other gifts were never disclosed.

The Finance Act, introduced earlier this year, has dealt Lord Astor a terrible blow for it requires people domiciled in England to pay estate duty on assets abroad as well as those in the UK.

Realising the Hever estate would be crippled on his death and *The Times* would certainly have to be sold, Lord Astor attempted to resign from the Trust but under American law he has been unable to do so. As the benefiaries of the Trust are his children his only course of action is to emigrate and leave the chairmanship of the *The Times* in the capable hands of his son, Gavin.

Although the decision has shocked his friends and family it is in line with the bravery he showed as a soldier in the 1914-18 war when he won the Legion of Honour and was so badly wounded that a leg had to be amputated.

His father gave him Hever Castle so he should have a new interest in life and from that moment the estate, the village, the county of Kent and his constituency at Dover which he successfully won in 1922 became an integral part of his affections.

To this he added *The Times* which he acquired on the death of Lord Northcliffe in 1922. He began a long stewardship in Printing House Square, choosing editors with great care and guiding the newspaper through some of its greatest years. His peerage came in the New Year Honours of 1956.

September: **The shingle promontory jutting out into the English Channel on the approach to the Straits of Dover is now considered to be the most important bird observatory in Britain. This is because of the nearness of France, some 23 miles away and the attraction that Dungeness has for big streams of nocturnal and diurnal migrants. In addition there is a natural bird sanctuary on the marshes where various waders nest undisturbed. Few places can provide a bigger variety at migration time.**

The observatory headquarters are the old naval signalling station. The Dungeness Bird Observatory committee, with Mr R.E. Scott as warden, have erected a large number of Heligoland traps over the large area of shingle. In two years they have ringed more than 8,000 birds. One of the reasons for the large influx of nocturnal migrants is the attraction of the yellow illuminant of Dungeness lighthouse. No-one is certain if the blue daylight lamp of the new lighthouse will have the same effect.

Ministers angered by David Frost's Saturday satire show

December 17th: David Frost, born in Tenterden 23 years ago and the son of a Methodist minister, is the cheeky front man of the new Saturday night satire show, *That Was The Week That Was,* which has been in so much trouble for lampooning famous personalities.

The Prime Minister, court officials, such as the Lord Chamberlain, and other politicians have been on the receiving end of Frost's icy comments and what is described as his "aggressive attitude".

This week the Postmaster-General asked to see the script of the next programme and will seek the views of MPs. He says he has not watched the show himself but is aware of an item which caused offence to the Chancellor of the Exchequer, Mr Reginald Maudling. The programme showed him dismissing a delegation of the unemployed with the words: "I can't spend all day talking to you. I've got work to do."

Frost is very much a Kent lad. He moved from Tenterden to Gillingham when his father, the Rev Paradine Frost. became minister of the Byron Road Methodist Church. He attended Barnsole Road Primary School — admitting he was madly in love with his teacher — and then Gillingham Grammar School.

David Frost's friends in Gillingham know him as an intelligent, likeable young man who went to Cambridge and started work as a researcher for the television programme *This Week.* He then met Ned Sherrin, a BBC producer and they started the satirical show which has won great viewing figures but given Frost such a bad name. One critic said this week that his vindictiveness is the kind once reserved for the heavy-handed villains of the silent screen!

The BBC said this week they do not censor *That Was The Week That Was* (TW3) but last week they received 1,000 telephone calls, six to four in favour.

If the show is taken off the air it unlikely to affect Frost's television career or damage the reputations of the others including Millicent Martin, Lance Percival, Roy Kinnear and Willie Rushton.

Great Smog claims more lives

December 6th: So dense was the smog that descended over South London and North Kent last night that traffic moved at walking pace and many pedestrians wore face masks to protect themselves from poisonous industrial gases swirling in the atmosphere.

This was a genuine "peasouper" — a water fog similar to those of ten years ago which killed hundreds of people along the industrial banks of the Thames.

On this occasion the fog which has blanketed most of Kent has already claimed more than 40 lives.

Motorists made slow progress in the fog and many vehicles were abandoned. A policeman on duty at the Poverest traffic lights, Orpington said: "All I could hear were bangs all around me as cars hit each other. Passengers were very good. Those who had torches walked in front to show drivers the way."

The fog apparently contains localised pockets of poison due to the concentration of sulphur dioxide and associated gases emanating from factory chimneys and drifting along in the sluggish circulation of the watery blanket.

Two girls on their way home shield themselves from the deadly fumes.

'I have a dream that the sons of former slaves and the sons of former slave owners would one day sit together at the table of brotherhood' — Rev Martin Luther King speaking in Washington.

January 14th: President de Gaulle of France told a Paris news conference today that Britain neither thinks nor acts like a Continental nation and is not qualified for full membership of the European Economic Community.

January 18th: Hugh Gaitskell, leader of the Labour Party, died in hospital today after a short illness. He was 56.

February 14th: Harold Wilson has beaten George Brown in a ballot between Labour MPs to be the party's new leader.

March 22nd: John Profumo, Secretary of State for War, said today there had been "no impropriety whatsoever" in his relationship with Christine Keeler, the 21-year-old showgirl.

April 9th: Winston Churchill has been awarded honorary US citizenship by President Kennedy.

April 24th: Princess Alexandra, sister of the Duke of Kent, was married today to Angus Ogilvy.

May 1st: Kent author Ian Fleming's latest thriller, *From Russia With Love*, has become a big hit with cinema goers. Starring Sean Connery as James Bond, the agent "with a licence to kill", it shows a number of spectacular stunts. Last year Bond made his screen debut in Fleming's *Dr No.*

The unique Chislehurst water tower which has spanned the road to Bromley for more than 100 years, has been demolished to facilitate the flow of traffic.

June 5th: John Profumo admitted today that he lied to the Commons about his involvement with Christine Keeler. He has resigned from the Government.

June 19th: An oral contraceptive pill, made in Britain, is now available on prescription.

June 21st: Mrs D. Millson of Deacon Leas, Tonbridge has given birth to what are believed to be the heaviest twins ever born in England. The boys, whose combined weight is 19lbs 5 oz, will be christened Charles Edward and Hugh Stephen.

Dr Richard Beeching, on his first day as chairman of the British Transport Commission when he predicted some hard decisions on the future of our railways. See page101-102.

July 1st: The "Third Man" who tipped off Soviet spies Burgess and Maclean is Kim Philby, a former Foreign Office diplomat. He had been named by MP Marcus Lipton eight years ago but was cleared by Harold Macmillan after an inquiry.

July 22nd: Liverpool rock group The Beatles were guest performers at the Winter Gardens, Margate, although they did not top the bill. The Fab Four, John, Paul, Ringo and George, sang some of their hits, including *She Loves You* to an enthusiastic audience. Later this year they are due to appear at the Royal Variety Performance.

July 26th: The Yugoslav city of Skopje was destroyed today by an earthquake which produced 80 shock waves. More than 1,000 people were killed.

August 3rd: Dr Stephen Ward, a key figure in the Profumo affair, died today after taking a drugs overdose.

August 8th: Fifteen armed men wearing masks hijacked a train at a secluded spot in Buckinghamshire today and escaped with mailbags carrying more than £1 million. This well-planned crime has been dubbed "The Great Train Robbery".

The Wouldham to Halling ferry across the Medway has been closed ending all direct access to the works and the railway on the west bank.

September 9th: With seven Grand Prix victories, Scotsman Jim Clark has become the youngest driver to win the world championship.

A new telephone exchange has opened at Dartford — the first in south-east London area to adopt STD (subscriber trunk dialling).

September 26th: A report by Lord Denning, released today, blames Harold Macmillan and his cabinet for failure in their handling of the Profumo affair.

October 18th: The Earl of Home has been named as Britain's new Prime Minister following the resignation of Mr Macmillan. It had been widely expected that Rab Butler would get the job.

November 22nd: President Kennedy was assassinated today as he drove through Dallas, Texas in an open-top car. A few hours later Lyndon B. Johnson was sworn in as the 35th President of the United States.

See page 108.

November 24th: Lee Harvey Oswald, the man charged with the assassination of President Kennedy, was murdered today in Dallas. The killer was later identified as Jack Ruby, a striptease club owner.

OBITUARY

Sarah d'Avigdor Goldsmid of Somerhill, Tonbridge, daughter of the Conservative MP, Sir Henry d'Avigdor Goldsmid has been drowned at sea in a sailing accident. *See page 117*

Group Captain Sailor Malan, one of England's greatest fighter pilots and former CO at Biggin Hill died on September 17th in his native South Africa of Parkinson's Disease.

GREAT HITS OF 1963

She Loves You

From Me To You

1963

Great freeze shows no signs of ending

February 22nd: Meteorologists are already predicting this is going to be the coldest winter of the century, for the snow that fell in Kentish fields and gardens on Boxing Day last year shows no signs of thawing. At Herne Bay and Whitstable the frozen waters stretch two and a half miles out to sea, Margate Pier is surrounded by great chunks of pancake ice and the ice is two feet thick on most Kentish rivers. Today it's snowing again.

For seven weeks now the county has been battling against the worst conditions since 1947. Villages have been cut off, motorists stranded in drifts and trains abandoned.

Few people will forget the scenes which greeted them on the morning after the Boxing Day blizzard. In many places the snow was two feet deep, there was no wind to disturb the tumbling flakes and the world outside was strangely muffled.

February: The big freeze has immobilised most shipping activities on the Medway and the Thames. Here at Sun Pier, Chatham pack ice extends the full width of the river. The sea at Whitstable and Pegwell Bay is also frozen.

Two days later the sky changed colour — from grey to a yellow-brown and an arctic nightmare followed as masses of crystaline snow was driven into huge drifts more than 15 feet deep. County-wide a fleet of 300 snowploughs was mobilised but the task was too great.

As January arrived there was only a brief sign of milder air but that was followed by a renewed surge of freezing cold easterlies which sent fuel bills soaring and brought power cuts to homes and factories with redundancies in the building industry. Milkmen and postmen fought bravely to reach isolated homes and in the towns massive queues formed outside bakeries. All trains in the county stopped again.

Villages and hamlets throughout Kent were cut off by drifts of snow. Those on high ground, on the North Downs, were without fresh food and supplies for days. Helicopters dropped a few parcels and efforts were made by gangs of men to dig a path through the drifts. But then the wind increased as if in mockery of their vain attempts.

Rugby, football and hockey matches have been abandoned and golf is impossible. Many cinemas are still closed and hospital casualty departments have a regular flow of victims who have slipped on the ice.

The question everyone is asking this week is; "When will it end."

The day 'Our Enery' floored Cassius Clay

June 18th: *Henry Cooper, South London's popular British heavyweight champion, yesterday fought the extrovert American, Cassius Clay at Wembley and gave him the biggest surprise of his professional life by sending him sprawling onto the canvas in round four. The bell went before the count could take place, Clay recovered and went on to force Cooper to retire with a badly cut eye. The American, who is the idol of the blacks, has risen to prominence through his personality and his great speed around the ring. He has been matched against world champion Sonny Liston next year and predicts he will win in the fifth round.*

'I'll retire at the next election', says Winston Churchill

May 1st: Sir Winston Churchill said today that he will retire from the House of Commons at the next election.

Just a few days after being awarded honorary American citizenship by President John F. Kennedy, the great man has announced the end of his political career.

During the last few years Churchill has spent most of his time at Chartwell, visiting only occasionally his London house at Hyde Park Gate. He has also continued to visit France and spend time at the villa La Pausa, above Menton where he paints and relaxes. His host there is Emery Reeves.

Sir Winston is now 88 and by October he will have completed 60 years as an MP. He is still suffering from breaking his thigh during a fall in France and, reluctantly, uses a wheelchair.

Disaster mission

October: The earthquake disaster in the Yugoslav city of Skopje in which more than 1,000 people died and many more were made homeless prompted Round Tablers from Kent to drive across Europe to the stricken area with six caravans, one ambulance and a lorry carrying clothes, medical supplies and other vital equipment.

Dr Beeching's axe falls on Kent's branch railways

March 27th: Many of Kent's delightful branch lines, which were opened amid great celebrations during the latter part of the nineteenth century, have already closed — but a British Railways Board report published today proposes even more cuts in the county's rail network.

The chairman of British Railways and one of the authors of the report, Dr Richard Beeching says that, country-wide, he intends to close 2,128 stations, scrap 8,000 coaches and axe 67,700 jobs. Scotland, north and central Wales and the West Country will bear the brunt of the closures.

The Southern Region's electrified system will escape comparatively lightly. Among the casualties will be the diesel-electric services from Ashford to Hastings and New Romney, passenger services from Haywards Heath to Horsted Keynes and from Elmers End to Sanderstead. A number of stations will lose their good facilities and several unprofitable intermediate halts will close.

Uproar has greeted the publication of the report which is entitled "The Re-Shaping of British Railways". The fiercest opposition is coming from the unions and from Conservative MPs in the south-east who are accusing the chairman of gross misjudgement.

One railway line which has escaped the ruthless attention of Dr Beeching and Mr Marples, Transport Minister, is the privately-owned Romney, Hythe and Dymchurch light railway opened by the Duke of York in 1927. Sadly, Captain John Howey has died but he realised his great dream — to build, own and run the smallest public railway in the world. And he has seen it develop into a magnet for train enthusiasts and countless children.

Fifty years of fruit research at East Malling

East Malling Research Station celebrates its golden jubilee this year with the knowledge that, in the field of fruit research, it is a legend all over the world.

The idea of creating an experimental fruit station in Kent was born among the fertile brains of Wye College, the station's mother institute. It began in 1913 with a staff of one, 22 acres of land and £500. Today, there is a staff of 75, 514 acres of land and a quarter of a million pounds each year to pay for research. The station association has paid back £20,230 towards the loan on acquiring Ditton Court. It is on course to greater prosperity with opportunities to add even more lustre to an already famous name.

1963

Lines to remember

Kent and East Sussex Light Railway
As Britain's first light railway and one of the most attractive routes, the Robertsbridge to Tenterden section opened in 1900 with an extension to Headcorn five years later. Part of the line was closed in 1955 with the rest following in 1961.

East Kent Light Railway
Various branches were opened to serve the collieries between 1912 and 1925. The final route closed in 1951.

The Thanet Lines
The former SER and LCDR, opened between 1861 and 1865, became redundant when the two rail systems in Thanet were linked by a new connecting line in 1926.

Elham Valley Light Railway
This line which traversed the picturesque valley through the North Downs between Folkestone and Canterbury was completed in 1889. It closed altogether in 1947.

Faversham Quay
From the town centre to the industrial area of Faversham Creek, this line opened in 1860. It will close soon.

Chattenden and Upnor Light Railway
Built for army training purposes in 1898 and used later by the Admiralty, this line closed in 1961.

Stoke Junction to Allhallows
Built across the marshes in 1935 to serve new homes at Allhallows, it closed in 1961.

Hoo Junction to Port Victoria
Opened in 1882, it closed for passengers in 1961 and is now used to take freight only to cement factories, the refinery and super tankers.

Fawkham to Gravesend
Opened to passengers and goods in 1886, this line runs through the farmland of North Kent and is scheduled for closure.

Sandling to Hythe
This hilly route that involved heavy earthworks when it opened in 1874 closed in 1951. It was a branch from the main Ashford to Folkestone line.

Appledore to Dungeness
This line was opened to passenger traffic in 1884 and closure (to passengers only) is recommended. It will continue to service the new power station at Dungeness.

Paddock Wood to Hawkhurst
Opened in 1893 this line ran through some of Kent's most beautiful countryside servicing hop gardens and orchards. It closed in 1961.

The Westerham Flyer steams into Brasted on its final run.

Bid to save the Westerham Flyer

Although Dr Beeching, as chairman of British Railways, is the architect of the "re-shaping" report, he is not entirely reponsible for decimating Britain's famous, complex and much-loved railway system. Transport Minister, the Rt Hon Ernest Marples, had already made the decision to close many lines.

Among them was the route between Dunton Green, through the fertile Holmesdale Valley below the scarp of the North Downs to the old market town of Westerham and the home of Winston Churchill. Just under five miles long with a halt at Chevening and a station at Brasted, it was local enterprise that promoted the railway in 1881.

At its peak there were 22 departures daily from Dunton Green with 20 on Saturdays and 15 on Sundays. Traffic was mainly commuters but a number of housewives and businessmen travelled to nearby Sevenoaks on the "Westerham Flyer" as it was affectionately known.

When the line was first earmarked for closure the Transport Users Consultative Committee reacted strongly but Mr Marples overruled them. Closure took place in 1961 and attempts are now being made to float a preservation society. They may be too late as the proposed Sevenoaks by-pass will follow a part of the route of the line.

The new M2 bridge over the Medway at Rochester. It cost more than £2 million to build and the lives of five workmen.

M2 opens — no more traffic jams in the Medway Towns

May 31st: The people of the Medway Towns can hardly believe their eyes. Traffic is flowing freely through Rochester and Chatham for the first time in many years. There are no long queues at the traffic lights in Strood and the volume of cars on the old Rochester bridge is remarkably light. All North Kent knows the reason; the first half of the M2 motorway has been opened and the Medway Towns will never be gridlocked by traffic again.

The opening ceremony was performed by Transport Minister, Mr Ernest Marples on Wednesday who said that the remaining 12 miles of the road will be completed next summer. He also mentioned the remarkable engineering feat that went into the building of the vast span of the new Medway Bridge which still requires minor work.

1963

April 24th: *Princess Alexandra, Kent's own Fair Maid, was a figure of beauty and serenity amid the glittering pageantry in Westminster Abbey at her wedding to the Hon Angus Ogilvy today. Visitors from all over the world crowded into London for the marriage of Princess Marina, Duchess of Kent's daughter to the handsome Scot who is the son of the Earl and Countess of Airlie. There were more than 2,000 people in the Abbey to see the Princess given away by her brother, the Duke of Kent. This group wedding photograph taken at St James Palace after the service shows: Front row (l to r) Doune Ogilvy, the Archduchess Elisabeth of Austria (bridesmaids), David Ogilvy (pageboy), the bridegroom and his bride, Princess Anne (senior bridesmaid), Simon Hay (pageboy) and bridesmaids Georgina Butter and Emma Tennant. Second row (l to r) Prince Michael of Kent, the Countess of Airlie and the Earl of Airlie, Princess Marina, Duchess of Kent, the Duke of Edinburgh and the Queen, Queen Elizabeth, the Queen Mother, Prince Charles, the Duke of Kent and the Duchess of Kent. Back row (l to r) the Hon Peregrine Fairfax (best man), Lady Griselda Balfour, Ian Tennant, Lady Lloyd, the Hon James Ogilvy, Lady Ogilvy, Lord Ogilvy, Mrs James Ogilvy, Lord Lloyd, Lady Margaret Tennant and Mr Peter Balfour.*

Gliding Club flies to a new home at Challock

June 15th: **Kent Gliding Club, the first in England and founder member of the British Gliding Association, has at last found a permanent home on top of the North Downs at Challock.**

The club's gliders, towed by Tiger Moths, left West Malling aerodrome today for the historic flight to Challock — led by Chief Inspector Roy Hubble.

The club was re-formed after the war in April 1956 by amalgamating with the Royal Engineers Flying Club at Detling. A nomadic existence followed with flying taking place at Lympne, Stowting and finally West Malling.

In May 1961 contracts were signed for the land at Challock and the Royal Engineers were delighted to train their "Sappers" by preparing a real airfield from scratch. Members will now have to remove a wood and clear away thousands of huge flints before sowing grass and erecting a hangar.

Profumo sex scandal rocks Britain: Macmillan to resign as Prime Minister

June 30th: Mr Harold Macmillan, MP for Bromley, will resign as Prime Minister before the next general election. This shock decision, announced today, comes in the wake of the Profumo affair which has gripped the attention of the whole nation.

Speaking at a Conservative fete in the grounds of Holy Trinity Convent, Bromley, on Saturday, Mr Macmillan said the sex scandal involving John Profumo, Secretary of State for War and 21-year-old Christine Keeler had inflicted deep wounds. "As you can imagine", he said, "they have not broken my spirit but wounded my heart".

His decision to resign follows an opposition censure motion in the House of Commons over security aspects of the Profumo affair in which 30 Tory MPs refused to back the government.

The Government won but "Supermac", close to tears, said: "I acted honourably. I believed Mr Profumo's denial of impropriety with Christine Keeler."

Apart from the minister and the call-girl other key figures are involved in what newspapers describe as "the scandal of the century". One of them is Dr Stephen Ward, an osteopath, who has a country cottage on Lord Astor's Cliveden estate in Buckinghamshire and it was here that Profumo met Keeler as she frolicked naked in the swimming pool.

Daily Mirror

1d Saturday, June 29, 1963 No. 18,514

Sensational start to Stephen Ward case

CHRISTINE'S FAMOUS FRIENDS

'Money and presents'

By TOM TULLETT and BARRY STANLEY

FAMOUS names were mentioned in evidence given yesterday by 21-year-old Christine Keeler and her friend, Marilyn (Mandy) Rice-Davies, 18, in the case against society osteopath Stephen Ward.

The two girls, friends since they worked together as show-girls in a night-club cabaret, told of their association with 50-year-old Ward—and spoke of these men:

JOHN PROFUMO, 47, former War Minister. Miss Keeler said Mr. Profumo had made love to her and given her presents—and money "for my mother."

VISCOUNT ASTOR, 55, on whose estate at Cliveden, Bucks, Ward rented a cottage. Miss Keeler said Lord Astor paid the rent of a flat she and Miss Rice-Davies shared in London.

DOUGLAS FAIRBANKS, Jun., 53, the actor, who has appeared in many films and TV shows. Miss Rice-Davies said she met Mr. Fairbanks during her association with Ward.

'Indiscreet'

Among other men figuring in the evidence of the two girls were

★ Eugene Ivanov, former Russian Naval attache in London—with whom Miss Keeler said she made love on one occasion.

★ Mr. Jim Eynan—described by prosecuting counsel as "an indiscreet business man." Miss Keeler said Mr Eynan gave her money—"as a friend."

★ A man whom Miss Keeler said she knew as "Charles." He lived off Park-lane and gave her "about £50" on one occasion when they were intimate.

★ Wealthy Peter Rachman, now dead—who was said by Miss Rice-Davies to have had a mirror designed so that people could look into the bed-room of his flat.

Stephen Ward, son of a clergyman, faces eight charges including two of living on immoral earnings at London's Marylebone Court.

FULL REPORT—Pages 3, 4 and 5

I HOPE TO STAY ON, SAYS PREMIER

PREMIER Harold Macmillan spoke on television last night about his future.

And he said he still hoped to lead the Tory Party at the next General Election.

Right

Mr. Macmillan who was being interviewed on Independent Television News, said at one stage:

"I can only say I shall do what is right for the Government and the party."

Full story on Back Page.

SHE WAS WITNESS NUMBER 1

CHRISTINE KEELER—looking thoughtful, hand on knee—is pictured just before being driven away yesterday from the flat where her friend Paula Marshall lives, at Devonshire-street, Marylebone. When she arrived at Marylebone Court, where she was Witness Number One in the case against Stephen Ward, she had to fight her way through the crowd outside. A policeman's helmet was knocked askew in the struggle.

June 29th: The front page of today's Daily Mirror.

Ward tipped off MI5 when he discovered that the showgirl was also having a liaison with Soviet naval attache, Eugene Ivanov. That was bad enough but then it emerged that Ward's shapely young mistress, Mandy Rice-Davies, once had an affair with Peter Rachman, the "slum landlord" and convicted racketeer.

Profumo has now confessed to his involvement and resigned from Parliament. Ward has appeared in court charged with living off immoral earnings and the Government's image has been so badly tarnished that commentators wonder if it can survive.

Certainly Mr Macmillan is a broken man. Bitter attacks were made last week by both the Liberal and Labour prospective parliamentary candidates for Bromley, John Mumby and John Bloom.

In a speech to Keston and Hayes Liberals, Mr Mumby said the Government had broken promises and abandoned moral standards. In a press statement, Mr Bloom accused the Government of distortion and Mr Macmillan of "incompetence that borders utter incredulity". The Bromley Communist Party said Mr Macmillan had led the country to "shame and disaster".

As the PM was walking around the Conservative fete today about 50 ban-the-bomb demonstrators were at the front gate shrieking "murderer resign". Their voices were drowned by most of the 2,000 crowd chanting: "Good old Mac."

The Veronica — a winner in this year's barge race. The number of working barges has so dwindled there is now little hope of the racing tradition continuing.

Cowdrey breaks arm but the Test Match is saved

June 25th: Kent and England captain Colin Cowdrey who lives at Hawthorne Road, Bickley, saved the day for his country in one of the most dramatic climaxes to a Test match ever known.

Cowdrey walked out to bat at Lords against the powerful West Indies team at number 11 with a broken arm. In the end he didn't have to face a ball but was quite prepared to do so for his country. The match was drawn.

Cowdrey's injury was caused by an express delivery from fast bowler Wes Hall when he had made 19. He will be out of cricket for the rest of the season.

September: If Kent's supporters have been disappointed with the absence of Colin Cowdrey this season, then they are delighted with the form of young Derek Underwood who made his debut a month before his 18th birthday and went on to become the youngest player to take 100 wickets in his first season.

Underwood's number one victim in first class cricket was Yorkshire's Ray Illingworth. He took 6-66 against the West Indians and ended with 101 wickets at an average of 21.12.

"One swallow does not make a summer", said a Kent spokesman this week about Derek Underwood "but his form is certainly an encouraging sign for the future".

Farewell, old ladies of the Thames

May: Gravesend, Dartford and other north Kent communities are preparing to say goodbye to the old ladies of the Thames — the sailing barges which have been competing in annual races for 100 years.

It was in 1863 that businessman, Henry Dodd (a refuse disposal merchant) had the idea of a race on the Thames between the sailing barges. At the time there were 8,000 of these slow, ponderous craft and one newspaper said to get them to race each other "was the idea of a madman".

The 'madman's' idea worked. More than 70 barges took part in the early races between Erith to the Nore Light and back and they were such a success that thousands of people lined the banks to cheer their favourite.

Henry Dodd died in 1880 and left £5,000 to a trust fund to provide prizes for the annual race as well as pensions for bargemen.

Although there was a gap in the early part of the century the matches continued to be an annual event until 1938 and were continued after the war. Sadly the number of working barges has so dwindled that there is little hope of this great tradition continuing after this year.

Christopher Cockerell, the 53-year-old inventor of the Hovercraft, has introduced another revolutionary method of transport — the Hovertrain. The vehicle can travel at speeds of 400 mph on concrete hovertracks, built over existing railways or alongside concrete highways. Mr Cockerell will demonstrate his Hovertrain to Ministry of Transport and British Railways officials early next year. Photograph above shows Cockerell (left) and engineer, Alan Pennington with a model of the Hovertrain at the Hovercraft headquarters in Hythe.

County stunned by news of Kennedy's death

November 25th: The tragic death of President Kennedy at the hands of an assassin on Friday (Nov 22) struck grief into the hearts of the people of Kent as they mourned with the rest of the world. Town hall flags throughout the county were flown at half-mast on Saturday and tributes were paid at many official functions.

The dreadful news was broadcast on radio and television in the early evening. John F. Kennedy was shot in the head as he drove through Dallas, Texas in an open car on his way to a political festival. The 46-year-old United States President slumped in his seat as his wife Jackie turned to help. She cradled him in her arms as the car sped to Parkland Hospital. He could not be saved; Kennedy died 25 minutes after being shot.

There was a television blackout immediately after the news was heard with the BBC returning to normal schedules after 24 minutes and ITV playing piano music for over an hour.

During the weekend hundreds of messages of sympathy poured in to the US base at West Malling, where, on Sunday morning, 300 officers men and their friends attended a service at the chapel conducted by Father Daly of West Malling assisted by seven priests from Aylesford Priory.

From his home at Chartwell, Sir Winston Churchill issued the following statement: "This monstrous act has taken from us a great statesman and a wise and valiant man. The loss to the United States and to the world is incalculable."

Requiems for Mr Kennedy are to be held in Kent churches during the week.

Farm hand murdered four members of his family in act of 'unparalleled horror'

July 25th: A 23-year-old Ugandan has been jailed for life for the murder of his middle-aged mother-in-law, Phyllis Waugh, her two young daughters and her baby grandson at their wooden bungalow home in isolated countryside near the hamlet of Hucking, six miles from Sittingbourne. The killings were described by the Assizes judge yesterday as being of "unparalleled horror".

The jury heard that Vincent King, a farm hand, lived with his wife, also Phyllis, at Bicknor Park Farm cottage, near Hollingbourne.

The bodies of Mrs Phyllis Waugh, aged 45, Rose Marie Waugh, aged 12, Mary Helen Waugh, aged 11 and Romali King, aged five months, were found at Volante, a bungalow in the narrow winding Hazel Street, near Hucking at 10. 20 pm on Friday by Margaret Waugh, aged 17, a pupil of Maidstone Girls Grammar School.

She was returning home from a cinema on a scooter ridden by her father, Mr Tom Waugh. He had been working on a late shift at the Sittingbourne paper mill where he was an electrician.

King was arrested by Detective Chief Inspector Albert Pritchard of Maidstone CID in Devon two days later. On being charged he said: "I can't remember murdering anybody, sir."

The case at Kent Assizes lasted two days. Just after the jury retired Mr Justice McNair upheld a submission by Mr Edward Sutcliffe QC, defending counsel, that the murders were not committed on different occasions. If the submission had failed King would have faced the death penalty.

***September 20th:** Princess Anne, aged 13, meets her new headmistress Miss Elizabeth Clarke today as she arrives at Benenden School to begin her first term there. The Princess was with her mother, Queen Elizabeth and most of the 300 girls were waiting under the oak trees at the school entrance to greet their new royal friend. Benenden was formerly Hempsted, the home of Viscount Rothermere. Also enrolled this term are four other princesses, including two granddaughters of King Haile Selassie of Ethiopia.*

Dartford Tunnel completed: 2s 6d toll faces motorists

November 18th: The long-awaited Dartford to Purfleet tunnel under the River Thames has opened at last. Linking the A2 in Kent with the A13 in Essex it has cost £11million and means motorists will no longer have to take the Tilbury or Woolwich ferry, or the longer route through the Blackwall tunnel.

It is estimated that six million drivers will use the 4,700-foot long tunnel every year but only motor vehicles will be allowed through. Cyclists will have to travel on a transporter and pedestrians by special bus services.

It was in 1799 that an Act of Parliament was passed for a tunnel to be provided between Tilbury Fort and Gravesend. Boreholes were drilled but the venture was abandoned in 1803 because the capital of the sponsoring company had already been exhausted.

More than a century lapsed. In 1924 the Gravesend-Tilbury route was rejected in favour of a Dartford tunnel because of the link with the 20th century network of roads. In 1929 the Essex and Kent County Councils promoted a Bill for the construction of the tunnel but this was deferred because of the financial crisis of 1931.

In 1936 the construction of a pilot tunnel was authorised and completed but the second world war came as another brake on progress. Preparations were revived in 1955 when the pilot tunnel was reopened.

Excavation of the main tunnel began in 1956 when engineers were required to burrow through silt and gravel, 14 feet below the bed of the river. The end product of seven years endeavour is a tunnel of which the whole nation may be proud.

Kent and Essex County Councils and the Ministry of Transport have shared £3 million of the cost. The rest will be repaid from tolls. They range from 6s for a heavy lorry, 2s 6d for a private motorist and 6d for a cyclist.

When the Beatles appear in Maidstone later this year — they have been booked to appear at the Granada — there will be a big crowd of adoring fans. The four boys from Liverpool have already made four number one pop hits and their first film A Hard Day's Night *will soon be released.*

Look what's happening to the 'silver screen'

When the first "talkie" was shown in 1929 and Kent's super cinemas entered the much-heralded golden age of glamour and excitement, no-one could have predicted that it would last less than 40 years.

But that is the case. Television is now rapidly taking over as the prime medium of entertainment; most homes have a TV set and former cinema patrons would rather stay in their own homes than queue up at the Odeon or Plaza for a ticket to the flicks.

In the past few years scores of cinemas in Kent have closed and many towns now have one "picture palace" where once there were four or five.

Those which have closed this year include **The Capitol, Tonbridge.** The last audience, admitted free of charge on March 28th, saw Kenneth Moore in *We Joined the Navy.* The building is now for sale.

The Rex, Borough Green has also closed, the proprietor, Frank Davies, unable to raise the £5,000 required to upgrade equipment and seating.

In the last three years the doors have closed on the **Empire, Chatham; Regal, Lydd; Playhouse, Folkestone; Kosmos, Tunbridge Wells; Savoy, Snodland; Ritz, Birchington; Tudor, Westerham and the Granada, Sevenoaks.**

The first sign that cinemas were in trouble came in the mid-fifties when the Odeon group (Oscar Deutche Entertains Our Nation) decided that 40 cinemas across the country would have to close in a severe rationalisation programme. The **Odeon, Broadstairs**, heavily damaged in the war and reopened by Jack Warner in 1950, was one of the first. It closed alongside **Ramsgate Picture House,** the **Hippodrome, Margate,** the **Tonbridge Empire Pool, Carlton, Sevenoaks** and the **Negresco, Edenbridge.**

During the late fifties many cinema proprietors, anticipating a grim future, rang the changes to stay afloat and introduced live shows and pantomime or Continental, art and revival films. In most cases they were unable to halt the flagging interest in the cinema. With heating, projection and seating showing signs of great use and considerable age there was no alternative but to close the doors.

Folkestone has lost two of the county's most famous cinemas. **The Savoy,** rebuilt in the twenties with 954 seats, a first-floor cafe, aerated soda fountain and palm lounge, has become a bingo parlour. *The Broadway Melody* — one of the first talkies to be shown in Kent — played at the Savoy in 1929.

The **Folkestone Playhouse**, once floodlit by night, faced in Bath stone and the first cinema in Kent to introduce tip-up seats, closed in August 1962 and will soon become the site of a supermarket.

'I love the early morning song of the lark...the rich fragrance of wild garlic...the rigour of the game in general and the prestige of St George's in particular' — Ian Fleming who died this year.

January 13th: British designer, Mary Quant opened her new boutique in Chelsea today and said young girls are tired of wearing the same things as their mothers. They prefer bold designs and very short skirts.

January 23rd: The *Daily Herald* newspaper will be relaunched as *The Sun*, Cecil King said today.

January 26th: A comedy series about a rag and bone man and his son, *Steptoe and Son,* has become Britain's most popular television show.

February 6th: Britain and France agreed today to build a Channel Tunnel costing £160 million.

February 8th: Thousands of American teenagers gave The Beatles an ecstatic reception when they flew into Kennedy Airport, New York today for the start of their American tour.

February 25th: Cassius Clay produced one of boxing's greatest surprises today by beating the "invincible" Sonny Liston. The heavyweight champion of the world retired in the seventh round.

March 28th: *Radio Caroline* began transmission today from a ship in the North Sea.

March 27th: Ten members of the so-called "Great Train Robbery" gang have been found guilty of plotting to steal mailbags with contents worth £2.5 million. Twenty others are still at large.

April 9th: Labour has won the first elections to the Greater London Council.

Pop music fever hit Ramsgate today when nearly 1,000 screaming teenagers crammed the West Cliff Hall for a dance at which the Rolling Stones group played. Hundreds more girls were left outside claiming they could not get in.

April 13th: Ian Smith, a fighter pilot during the second world war, today became Prime Minister of Southern Rhodesia.

Sir Garrard Tyrwitt Drake, the charismatic former owner of Maidstone Zoo, has died and left Cobtree Manor to the nation. Famous for his yellow Rolls Royce and wonderful collection of animals, Sir Garrard closed the zoo five years ago, keeping only his llamas and collection of Royal Cream ponies. They have now been presented to Whipsnade. He is seen here on his white horse at the head of Maidstone Carnival.

May 28th: Jawaharlal Nehru, Prime Minister of India since Independence in 1947, died at his home in New Delhi yesterday after a heart attack. He was 74.

May 30th: Another "pirate" radio station has started to broadcast pop music from "somewhere off the East Coast". *Radio Atlanta,* like *Radio Caroline,* operates legally from international waters.

Following the death of Vita Sackville-West in 1962 the Treasury has accepted Sissinghurst as part payment for estate duty from the Nicolson family. Compulsory self-destruction of British heritage by the imposition of death duties was avoided by the National Trust.

June 14th: Nelson Mandela, who took up the black nationalist cause in 1944, has been sentenced to life imprisonment for plotting to overthrow the South African Government. Among those who protested outside the South African embassy was Labour MP, Anthony Wedgwood Benn.

July 2nd: *Radio Caroline* and *Radio Atlanta* have amalgamated.

July 16th: Donald Campbell today set a new world land speed record of 403.1mph in *Bluebird.*

July 28th: Sir Winston Churchill, 89 and very frail, made his last appearance in the House of Commons today.

August 2nd: Mods and Rockers clashed today at Hastings. Police reinforcements had to be flown in from Kent.

August 7th: Congress has approved President Johnson's call for the United States to take action against the Communist regime in North Vietnam.

August 21st: Three women have been found guilty of indecency for wearing topless dresses in London.

September 28th: A survey has shown that *Radio Caroline* has more listeners than BBC Radio.

October 15th: The Soviet leader, Nikita Khrushchev, 70, was ousted from office today in a coup.

October 24th: Dr Martin Luther King, 35-year-old American black integration leader, has been awarded the Nobel Peace Prize.

October 25th: Long jumper Lynn Davies, a South Wales schoolteacher, has won a gold medal for Britain in the Olympic Games at Tokyo.

December 21st: The death penalty for murder has been abolished. The vote was so overwhelmingly in favour of abolition that the House of Lords will not discuss it.

December 23rd: Dr Richard Beeching, chairman of British Railways, has been sacked.

December 31st: Donald Campbell today added the world water speed record to his land record with 276.33 mph.

The Chatham Marine Cadets Unit, under the chairmanship of Col Archibald Wright, has been told by the courts that they cannot establish a legal charity out of the money donated following Britain's worst-ever road disaster.

OBITUARY

Sir Harry Mackeson, former MP for Folkestone and Hythe and director of the family brewing business which bears his name, died this year aged 58. Sir Harry, who became a baronet in 1954, lived at Great Mongeham, Deal.

GREAT HITS OF 1964

I Love You Because

I Won't Forget You

1964

Terrified villagers declare gorilla warfare

January 24th: Two gorillas, who escaped from John Aspinall's private zoo at Bekesbourne yesterday, roamed the area for five hours, defied all attempts to catch them and caused terrified villagers to demand tighter security immediately.

The gorillas are Kula (a male weighing 16 stone) and his mate Shamba. They just walked out of their cage while it was being cleaned and played happily on the lawn in front of Howlett's Cottage by the drive leading to Aspinall's mansion.

Nine policemen arrived from Canterbury, followed by the fire brigade but the animals resisted all attempts to lure them back to their cages with oranges, preferring to drink milk left on the cottage doorstep.

The firemen fixed up their jets and sprayed the gorillas with ice-cold water. Kula quickly ran back to his cage but Shamba disappeared. Minutes later an attic window in the cottage was flung open and Shamba peered out. Leaning on one elbow she waved gracefully to the crowd which had gathered below. Then deftly she clambered out of the window, dropped down on to a wall and, encouraged by the jets of water, lumbered off to her cage. Inside the cottage there was chaos. Shamba had knocked over furniture, pulled books from the bookshelves and broken several bottles.

Chairman of the parish council, Mr William Wallis said today: "There is something wrong with security at the zoo and we are demanding action now. It is a terrifying thought that they can escape like this. A few weeks ago a council tenant heard a knock at his door and there was a gorilla outside."

First flyer says farewell as supersonic age approaches

May 18th: In about three months time Britain will say hello to the supersonic age when the TSR-2 tactical strike plane makes its much-publicised maiden flight. Yesterday the country said goodbye to the man who started it all, Baron Brabazon of Tara — the first Englishman to pilot a heavier-than-air machine under power in England. He was 80.

John Theodore Cuthbert Moore-Brabazon was once the unpaid mechanic to Charles Rolls, the motorcar pioneer. He later became an international racing driver and balloonist, exchanging those tranquil pleasures for a Voisin aircraft in which he made his famous flight on the Isle of Sheppey in 1909.

Later that year, piloting a machine made by Short Brothers, he won a prize of £1,000 offered by the Daily Mail for the first English aircraft to fly one mile.

Moore-Brabazon served with the Royal Flying Corps on the western front and was awarded the MC. After the Great War he became the Conservative member for Rochester which he held until his defeat in 1929. During part of that time he was Churchill's private secretary and supported his policy of rearmament.

He represented Wallasey in the 1930s and was one of the last politicians to wear a top hat in the House of Commons.

Moore-Brabazon excelled at several sports and braved the Cresta Run at St Moritz every year from 1907 to 1963.

Canterbury's special tribute to the son of a shoemaker

February 22nd: Canterbury today will pay special tribute to Christopher Marlowe, one of England's greatest playwrights and poets — who was born in the city exactly 400 years ago.

The celebrations will begin with the unveiling of a plaque on the tower of the former St George's Church which remains as a symbol to Canterbury's greatest ordeal. Marlowe's home was also one of the buildings destroyed in the 'Baedeker raid' of 1942.

Later in the day tributes will be placed at the poet's monument in the Dane John Gardens and a recital of Elizabethan music will be given in the Chapter House by the Marlowe Society.

Tonight the mayor, the dean, the master of Corpus Christi College at Cambridge, the headmaster of King's School and the president of the County Society will be among the guests at a banquet at the County Hotel.

Marlowe, the son of a Canterbury shoemaker, lived in the city in the sixteenth century and later at Scadbury Hall, Chislehurst. He was murdered in 1593, aged 29.

Daily Mirror

3d. Monday, May 18, 1964 No. 18,788

After Clacton . . a new battlefield

WILD ONES 'BEAT UP' MARGATE

40 arrested in all-day clashes

THE GIRLS FIGHT IT OUT A girl Mod and a girl Rocker stage a hair-pulling battle outside Margate Station, while their friends stand looking on. The fight lasted three minutes, with the girls rolling over and over on the ground.

MIRROR REPORTER

THE Wild Ones — self-styled Mods and Rockers — picked the Kent resort of Margate to beat up for Whitsun.

All day yesterday the rival teenagers fought and smashed their way around the town.

They clashed with police, who went into action with truncheons drawn.

When it got dark, about 300 Mods were parading around Margate. Two hundred Rockers were lurking in a quiet corner of the town.

Blood

At least forty youths had been arrested. And there was blood on the sands.

About 1,000 warring Mods and Rockers were in town. Most of the Mods had arrived on scooters bristling with headlights and badges.

Most of the leather-jacketed Rockers had roared into town on shiny motor-cycles.

Many of the teenagers turned up late on Saturday night. They got down to the wrecking and smashing right away.

At 10.30 yesterday morning, the big battle broke out—as 500 Mods attacked 100 Rockers.

Six policemen stepped in truncheons waving — and both mobs turned on them.

Shouting

Then the Mods streamed across to the huge Dreamland amusement centre. They marched among the pintables, chanting, shouting and clapping hands.

Soon after that, raging Mods swarmed along Margate's High-street.

Later, the rival gangs again faced each other on the crowded beach, but there were only isolated outbreaks of fighting.

Late last night, one group of youths set light to a pile of deckchairs on the beach, then sang and danced around the bonfire.

A twelve-strong squad of policemen surrounded the youths. Some officers questioned the youngsters, while others put out the fire with sand.

At Brighton last night, hundreds of Mods roamed the sea front hunting for Rockers and breaking windows.

Practically all of Brighton's police force was on duty and more than 100 officers rushed to the sea-front cinema where gangs of Mods were attacking a dozen Rockers.

The Rockers, bruised and shaken, escaped on their motor bikes.

At Clacton, Essex—beaten up by 1,000 teenagers at Easter—no trouble was reported yesterday.

Girls behind the Wild Ones—Page 4. Charge of the Mods at Margate—Centre Pages.

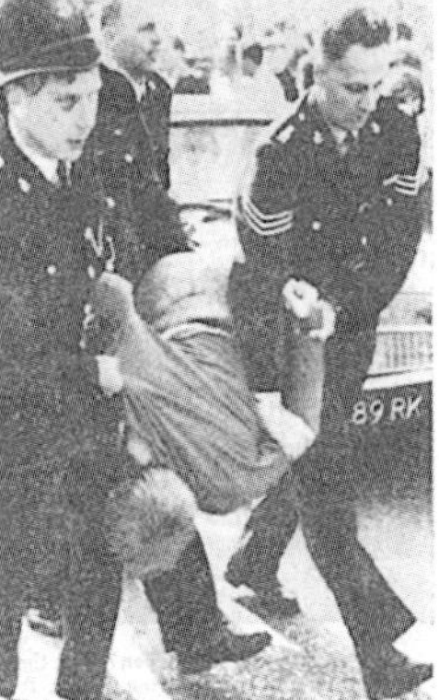

BLACK EYE A constable with a black eye and a sergeant who has lost his helmet carry a youth away to a police car.

Picture by Alisdair Macdonald.

***May 18th:** Girls fighting outside Margate station and a policeman with a black eye — this was today's Daily Mirror front page report about the "wild ones".*

May 18th: During two successive days of unprecedented violence hordes of Mods and Rockers disrupted normal holiday business in Margate over the Whitsun weekend. The "wild ones" clashed in the town centre and brawls erupted on the beach and along the promenade. Windows were broken in the High Street and along Marine Terrace and at least two young men were taken to hospital with knife wounds.

Police from many parts of Kent were drafted in to Margate to deal with the troublemakers who first clashed on Sunday morning when police had to use staves to keep two rival factions apart.

There were fights in the Silver Slipper coffee bar, the buffet at Margate station and near the Clock Tower where holidaymakers scurried to get out of the way of youths on scooters and motorbikes.

There was further violence on Monday but the day ended in retribution when 51 hooligans appeared before magistrates at two special courts. Under special police escort the youths appeared one by one and many were given prison and detention centre sentences.

A plea by the Mayor of Margate to make no mention of the Whitsun violence on the basis that publicity was giving "these mentally unstable young people some false sense of their own importance" has been ignored by the *Isle of Thanet Gazette.*

The editor said today: "Those who believe that a Press boycott would put an end to the kind of trouble that has spoilt Margate's holiday weekend are merely skimming the surface of the problem. The heavy fines and sentences imposed by magistrates should be a deterrent to future outbreaks of this kind. The Press has a responsibility to report factual events such as this."

Apart from the police who maintained a round-the-clock vigil in Margate during the weekend, one heroic figure emerged in the shape of Mr George Simpson, chairman of Margate magistrates. For the sentences he imposed on the Mods and Rockers he received more than 50 fan mail letters from people all over England praising his efforts to stamp out this alarming new brand of hooliganism.

1964

Kent's goodbye to traditional boundaries

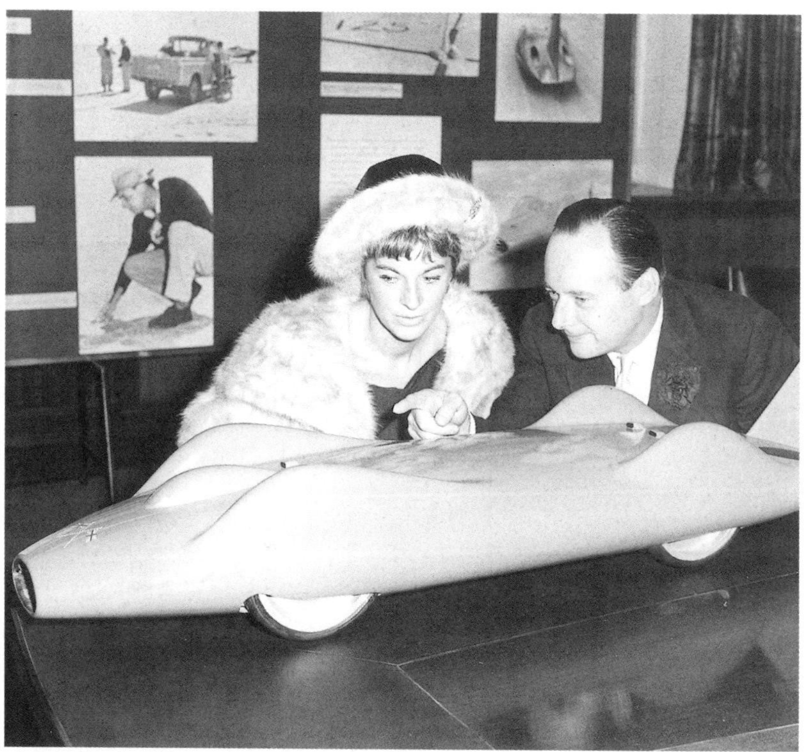

July: This is a sad moment in Kent's long history. In a few months the county will say goodbye to its metropolitan boroughs. Fast-growing towns such as Bromley, Orpington, Bexley and Beckenham will soon become part of the new administrative area of Greater London. The decision follows many months of heated arguments and debates which have lasted well into the night. Along with the County of London, Kent's traditional boundaries have been demolished.

Sir Keith Joseph, Minister of Housing and Local Government has announced the following: "The metropolitan boroughs of Lewisham and Deptford will be combined to form the London Borough of **Greenwich.** Beckenham, Bromley, Orpington, Penge, Chislehurst and Sidcup will become the London Borough of **Bromley**. Bexley, Crayford, Erith and Sidcup will be the London Borough of **Bexley.**"

When the boundaries become effective from April next year Kent will be left with 1,432 square miles and a population of approximately 1,292,000. *See page 123.*

July 16th: *Donald Campbell, who inherited his father's desire to break world records on land and water, today set a new land speed record of 403.1 mph in his jet-powered Bluebird. His father Malcolm Campbell, who was born in Chislehurst, was a champion in the 1930s.*
Donald Campbell is seen here with his wife Tonia looking at a model of the new Bluebird in which he broke the record. He now intends to increase his own waterspeed world record at Coniston Water. See page 133.

Permanent home for County Show

After investigating a number of sites for a permanent showground, Kent County Agricultural Society has found the ideal location — 120 acres of flat ground next to the A249, alongside the former RAF fighter base at Detling.

For a number of years now the annual Kent show has increased in both popularity and reputation and the 30 acres of Mote Park is no longer suitable. A massive landscaping project is underway and Detling will be used for the first time in July. It is hoped eventually to attract 100,000 people to "the best agricultural show in England".

Pioneer TV company ready for colour

October 23rd: A Thanet company which introduced the first proper television service for the public said this week they are ready to convert to colour TV when it is introduced by the BBC in about two years time.

Rediffusion Ltd was the brainchild of Mr Frank Austin of Pembroke Avenue, Margate who relayed sound radio to a friend's house way back in 1934, more as a fascinating experiment than a commercial idea.

This one-man, one-house relay service expanded so successfully that Mr Austin was soon supplying sound to most homes in Thanet under the operating name of Rediffusion. In 1951 he converted to television and now supplies more than 50 per cent of the homes on the island.

Rediffusion (South East) Ltd of Relay House, Westwood, Broadstairs has branches in six Kent towns with a staff of several hundred.

It was in 1960 that Mr Austin was appointed MBE, the citation referring to him as one of the country's foremost pioneers in wireless relay service.

James Bond's creator dies in Canterbury

August 13th: With the death of Ian Fleming at the early age of 56, James Bond (secret agent 007) has enjoyed his last great adventure. The writer died in the Kent and Canterbury Hospital yesterday; unable to take up his appointment as captain of the Royal St George's Golf Club, Sandwich to which he was recently elected.

Fleming, banker, stockbroker, Commander in naval intelligence during the war and, later, foreign correspondent with Reuters, introduced Bond to a delighted public in 1953. Beginning with *Casino Royale* one book about this handsome, tough, predatory and yet chivalrous character appeared every year until 1966.

In those 13 years Fleming published a string of absorbing and remarkable adventure stories including *Goldfinger, Dr No, You Only Live Twice, Moonraker, On Her Majesty's Secret Service, The Spy Who Loved Me* and *The Man With The Golden Gun.*

His friend Kingsley Amis recently said that Fleming's style is plain and flexible, serving equally well for fast action, lucid technical exposition and sensuous evocation of place and climate. "The strength of his work", he said, "lies in its command of pace and profound latent romanticism."

Fleming travelled widely from an early age but Kent was always his English home. He married Anne, the divorced wife of the second Viscount Rothermere in 1952 and lived in houses near Dover and at the Old Palace, Bekesbourne, where his pursuits included motoring, golf, bridge and underwater swimming.

He never took himself seriously as a literary figure and the success of his Bond series was not overwhelming until the publication in 1958 of *Dr No,* the first of his books to be filmed. This gave him both economic freedom and worldwide fame.

More Bond films will follow allowing cinema goers to understand Fleming's familiarity with secret service activities and his obsessive interest in gambling, gadgets, smart restaurants, exotic settings and repulsive villains.

"Bond", says Amis, "is a carefully constructed amalgam of what many men would like to be and of what perhaps fewer women would like to meet".

James Bond (alias Sean Connery) who also knows the Royal St George's.

Tories lose three Kent seats

October 16th: As widely predicted, Labour are in power again — by an overall majority of just four. Harold Wilson, the first Prime Minister to be born this century, says there are exciting times ahead.

The national situation is reflected by the results in Kent. Labour gained Gravesend, Rochester and Chatham and Dover, held on to Dartford and Erith and took votes from the Tories in most of the constituencies. With the charismatic Eric Lubbock leading the charge, the Liberals held on to Orpington with a reduced majority.

Mr Edward Heath's popularity at Bexley slipped considerably. He received more than 4,000 fewer votes than at the previous general election.

At Sevenoaks and Ashford, however, the long-serving members Sir John Rodgers and Mr Bill Deedes easily held on to their respective majorities — although the latter loses his cabinet minister's salary.

The most interesting Labour gains are at Dover where Mr David Ennals unseated Sir John Arbuthnot after a recount and at Rochester, where 39-year-old housewife Mrs Anne Kerr defeated Mr Julian Critchley.

Flashback to 1958 when Formula Two meetings for the popular Kent Trophy were held at Brands Hatch. Here, waiting for the event to start is Jack Brabham (extreme left), the eventual winner and Lewis-Evans (extreme right) who was runner-up.

Bumpy grass cycle track becomes Grand Prix circuit

July 12th: The great dream of bringing the prestigious British Grand Prix to Kent has been realised at last. Yesterday, on the challenging Brands Hatch circuit, the flying Scot Jim Clark continued his phenomenally successful partnership with Lotus by taking the chequered flag ahead of his English friend and rival Graham Hill who was driving for BRM.

By staging the Grand Prix for the first time, Brands Hatch is set to become another "Brooklands" where the international contest first began in 1926. Since the war there have been Grand Prix meetings at Donington Park, Aintree and Silverstone but the organisers are now keen to establish a regular fixture on the 2.65-mile circuit in the village of West Kingsdown.

It has certainly come a long way since Ron Argent and a group of friends organised cycling and pacemaking competitions in 1926. Then it was a bumpy grass track which quickly became the venue for informal motorcycle events. These were so successful that a complete circuit was marked out using all of the field, a distance of about three-quarters of a mile.

The first organised motorbike meeting was held in March 1932 by a conglomerate of the Bermondsey, Owls, Sidcup and West Kent clubs. With a natural amphitheatre, which proved ideal for spectators, a promising future for Brands Hatch was established.

Brands Hatch Stadium Ltd was created in 1947 and the grass track extended to a full mile. Two years later tarmac was laid on the kidney-shaped circuit and motorcar racing came into being with Formula Three events.

With both motor cars and motor bikes now meeting regularly the circuit began to gain a national reputation and an interesting decision took place in 1954 when, for the interests of safety, it was agreed that all cars should run in a clockwise direction, especially with the tricky Paddock Bend to negotiate. The track was then extended to 1.24 miles with the addition of a loop up to Druid's Hairpin.

The new grandstand was built in 1955 and, in 1960, Brands Hatch was upgraded to full Grand Prix status of 2.65 miles.

Margate pier blaze seen 15 miles out to sea

November 8th: Thanks to a party of 40 Royal Engineers on a coach outing to Margate and the vigilance of local firemen, the town's famous pier was saved from complete destruction last night.

The flames could be seen by ships' crews 15 miles out to sea and, believing that a ship was on fire, they bombarded the local coastguard station with SOS calls.

The fire severely damaged the pier pavilion and the flames, fanned by a strong east wind, spread rapidly, forcing lifeboatmen to remove rockets and explosives from their lifeboat which was lying in the harbour nearby.

Hundreds of people crowded onto the promenade to watch the blaze. They were controlled by the soldiers who also helped in carrying hoses.

'There are moments when I have such an eagerness for death that I could fly to it as to the arms of a lover'— Somerset Maugham, shortly before he died this year aged 91.

January 1st: Stanley Matthews has been knighted in the New Year Honours, the first footballer to receive the honour.

Dover's Promenade Railway between the harbour and the eastern docks has closed after 46 years. The last train ran yesterday (December 31st).

January 27th: Extra train services have been laid on from the Kent stations to accommodate the thousands of people on their way to Westminster Hall for Churchill's lying-in-state.

February 8th: From today cigarette advertising is to be banned from television.

February 22nd: The TSR-2 today flew faster than the speed of sound for the first time.

February 23rd: Stan Laurel, the partner of the late Oliver Hardy, died today. He was born Arthur Stanley Jefferson in South London.

March 2nd: Actors Roger Moore and Patrick McGoohan have been reported as earning £2,000 a week.

March 28th: Dr Martin Luther King led 25,000 marchers on a protest march today to present a petition of black grievances to Alabama's Governor Wallace.

April 6th: Reggie and Ronnie Kray have been cleared at the Old Bailey of running a protection racket in East London.

British actress Julie Andrews has won a Hollywood Oscar for her role in the film *Mary Poppins. My Fair Lady*, starring Rex Harrison, won eight Oscars, including the Best Film of the Year. MC Bob Hope, who was born in Kent, opened the Oscar proceedings by remarking: "Welcome to Santa Monica-on-Thames".

April 15th: The Queen dispensed the royal Maundy money in Canterbury Cathedral today in the presence of a 3,000 congregation.

May 14th: The Queen has dedicated an acre of wood and grassland in memory of President Kennedy. It is situated close to the spot where the Magna Carta was signed at Runnymede.

Honor Blackman, who plays Pussy Galore in Goldfinger *and stars in the TV thriller series,* The Avengers, *has discovered a new adventure — learning to fly from Biggin Hill.*

June 3rd: Astronaut Major Edward White today became the first American to walk in space.

June 14th: The Queen's birthday honours have included an OBE for Jack Warner, Dixon of Dock Green. Two people have returned their OBEs in protest at the award of MBEs to The Beatles.

June 18th: The Government announced today it will introduce a legal blood alcohol limit for motorists.

July 19th: Sir Robert Menzies, the retiring Prime Minister of Australia, was today installed as the 117th Lord Warden of the Cinque Ports. He was welcomed by the Archbishop, Dr Michael Ramsay, who said the office was older than the British Parliament.

July 20th: The House of Lords today approved the Bill to abolish hanging.

July 24th: The former world light-heavyweight champion, Freddie Mills, was found shot dead in a car today. He was 43.

July 28th: US troop strength in Vietnam is to be raised to 125,000. It is reported that 35,000 are being called up each month.

August 2nd: A plaque has been unveiled at St Lawrence Ground, Canterbury in honour of "Tich" Freeman, the Kent and England slow bowler who took a record 3,776 wickets.

August 18th: With Dartford's Mick Jagger as best man, photographer David Bailey was married today to French actress, Catherine Deneuve.

A Kent River Authority has been formed with Mr A.B. Long, the first chairman.

September 22nd: In another threat to world peace India and Pakistan today declared war over rival claims on the border state of Kashmir.

It is reported that *Coronation Street* is still Britain's most popular TV series while *Ready Steady Go* is the most influential live music show. Both are screened by ITV.

October 28th: Ian Brady, aged 27 and Myra Hindley, aged 23, have been charged with the murder of a 10-year-old girl Lesley Ann Downey. Her body was found on Saddlesworth Moor 13 days ago.

November 8th: The Murder Bill (abolition of the death penalty) and the Race Relations Bill both became law today.

November 11th: Ian Smith, Prime Minister of Rhodesia, chose Remembrance Day to issue a Unilateral Declaration of Independence. Commonwealth leaders in black Africa are calling on Britain to take decisive action to crush the regime.

November 16th: Parliament met today to draw up economic sanctions against Ian Smith's Rhodesia.

December 22nd: The British journalist and broadcaster, Richard Dimbleby, died of cancer today. He was 52.

Ted Burbury, Gravesend's last shrimper has retired. The shrimping boats were called 'bawleys' and their moorings were on the foreshore around St Andrews Waterside Mission church, known as Bawley Bay.

GREAT HITS OF 1965

Tears

A Walk In The Black Forest

Another new landmark which dominates the skyline around the flat marshland of East Kent is the Richborough Electricity Power Station which came into operation last year. The building of this modern structure was preceded by great controversy among those who believed "the great concrete scar would turn Kent into a new Black Country". The huge chimneys are sited close to the spot where Hengist and Horsa landed and, later, St Augustine and his 40 monks brought Christianity to the Court of St Ethelbert.

World bids farewell to Winston Churchill

January 23rd: After lying unconscious in the bedroom of his house at Hyde Park Gate for nine days, the soul finally quit the body of Sir Winston Churchill on this wet and blustery Sunday morning. The old warrior left no last word; he died without pain in a quiet cul-de-sac, leaving the world to grieve the passing of the outstanding statesman of the century.

In the small town of Westerham where Churchill made his home, the mourning is not only for a national hero but for one who was part of the community and a friend to many.

Local people recall the occasion in 1938 when he opened the British Legion fete and made a comparison between that carefree British Bank Holiday and the terrible life in Europe under the Nazi regime. They remember the time he came home to Chartwell soon after VE Day in May 1945 and stepped out on the village green to receive a hero's welcome and the occasions when, with the affairs of State upon him again, he visited the Whit Monday carnival on several successive years, clearly relishing the uninhibited spectacle with his special verve for life.

After the lying-in-state at Westminster Hall the funeral service will take place on Saturday when Sir Winston's body will be borne in solemn procession to St Paul's Cathedral via his beloved Whitehall.

Among the representatives of 110 nations will be two members of Westerham British Legion. Branch standard bearer Ron Ayres will walk alongside Captain Robert Evans. Inside the Cathedral they will meet up with the staff of Chartwell who have also received invitations to the funeral.

The Greatest Englishman could have selected a final resting place in Westminster Cathedral but he chose to be buried in the village churchyard near his family's ancestral home at Blenheim Palace, Oxfordshire.

Tributes to Churchill are already pouring in to Chartwell and Hyde Park Gate from all over the world. In the House of Commons on Monday there will be more veterans recalling his finest hours. The tributes will be eloquent. There is a void in the nation.

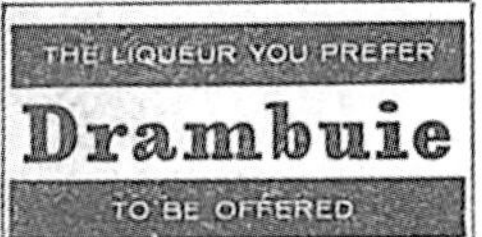

Evening Standard
43,731 MONDAY, JANUARY 25, 1965 4d. 3

LYING-IN-STATE For 23 hours a day you can file by

The funeral plans

By ROBERT CARVEL

It was the turn of Parliament today to pay its tributes to Sir Winston Churchill in acceding to the Queen's request that he should be accorded the

By MICHAEL F. KING

Official details of the three-day lying-in-state in Westminster Hall for Sir Winston Churchill were announced today from the Office of the Lord Great Chamberlain, the Marquess of Cholmondeley. The announcement confirms that the lying-in-state will last from Wednesday until Friday.

The following are the times of admission:

WEDNESDAY: 9 a.m. to 10 a.m.: Peers and Members of Parliament. Ten a.m. to 10.30 a.m.: Members of the Royal Household, Diplomatic Corps,

The world's leaders will be there

BACK PAGE

Churchill by his lieutenants

PAGE EIGHT

SUNDAY EXPRESS

JANUARY 31 1965 Lighting-up Time 5.17 p.m. to 7.9 a.m. (Mon.). Founded by LORD BEAVERBROOK Moon Rises 7.31 a.m. Sets 3.15 p.m. PRICE 6d.

CHURCHILL SPECIAL ISSUE

On the steps of St. Paul's . . . a family filled with sorrow

THE FAMILY at St. Paul's. Grandson Winston walks with Mr. Soames behind Lady Audley (daughter Sarah) and Mrs. Soames (daughter Mary), Lady Churchill and Randolph

GOODBYE, SIR WINSTON

Sometimes a baby's cry broke the stillness

KINGS and Queens, Presidents and Prime

The Golden Arrow Service leaving Dover for Calais, en route for Paris. The journey from London to the French capital takes just over six hours. The sea journey is one hour and 45 minutes. See page158

Broadstairs boy, Ted Heath, is new leader of the Tory Party

July 27th: Edward Heath today became the first Grammar School boy to land the job as leader of the Conservative Party. The MP for Bexley who was born in Broadstairs and attended Chatham House School, Ramsgate, beat Reginald Maudling and Enoch Powell in a contest among fellow MPs.

Heath, at 49, is the party's youngest leader for almost 100 years. His first task is to restore party morale which has been sagging badly. Sir Alec Douglas-Home decided some weeks ago that it was time for him to make way "for more vigorous management".

A preservation group has been formed to restore the Kent and East Sussex Railway from Tenterden towards Robertsbridge. It was closed to passengers in 1954 but freight transport continued for a few more years. Steam enthusiasts now have the difficult but rewarding task of repairing much of the track and restoring the stations and halts. The section first opened in 1903 as the Rother Valley Railway but changed its name to the Kent and East Sussex when Tenterden to Headcorn opened in 1905.

Maidstone has become the fourth Kent town to bestow the Freedom of the Borough on the Corps of Royal Engineers when 250 soldiers, with bayonets fixed, marched through the town. It followed the opening of their new home, Invicta Park Barracks, by the mayor, Cllr Capt John Evans. The three other boroughs to confer the honour on the Corps of R.E.'s are Chatham, Gillingham and Rochester.

To mark the bicentenary of the launching at Chatham on May 7th, 1665, of history's most famous warship, HMS Victory, the Royal Navy, HM Dockyard and the town of Chatham have organised a week of celebrations.

Archaeologists have excavated the site of the Faversham Abbey's Royal Chapel (under a school playing field) hoping to find the two vaults which contained the remains of King Stephen (who founded the Abbey) and his wife Matilda. They were disappointed. They discovered the mausoleum — seven ft by seven — but inside there was no trace of the bodies or the coffins. It was assumed that the coffins were robbed after the dissolution of the monasteries in 1538. In the Trinity Chapel of St Mary's Church a brass plate above a stone tomb states "In memory of Stephen, King of England, buried at Faversham".

The opening of the Dartford tunnel has caused the closure of the car ferry between Gravesend and Tilbury. The last two boats were the *Minnie* (1927) and the *Tessa* (1924).

Knockholt is the highest placed village in Kent, built on the chalk hills of the North Downs. It has a green, old houses, delightful villas and is surrounded by farmland. Residents are seething over their new status as ratepayers of Greater London and vow to fight with all the character and pride for which the village is famous.

Anguish over new name as Big Bromley takes over

April 1st: The newly formed, much despised, Greater London Council officially came into being today. Not only has it taken over such historic Kentish towns as Bromley, Beckenham and Bexley but extended its greedy fingers into the countryside to gather in Knockholt, Downe and Farnborough — idyllic villages all.

The new London boroughs, however, are still part of Kent. Dame Patricia Hornsby-Smith made this clear on Monday when she told members of the county society that the area is being taken over for administrative purposes only. "We are still Kentish Men and Fair Maids", she said, "and always will be".

These comments were endorsed by Kent County Council last week as they said goodbye to six aldermen and 17 councillors. "It will take more than an Act of Parliament to damp down the spirit of Kent", the chairman, Major Sir Charles Pym told them.

By merging with Beckenham, Orpington, Chislehurst Sidcup and Penge, little Bromley has now become Big Bromley with 39,266 acres — the largest in area of the new 32 London boroughs.

Alderman H.T. Parkin, a Beckenham man, is the first mayor but many of the former council officers will be leaving the authority — now known at County Hall as Borough 19.

The name Bromley was decided after much anguish. Orpington wanted the name Kentgate to be adopted but was told artificial hybrids should be avoided. Beckenham also rejected Bromley and suggested Ravensbourne but as that was a constituent name it was quickly dropped.

It was the Minister of Housing and Local Government Sir Keith Joseph who made the final choice, despite great opposition in the House from Mr Eric Lubbock, Liberal member for Orpington, who showed such dissent that he was ruled out of order by the Speaker.

Also showing dissent is the woodland village of Knockholt, 770 feet high on the North Downs and famous for its views, beeches and 13th century church. Villagers want to be transferred to the Sevenoaks authority and vow they will fight until they get their way.

The burning deck of the Yousof Baksh. For Kent's firefighters it was one of the biggest conflagrations at sea ever experienced.

Crew rescued but fireman dies as huge blaze engulfs freighter

May 8th: Kent firemen, working in shifts, have taken four days to control a fire on board the Pakistani freighter, *Yousof Baksh.* The drama at sea began when the vessel, carrying a highly inflammable cargo of jute, cotton and oil cake, caught fire and blazed so furiously from bow to stern that a lifeboat and helicopter were called to rescue the crew, women and children.

The freighter, in danger of sinking, had to be beached about 300 yards off Deal. Meanwhile firemen with their equipment were ferried out to the burning ship while privately-owned motor boats were requisitioned to take reinforcements to those already on board. An SOS went out to fire fighting tugs and two arrived, one from Germany almost 300 miles away.

Thousands of people stood on the seafront to watch the ship, burning so furiously that it could be clearly seen on the French coast. Kent firemen worked in relays and, on the third day, Retained Fireman Reginald Deveson collapsed and died from the heat and exhaustion.

Eventually the flames were brought under control, the vessel refloated and towed, badly damaged to Germany.

July 20th: *John Surtees (right) world motor racing champion was delighted yesterday to receive a special commemorative plaque to mark his success on four wheels. Seven times world motorcycle champion and a former two-wheeled Brands Hatch champion, Surtees is now a household name throughout Europe. The plaque was presented to him by the reigning "King of Brands" —motorcycle champion, Derek Minter —at the clubhouse on the new Grand Prix circuit. In return Surtees presented the clubhouse with the steering wheel from his championship-winning Ferrari and that will be placed alongside the steering wheel from Jim Clark's Lotus in which he won the 1965 European Grand Prix.*

News this year that the paddle steamer, the Medway Queen, *is being preserved at Newport, Isle of Wight, will delight all those holidaymakers and daytrippers who sailed on Kent's most famous ship. The latter includes the 7,000 hungry, exhausted troops of the British Expeditionary Force who were rescued from the beaches of Dunkirk in 1940. Day after day the* Medway Queen *refuelled and came back for more men. With a 12-pounder on her bows she sailed through minefields and shelling from the German batteries and eventually received an ecstatic welcome at Dover.*

Magnificent university on a green hill in Canterbury

October: The University of Kent, built with great foresight on open land on St Thomas's Hill, overlooking Canterbury Cathedral, will soon welcome its first students. Eliot College, named after the American-born poet T.S. Eliot, opened this month. Rutherford (eminent scientist) and Keynes (historian and economist) colleges will follow next year.

Much has happened since 1961 when the Government decreed that six new universities should be established in various parts of the country and Kent was invited to find a suitable site.

There were several contenders for the privilege. Half-empty hotel buildings in Thanet were considered and so was a site at Bridge where a fine old mansion seemed perfect for conversion.

In the end the Interim Committee agreed to continue with educational tradition and base the new university in the city of Canterbury. The site chosen was 267 acres on the crest and southern slopes of St Thomas's Hill and the project forged ahead with great speed.

The Interim Committee has now been superseded by the Council of the University. Its members have great faith in the collegiate system and want the ecclesiastical influence to be strong.

The buildings have been designed by Lord Holford, who is no stranger to Canterbury. The colleges will be cruciform in shape with a large central dining hall rising to full length of the building and large windows which frame the great tower of Bell Harry in the distance.

The University of Kent has opened with three faculties — natural sciences, social sciences and humanities. An appeal for £2 million has been launched to provide amenities for residential accommodation for students to supplement the Government's provision of the essential academic buildings.

H.R.H. Princess Marina, Duchess of Kent, will be installed as the first Chancellor next year (1966). Accepting the invitation she said this week that "to belong to the first generation of students at this University will be a unique experience which carries a special responsibility".

Lord Cornwallis will be Pro-Chancellor and Dr Geoffrey Templeman, Vice-Chancellor.

May 21st: **More than £3,000 in cheques have been returned to nearly 300 homes in the Medway Towns this week as repayment to some of the thousands who contributed to the Marine Cadet Fund, set up in 1951 after 24 boy cadets were killed by a bus.**

It marked the final step in a legal wrangle which began in 1957 when the High Court ruled the fund was not a valid charitable trust and directed that money should be returned to donors where they could be traced.

'It is a place of unknown age and infinite mystery. One cannot imagine anywhere comparable in the country' — author Anne Roper about Dungeness — now the site of a massive new power station.

January 8th: A Viet Cong jungle stronghold north of Saigon was attacked today by 8,000 US troops in the biggest American offensive of the Vietnam war.

January 19th: Mrs Indira Ghandi, 48, daughter of Pandit Nehru is the newly-elected Prime Minister of India. She has taken the place of Lal Bahadur Shastri who died of a heart attack last week.

January 29th: The new breathalyser bill, setting a limit of 80 milligrammes of alcohol in 10cc of blood, has been published. Motoring organisations say it is "an infringement of liberty".

February 8th: Former BUA supremo, Freddie Laker, has set up his own all-jet airline company by buying three BAC One-Elevens at a cost of £4 million. He will now cater for the booming package holiday trade.

After many years of successful trials the first public hovercraft service in the world has opened at Pegwell Bay. A small Westland SRN 6 hovercraft uses a hoverport apron within the harbour and takes passengers to Calais or on pleasure trips to the Goodwin Sands. *See page 153*

March 4th: The second commissioning ceremony of *HMS Kent,* the ninth took place today with a service conducted by the Rev R.W. Pope. The cruiser "dressed ship" for the occasion.

March 17th: The Cheltenham Gold Cup was won today by the Irish steeplechaser Arkle who many now believe to be the greatest jumper of all time.

March 23rd: The first official meeting for 400 years between the heads of the Roman Catholic and Anglican churches took place in Rome today when the Pope and Archbishop Michael Ramsay exchanged a "kiss of peace" in the Sistine Chapel. The meeting in 1960 between Archbishop Fisher and the Pope was unofficial.

April 1st: Princess Marina has been installed as Chancellor of the University of Kent at Canterbury. She becomes the University's first Graduate with an Honorary Degree of Doctor of Civil Law.

Laura Ashley, whose entrepreneurial skills in the design business has made her a household name, is advocating that women wear the maxi skirt which she considers infinitely more attractive than the mini. Laura's burgeoning empire began in a small way when she and husband Bernard opened a small mill in Brasted, near Westerham and installed a machine to print tea towels. The disastrous flood of 1960 put an end to this enterprise so the couple moved to their native Wales.

May 6th: Ian Brady and Myra Hindley have been sentenced to three concurrent terms of life imprisonment for the murders of Edward Evans, aged 17, and two children Lesley Ann Downey, 10 and John Kilbride, 12. Police are still searching for the bodies of two other children on the Moors.

June 2nd: A gas flow of up to 17 million cubic feet a day has been found in the North Sea. More big gas finds are expected.

Summer: Kentish wine, which was so popular in the years during the Roman occupation, will soon be available once more in the county. A vineyard has been sown in a former cherry orchard at Wateringbury and, if successful, may well be the forerunner of more commercial Kentish vineyards. Cherry Hill sits on the slopes around the Medway Valley. *See page 151*

June 30th: Swanley bypass (part of the new A20) opened today .

July 19th: Frank Sinatra married Mia Farrow in Las Vegas today (Tuesday). Last week Brigitte Bardot married Gunther Sachs.

The village of Hoo (Hoh in Old English meaning a piece of land jutting out) has become officially known as Hoo St Werburgh to differentiate it from St Mary's Hoo. The name was taken from the name of the 13th century ragstone church. St Werburgh was a Saxon princess who became a nun and was buried on the site about AD 700. The remains were removed and taken to Chester Cathedral.

July 20th: Prime Minister Harold Wilson has imposed a six-month standstill on wages, prices and dividends, followed by another six months of severe restraint.

September 6th: South African Prime Minister Dr Hendrik Verwoerd was assassinated today in the House of Assembly. Demetrio Tsafendas stabbed Verwoerd four times in the chest with a long stiletto.

October 11th: The Post Office announced today that postcodes will be introduced to all homes starting on November 5th.

October 21st: 116 children and 28 adults were killed today when a slag heap moved down the hillside at Aberfan and engulfed the school and part of the village. The avalanche of black slag demolished the school within seconds. The disaster has shocked the world.

November 9th: The Rootes Group which began in Maidstone earlier in the century today launched their latest model, the Hillman Hunter.

November 24th: Figures released today show that unemployment has risen to 531,000 — almost 100,000 in a month.

November 25th: Warren Mitchell has been named best TV actor of 1966 for his part in the series *'Till Death Us Do Part.*

December 2nd: Harold Wilson and Ian Smith met on *HMS Tiger* for talks on the future of Rhodesia.

GREAT HITS OF 1966

Strangers In The Night

Distant Drums

3,500 Sikhs establish township in Gravesend

Despite the restrictions imposed by the Commonwealth Immigration Act, which became law almost four years ago, more and more members of the Sikh community are choosing to live in the riverside towns of Gravesend and Northfleet, bringing with them great problems of integration.

Since 1956, when the first wave of immigrants arrived, 3,500 Indian Sikhs and a few Pakistanis are now living in North Kent. Their tightly-knit family and village ties have created an almost impenetrable barrier against the outsider.

They were drawn to the borough by the availability of sub-standard houses found mainly near the river. The rehousing programme gave local residents an opportunity to leave the area and landlords were only too ready to sell the then-threatened homes at rock-bottom prices to the immigrants.

Tilbury, a 1/- fare across the Thames, was the landing stage and very quickly the area became an Indian township. Others arrived aboard a mystery yacht which belonged to a wealthy Asian who financed the mass-settlement of his fellow countrymen in Gravesend.

Today the problems are acute, with accusations of overcrowding, devaluation of property, exploitation and language barriers. Local residents have been accused of blind prejudice and the creation of ill-feeling; the immigrants of an inability to mix freely. They have established a separate existence for themselves, setting up their own shops and a cinema and walking together only in groups.

Fights in local pubs, an outbreak of tuberculosis and incidents of prostitution are adding fuel to the fire of those who have shown antagonism towards the Sikhs.

A recent letter to the Reporter urges the citizens of Gravesend to treat everyone equally regardless of religion or race. "Gravesend is one of Britain's most ancient ports with a reputation for hospitality to all newcomers. Let us not see this reputation marred."

Pickles find the World Cup and then England wins it

July 30th: England's football team, captained by Bobby Moore and managed by Alf Ramsay, has won the World Cup for the first time.

In a superb, fluctuating final at Wembley, the red-shirted England team beat an organised West German side by 4-2 in extra time.

Sixteen nations reached the final stages and surpisingly the two favourites, Brazil and Hungary, were quickly eliminated leaving Portugal, England, Russia and West Germany to fight it out in the semi-finals.

West Germany won 2-1 and England also qualified for the final by the same score, thanks to an outstanding performance by Bobby Charlton — setting the stage for the showpiece at Wembley.

The score at full-time was 2-2 and in a nail-biting, frenetic extra time Geoff Hurst scored two goals (one hotly contested) and it was all over.

England were lucky to win the Jules Rimet trophy — not because of the quality of their football but because the cup was stolen in March and a ransom demand received by the F.A.

It was found in a South London garden and the hero was a mongrel dog called Pickles. David Corbett, a Thames lighterman, saw Pickles tearing at an object wrapped in a newspaper. The bundle contained the solid gold Jules Rimet trophy.

Election shock at Bexley for Tory leader Edward Heath

April 1st: Tory Party leader Ted Heath has been re-elected MP for Bexley following yesterday's general election — but not without a big fright.

His majority was cut to just over 2,000 and he had the disappointment of seeing his friend, Patricia Hornsby-Smith, a junior Minister in the previous Conservative administration, lose her seat in the one-time Tory stronghold of Chislehurst and Sidcup.

It was a good day for Labour. The party held onto the north Kent seats of Dartford, Gillingham, Gravesend and Rochester which all followed the national trend.

Labour now has a secure grip on power with an overall majority of 96. It gives Harold Wilson a clear mandate, although the crisis in Rhodesia continues to top his political agenda.

Mr Heath has five years to win the confidence of the people and re-capture the middle ground. With incomes' restraint continuing and the unions showing every sign of rebellion, Mr Heath is confident that his best chance lies on the economic front.

These mini-skirted beauty queens from Medway villages are competing for the title of Miss Strood Rural. Here they are at the Corn Exchange, Rochester.

A symbol of the sixties — mini dresses are turning heads everywhere

More and more girls — and they are certainly not all teenagers — are now wearing the mini dress, condemned by moral watchdogs as an example of the "new permissive society" which, they claim, is rampant in Britain. But as eyebrows and hemlines rise together the young women say they do not care. They see the mini as a symbol of sexual freedom, particularly since the advent of the contraceptive pill. The mini dress was launched by the French designer, Courreges a few years ago and then popularised by Mary Quant and models such as Jean Shrimpton and Twiggy, a waif-like Cockney who weighs 6½ stone and can earn as much as 10 guineas an hour.

Nuclear power station opens at Dungeness

May 26th: The nuclear age reached Kent this week when Lord Hinton of Bankside opened the massive power station at Dungeness which had been commissioned in September last year.

It was almost 20 years ago that scientists at Harwell, Oxfordshire devised a gas-cooled reactor using uranium rods housed in a casing of magnesium (magnox) which produced electrical power, and the plutonium needed for the atomic weapon establishment at Aldermaston.

A magnox reactor, designed to achieve both these purposes, was built at Calder Hall on the Sellafield site, opening in 1956 as the country's first large-scale nuclear powerplant.

Dungeness is the fifth station in the nuclear power programme and is linked to the National Grid by volt lines, supplying the south coast and London via the Canterbury-Northfleet connection.

Nuclear power is now a major source of the country's electric energy and scientists are predicting that, one day, it may even exceed coal as the largest. Certainly Dungeness is considered to be one of the best in the country as it is close to deep water for cooling purposes and the land utilised for the project was of minimal value to agriculture.

The huge cooling towers of the completed power station now dominate the flat marshland for many miles around.

'Red Dean' of Canterbury dies at 92

The Very Reverend Dr Hewlett Johnson, Dean of Canterbury and one of the most controversial figures in the Church of England, has died just three weeks after the publication of his autobiography *Searching for Light.* He was 92.

Because of his outspoken views on socialism which made him a hated figure among his fellow Canons and his Chapter, Dr Johnson has been denied a memorial service or burial in the Cathedral for which he fought so hard. Instead he will be laid to rest in the Cloister Garth in the precincts.

Known as the Red Dean because of his books, speeches and well-publicised tours across China, Russia and Central Asia, Dr Johnson was a star performer in the Cathedral and the people of Canterbury had a soft spot for him.

He raised the standard of ceremonial and music in the Cathedral, he travelled widely raising funds and in one tour of New Zealand, he preached 98 sermons in 38 days.

Before the war he demanded better nutrition for England's malnourished children. When the Blitz was over he gave shelter to the homeless in his damaged Deanery, held recitals for homesick troops and entertained many officers including General Montgomery.

His first book *The Socialist Sixth of the World* ran to 22 editions in 24 languages. His collected sermons *Christians and Communism* sold out in Moscow within seven hours of publication. He was awarded both the Stalin Peace Prize and the Star of Mongolia.

Archbishop Geoffrey Fisher who knew him well admired him greatly as a man but was opposed to his views.

September 12th: *Scores of friends and wellwishers travelled to Caxton Hall, London today to see popular Chislehurst GP, Dr Emmanuel Cowan marry the singing star Joan Regan.*

Front page news for *The Times!*

November: *The Times* may soon have a new owner — Canadian-born Roy Thomson who is trying to build a newspaper empire in Britain.

This month Gavin Astor of Hever, who has held a 90 per cent holding in *The Times* since his father became domiciled in the south of France announced his intention to set up a new company in which Lord Thomson of Fleet will have an 85 per cent interest but he, Astor, will remain on the board.

Mr Astor has been convinced for many years that only a large injection of capital will save *The Times*. Ownership of the prestige newspaper has brought his family much honour if little profit and he regards his decision to sell as a cruel necessity.

continued on page 131

County infantry regiment is absorbed with The Queen's

December 31st: After a lifespan of just five years and ten months, Kent's single county regiment, The Queen's Own Buffs, The Royal Kent Regiment exists no longer. Today, at a short but moving parade at Gun Club Barracks, the blue and buff flag with its White Horse badge was lowered to be replaced by the colours of the new Queen's Regiment.

The former county regiment thus becomes the 2nd Battalion, the Queen's Regiment (Queen's Own Buffs) with Princess Marina as Colonel-in-Chief and King Frederick of Denmark as Allied Colonel-in-Chief.

Since the amalgamation in 1961 controversy has never been far away, with prolonged and heated bargaining over the title and other marks of identity. But the infantry has travelled extensively — England, Kenya, Cyprus, Canada, British Guiana, Denmark, Germany, Hong Kong, Sabah and Sarawak. Many of these successful missions have been in troubled lands in which the county regiment had to act as a stabilising influence.

Freddie Laker with his mother. In the background is a DC10.

continued from previous page

He said recently that the world of the 1960s is far removed from that of the 1920s when his father acquired the paper. "The age when proprietors could successfully run their newspapers as a sideline is fading. Survival and prosperity today depend upon brilliant commercial and professional management."

One revolution introduced on May 3rd this year was to put news on the front page for the first time but its immediate effect has been to increase costs rather than revenue. Mr Astor will remain close to *The Times* but he will now concentrate on opening Hever Castle to the public to defray the burden of costly upkeep. ***See page 167***

Freddie Laker — king of the holiday trade

February 8th: Ramsgate's popular aviation entrepreneur Freddie Laker has bought three BAC One-Eleven 75-seater airlines at a cost of £4 million and promises he will make holidays abroad even cheaper and longer.

A hero now among thousands of the travelling public outside the Isle of Thanet, Freddie has taken full advantage of the booming package holiday trade to pioneer cheap air travel. He has also set up a new company called Laker Airways.

Mr Laker is 43. He was educated at the Simon Langton School, Canterbury, where an interest in aviation first developed. In 1938 he joined Short Brothers at Rochester and worked with the Air Transport Auxiliary during the war. For many years he was employed by Aviation Traders before joining British United Airways in 1960 as managing director. Within five years he had turned the company into Britain's largest independent carrier.

This week he said that he started his career with a £46 RAF demob pay and is now able to spend millions of pounds in setting up Laker Airways.

September 26th: Jack Warner with the cast of Dixon of Dock Green. *The popular TV series is now in its 12th year.*

The wise old copper who solves a crime each week

September: Evening all! The well-known catch phrase belongs to George Dixon (alias Jack Warner), an avuncular old East End copper who applies reassuring and traditional wisdom as he helps to solve a crime every week.

Before he evolved into the reliable London bobby in BBC Television's *Dixon of Dock Green*, Jack Warner was a cabaret singer, cockney comedian and star of several films including the *Blue Lamp*. He had no formal training as an actor and performed rather than acted in a style that was ideal for radio and film.

He lived for many years at Kingsgate and appeared regularly in the Winter Garden, Margate and other Kent seaside venues.

He was born Horace John Waters in Bromley in 1895 and his two sisters Elsie and Doris became successful as radio and variety comediennes, Gert and Daisy, before the war.

Warner, however, will always be best known for PC Dixon. This first television police series which began in 1955 was written by Ted Willis, the prolific play and screenwriter who lives at Chislehurst.

Ted Willis began his writing career in 1936 while he was a tramp. He and his friend Joe were sleeping rough and odd-jobbing here and there and were so short of cash that Ted committed his adventures to paper. He was paid 7s 6d — a fortune for a gentleman of the road.

Since then Ted has gone from strength to strength. At the end of the war he was appointed artistic director of the Unity Theatre.

'In a decade dominated by youth, London has burst into bloom. It swings; it is The Scene' — Time Magazine, New York.

January 1st: Alf Ramsay, manager of England's World Cup winning football team, has been knighted in the New Year honours.

January 4th: Donald Campbell died today when his jet-powered Bluebird somersaulted and plunged into Coniston Water during an attempt to break his own water speed record.

January 12th: Britain's largest new town, built on 22,000 acres of Buckinghamshire countryside, will be called Milton Keynes.

January 13th: The London Borough of Bromley is to enter negotiations to buy Biggin Hill aerodrome.

January 18th: Jeremy Thorpe, extrovert Old Etonian, has been chosen as the new leader of the Liberal Party in place of Jo Grimond who has retired.

March 14th: Nine executives of the German company that launched the drug known as thalidomide have been charged with causing death by negligence and contravening drug laws.

March 19th: An oil tanker, *The Torrey Canyon,* ran aground off Lands End today spilling her oil cargo which is fouling the Cornish beaches.

April 8th: Foinavon, a rank outsider at 100-1, today won the Grand National when most of the horses fell at the 23rd fence.

April 10th: Actress Elizabeth Taylor, who lived, as a child, at Manor Farm in the grounds of Great Swifts, Cranbrook, has won an Oscar for her role in *Who's Afraid of Virginia Woolf.*

April 30th: Cassius Clay, the boxer who now calls himself Muhammad Ali, has been stripped of his world title for refusing military service.

May 1st: Sandie Shaw, the barefooted British singer, has won the Eurovision Song Contest.

May 4th: Folkestone's new civic centre was opened today by Princess Alexandra in the presence of the mayors of Folkestone and Boulogne and the Burgomaster of Middleburg.

The seventh Earl Stanhope, of Chevening House near Sevenoaks, who died this year. The Lennards and the Stanhopes have lived at Chevening for several hundred years and the famous traveller, Lady Hester, niece of William Pitt the younger, was born there in 1776. See page 135

June 2nd: Kent Cricket Club held a dinner yesterday at the Royal Star Hotel, Maidstone, in honour of their great all-rounder Frank Woolley who was celebrating his 80th birthday.

June 4th: 78 people, returning from Majorca, were killed today when a British Midlands Argonaut crashed four miles from Manchester. Yesterday, a DC-4 carrying 83 passengers to the Costa Brava crashed into the Pyrenees.

June 10th: The six-day war between Israel and the Arab states ended today when Israel observed the UN ceasefire. Casualties are estimated to be more than 100,000.

The White Hart public house at Newenden has come first in the Evening Standard's "Pub of the Year" contest.

July 3rd: ITV today launched a regular daily news programme called *News at Ten.*

July 8th: Vivien Leigh, former wife of Laurence Olivier and best known for her performance as Scarlet O'Hara in *Gone With the Wind,* died today aged 53 from tuberculosis.

Kent archaeological unit has excavated a Roman barrack block at Reculver.

July 14th: The controversial Bill to legalise abortion is expected to become law later this year.

August 27th: Brian Epstein, manager of The Beatles, was found dead today in his house in Belgravia. Foul play is not suspected.

The first comprehensive school in Kent has been opened at Swanley.

September 30th: BBC's Light and Third programmes and the Home Service have been abolished to make way for Radios One, Two, Three and Four.

October 8th: Former Prime Minister Clement (later Earl) Attlee died today aged 84. From 1945 to 1951 he led Labour's first majority government.

October 10th: Among six guerrillas killed in Bolivia is Ernesto "Che" Guevara, the Argentine-born hero of Latin American revolutionaries.

November 19th: The pound has been devalued. In the worst financial crisis for 20 years the exchange rate was brought down today from two dollars 80 cents to two dollars 40 cents — a fall of 14.3%.

December 3rd: A team of 30 Cape Town doctors led by Professor Christian Barnard gave a new heart today to a man suffering from heart failure.

December 11th: England and France celebrated a triumph of international co-operation today by introducing Concorde — the world's first supersonic airliner.

December 14th: The Lawn Tennis Association has ended the distinction between amateurs and professionals. Wimbledon will be an open championship next year.

December 26th: Tommy Steele's musical Half a Sixpence was premiered today in London.

GREAT HITS OF 1967

The Last Waltz

Please Release Me

There Goes My Everything

The famous four in Knole Park, Sevenoaks where they were making a film to accompany their new songs. It will soon be shown on television.

What's this? Beatlemania in Sevenoaks

February 6th: Scores of children from schools in the Sevenoaks area played truant yesterday (Tuesday) in order to grab a ringside seat in Knole Park where the Fab Four, as they are known, were making a television film to illustrate their new songs, *Penny Lane* and *Strawberry Fields For Ever.*

John, Paul, George and Ringo — whose music is having such a remarkable effect on modern popular culture and permeating every level of society — appeared quietly in the deer park hoping there would be no scenes of the mass hysteria — which they always seem to attract.

For a while five girls had the Beatles to themselves and they were all given autographs if they promised not to tell their friends. On Tuesday, however, the scene changed and the supposedly deserted hillside became a sea of straw boaters as pupils from Sevenoaks School joined those who were already there.

One of the girls who watched the entire shooting for the promotional film which will be played on *Top of The Pops* said: "I fainted three times yesterday. None of us have ever had such a wonderful thing happen." Another said: "I don't care if my headmistress turns up. I'm not leaving. I will stay here all night."

A sequence in the film will show Paul McCartney dropping out of a tree and running backwards to a battered piano which he will then start playing.

The filming was intended to be in Richmond Park but John Lennon said: "This is better. It's gorgeous here."

The beautiful Chevening House, near Sevenoaks, along with its great park and wonderful treasures has been left to the nation in the will of the seventh Earl Stanhope, who has died without an heir. Stanhope, a one-time Leader of the House of Lords, had been anxious for some years that Chevening should continue to be a family home and a worthy part of our heritage.

An Act of Parliament, drawn up in 1959, made the Prime Minister as the first choice, a cabinet minister as the second while "a lineal descendant of George VI, or the spouse, widow or widower of such a descendant" as the third choice from whom the Prime Minister may nominate.

The estate will now be administered by the Trust until a decision is made as to the next occupant but it is no secret that Prince Charles, nineteen on November 14th, must be among the possible candidates. There is no lovelier corner so near to London and this impressive house on the slopes of the North Downs and at the bottom of a lane that has no turning, would make an ideal home for the heir to the throne — and his future wife and family.

December 29th: Tilmanstone Quarry — the oldest, smallest and most troubled of the four Kent pits — may be closed by June, putting more than 800 men out of work. This is the grim implication in a decision revealed by the National Coal Board yesterday (Thursday). The news broke after a day of talks between National Coal Board chiefs and miners' representatives who learned that the Tilmanstone has just three months to meet a target imposed by the Board. Miners will have to step up output per manshift overall from between 25-30 cwt to 49 cwt...because the pit is currently losing money at the rate of £500,000 a year.

Norman Dodds — champion of the gipsy cause

It appears that the gipsies of Kent, who are camped in woods, marshes, roadside verges, slum clearance areas and even refuse dumps all over the county, have at least one influential friend. For 22 years Mr Norman Dodds, MP for Dartford and later Erith and Belvedere, has conducted a one-man campaign exposing the hard facts of nomadic life and attempting to persuade the authorities to treat all travellers as human beings.

His crusade has culminated in a book highlighting stories of neglect and persecution which, he says, have disgraced our treatment of these unfortunate people for years.

The book called *Gipsies, Didikois and Other Travellers* has received much publicity, stimulating Mr Dodds' cause and showing the inhuman way in which the problem had been tackled by almost every council in Kent.

Mr Dodds has visited most camps, including the largest in Britain at Belvedere Marshes on the south side of the Thames where children and dogs play together in a sea of mud. He has visited Corkes Meadow, St Mary Cray, Hever Road, Edenbridge, King Hill, West Malling, Cobham Camp and Darenth Wood, near Dartford where, he says, 200 gipsies were martyred by a brutal and ruthless eviction covered by both television channels when they were forced to move to the wilderness of the verges of the A2.

In a leader the *Times* wrote: "A bureaucratic machine has been marshalled against victims whose helplessness merits sympathy. The two councils concerned (Darenth Parish and Dartford Rural) do not even have the excuse that their action was taken in the heat of the moment..."

Mr Dodds has attended public inquiries, spoken at parish meetings across the county, addressed parliament on numerous occasions, lobbied ministers and even spoken to Labour leader Harold Wilson who took up the campaign. In many cases he has won considerable respite.

The problem, he says, is not insoluble. "Once a national policy has been implemented, it is up to local authorities to shoulder responsibility and establish the integration of the gipsies into the community to which they rightly belong."

1967

Rolling Stones sent to jail on drugs charges

June 29th: Drugs may prove be the downfall of *The Rolling Stones,* the successful rock group which was formed in Kent in 1962 by the former Dartford Grammar School boy Mick Jagger and his friends Keith Richards, rhythm guitar, and Brian Jones, lead guitar.

All three have been sent to prison for various terms after a jury found them guilty of drug offences following a police raid on Richards' home in Sussex. Richards has been jailed for a year and Jagger, three months. Jones will be sentenced later.

Left to right: Charlie Watts, Mick Jagger, Keith Richard, Brian Jones and Bill Wyman.

The Dartford boys who share, with *The Beatles*, the leading position in the British pop scene, burst into prominence in 1963 when they introduced the sound of black rhythm and blues which carried their first LP (called *The Rolling Stones*) to the top of the UK charts.

By then they had been joined by Bill Wyman, bass, and Charlie Watts, drums, and acquired a manager in Andrew Loog Oldham who saw their potential as a wild and rebellious alternative to the clean-cut group from Liverpool.

The *Rolling Stones* are noisier and scruffier with perhaps more sex appeal. Their first single to reach the top of the charts in both the UK and the USA was *I Can't Get No Satisfaction,* in 1965.

Mick Jagger, who writes most of the lyrics, left Dartford Grammar School in 1960 with A Levels in English, History and French. He was then living with his parents, Basil Joe and Eva in Wilmington and took on a summer job selling ice creams outside Dartford Library.

At the London School of Economics he teamed up again with his old choirboy chum, Keith Richards who had been at Wilmington Primary School at the same time as Jagger. The two persuaded commercial artist and occasional jazz drummer, Charlie Watts to change his day job and, with Brian Jones, from Cheltenham and Bill Perks (later Wyman) from Beckenham completing the line-up, this London beat combo was formed. They called themselves *Rollin' Stones* after a song by their hero, American blues legend Muddy Waters — and then changed to *Rolling Stones.*

The story then jumps from one success to another. Manager Oldham encouraged the Stones to adopt an attitude of anti-establishment. They appeared to have little difficulty in producing an aggressive reputation which the fans love.

During the last few years newspapers have been full of reports of rioting fans. There has been a paternity suit against Jagger and a charge of urinating against a petrol station wall. Their performances have been described as one big sexual assault by Mick Jagger on a huge screaming audience of willing girls. As their music got wilder they even decided they could do without a manager.

The recent drug trial has badly affected their standing among the thousands of loyal fans. Older people suggest they are "fallen idols" — folk heroes who will never recover their former identity. "The Rolling Stones", they say, "are finished".

Jagger and Co were with art gallery owner Robert Fraser when they were arrested and initially charged at Chichester magistrates court where they pleaded not guilty. The trial and the sentences followed.

July 31st: Mick Jagger and Keith Richard (he has now dropped the 's') walked free today after appeal court judges quashed the prison sentences that followed their recent trial. After leaving the court Jagger was whisked away by helicopter to an unknown destination where he will give a television interview.

Chagall church window in memory of Sarah

December: Marc Chagall, the Russian-born French Jew, who is considered to be one of the greatest living artists, saw his latest masterpiece dedicated this month in the tiny village church of Tudeley, near Tonbridge. His design, brilliantly translated into stained glass, of the memorial east window commemorates the tragic death of a 21-year-old girl who lived nearby.

Sarah Venetia was the daughter of Sir Henry and Lady d'Avigdor-Goldsmid of Somerhill, Tonbridge. In 1963 she and two of her companions were drowned in a sailing accident off the coast of Rye.

In her memory, her family and many friends subscribed to the restoration of the interior of All Saints' Church where they worshipped and her father, a Member of Parliament, commissioned Chagall to design the window.

Sarah, on a visit to Paris in the summer of 1961, had visited the Chagall exhibition at the Louvre — the first living artist to be exhibited there — and had been enraptured by the great windows Chagall had designed for the synagogue of the Hadassah Medical Centre in Jerusalem,.

The recollection of their daughter's admiration of Chagall's stained glass became the inspiration which led Sir Henry to commission Marc Chagall to design a memorial window at Tudeley. Seeing his completed work for the first time this week, Chagall, who is aged 74, said: *"C'est magnifique, je ferai les tous"*. Tudeley is his only commission in England and he has said he would now like to prepare designs for the entire church.

The memorial east window of All Saints' Church, Tudeley shows the drama of a young girl drowning in the swirling waters of the sea and angel figures waiting for the arrival of new young souls.

June 13th: Lone yachtsman Francis Chichester has been knighted by the Queen. A special ceremony took place today at Greenwich Naval College to honour the man who completed his epic 28,500-mile voyage round the world two weeks ago. Gipsy Moth IV received a tumultuous welcome from hundreds of small craft as it crossed the finishing line at Plymouth after 119 days at sea. There was another great welcome today for the 65-year-old lone sailor who hopes his now-famous yacht will eventually be preserved at Greenwich.

August 7th: High Elms, Downe, formerly the home of Sir John Lubbock, once Liberal MP for Maidstone, has been destroyed by fire. Lubbock was a scientific writer, sociologist and a friend of Charles Darwin. But he was best known as the begetter of "Lubbock's Day" — the national Bank Holiday which he introduced through a Bill in Parliament in 1871. Ironic that his great house should burn down on Bank Holiday Monday.

August 24th: Members of the County Society, the Earl of Guildford and officers of *HMS Kent* were among the guests today who commemorated the 750th anniversary of the great Battle of Sandwich which took place in the Channel in 1217. The celebration was held in the chapel of the Hospital of St Bartholomew at Sandwich.

Several members of the Great Train gang, the well-organised robbers who stole mailbags worth well in excess of £2.5 million in August 1963, are serving their sentences in Maidstone Prison.

November: Chartwell Manor, Westerham, the country home of Sir Winston Churchill from 1922, has completed its first full season as one of Britain's major showplaces. More than 200,000 people have visited the gardens and the house since they were first opened last year. Already it is second in popularity in the National Trust's properties.

An evangelical trust led by the charismatic Tom Rees has taken over Sir Oliver Lyle's great house on the North Downs above Kemsing. Built in 1930 in a competition for the most expensive house in Britain, it was the home of the sugar magnate for many years. The house will be renamed after Hildenborough Hall where the evangelical centre started.

Siegfried Sassoon, a brave Kentish Man

September 1st: Siegfried Sassoon, who became internationally known through his savagely realistic and compassionate first world war poems, has died aged 82.

Sassoon was born at Weirleigh, Paddock Wood and his first school was at Sevenoaks. As a commissioned officer in the Great War, nicknamed "Mad Jack", he won the VC for bravery. In 1917, while recovering from a wound, he wrote a violent attack on the conduct of the war, accusing the military authorities of deliberately prolonging it.

His letter was read out in the House of Commons and Sassoon expected a court martial. Instead he was declared to be suffering from shell shock and sent to a military hospital, from where, it is believed, there were attempts to move him on to a lunatic asylum.

The Kent squad of 1967. Back row (left to right): Alan Ealham, Brian Luckhurst, Derek Underwood, John Prodger, Norman Graham, John Dye, Alan Knott, David Nicholls. Front row: Mike Denness, Bob Wilson, Stuart Leary, Colin Cowdrey, Alan Dixon, Alan Brown, David Sayer.

At last — a cricket trophy for the hop county

September 2nd: Kent Cricket Club's barren years without a trophy is over at last. At Lord's today the county won the Gillette Cup knock-out contest beating Somerset by 32 runs. It was an exciting and memorable occasion.

Kent supporters, present in their thousands, were delighted to see the Lord's pavilion decorated by a garland of hops. They were even more delighted when Denness and Luckhurst put on 78 for the first wicket.

After a middle-order slump Kent were all out for 193. This was enough. Kent held their catches, the bowling was tight, Colin Cowdrey received the cup from the President of the MCC and Denness won the Man of the Match award.

September 20th: Patient team building over the previous 10 years is reaping its rewards. Kent have finished second to Yorkshire in the County Championship, despite the fact that Cowdrey, Knott and Underwood have been on Test duty.

Buckled railway lines, overturned coaches and a complete disruption of the train service — the scene at Hither Green on November 6th, after yet another tragedy on this stretch of line.

49 killed, 78 hurt in another rail tragedy

December 15th: Following an inquiry into the serious derailment of an express train at Hither Green in which 49 passengers were killed and 78 injured, it has now been confirmed that the tragedy was caused by a small piece of steel which had broken away from the railway line.

The crash occurred on Sunday November 5th — just a month short of the 10th anniversary of the Lewisham disaster. On this occasion the train was approaching Hither Green on the up-line at 70 mph when the third coach struck the offending steel wedge and became derailed. Four coaches overturned and were dragged along for some yards.

The scene was chillingly similar to that at St John's, 10 years earlier, with scores of dead and injured passengers trapped under tons of twisted metal. The train was packed with many standing in the corridors. These people stood no chance.

Calls for assistance were immediate. Within eight minutes of the accident, police, ambulances and firemen were on the scene and the first casualties reached hospital just 18 minutes after the crash at 9.16 pm.

The Salvation Army, Women's Voluntary Service and other welfare organisations helped local residents assist and comfort those who were injured or suffering from shock.

The train was the 7.43 fast from Hastings to Charing Cross. It had joined the electrified line at Tonbridge, travelling through Sevenoaks and Orpington before leaving the rails between Grove Park and Hither Green. Both the up and down fast lanes were blocked by the fallen coaches and these caused short circuits which cut off the traction current and created widespread dislocation of the train service.

The Ministry of Transport confirmed this week that the derailment was caused by the fracture of the rail at a joint. The coaches overturned because the derailed wheels struck a connection a short distance ahead. No blame was attached to either driver or guard.

'Enid Blyton was a tiresome, insecure, pretentious woman whose only interesting feature was the ability to pour out unlimited quantities of harmless drivel' — Rosemary Dinnage, Times Literary Supplement.

January 1st: A new movement called *I'm Backing Britain* has been started by five typists from Surbiton. Politicians and the press have joined in, suggesting that Britain could be great once more.

January 31st: Peter Hall has handed over the directorship of the Royal Shakespeare Company to Trevor Nunn.

February 22nd: There is to be new legislation to prevent Asian immigrants gaining such an easy entry into Britain. During the last few weeks at least 2,500 have arrived all holding British passports.

February 24th: The Americans and South Vietnamese have recaptured the city of Hue which had been seized by Viet Cong guerrillas.

March 15th: George Brown today resigned as Foreign Secretary, accusing Mr Wilson of running the Cabinet in a dictatorial fashion.

March 16th: President Johnson is to send another 50,000 troops to Vietnam.

Robert Kennedy, brother of John, announced today that he is a candidate for the Presidency of the United States.

March 21st: Road deaths in Kent have shown a sharp decline since the introduction of the breath test.

April 2nd: Today is the 100th anniversary of the last woman to be hanged in public — outside Maidstone Jail.

April 4th: Dr Martin Luther King was shot dead in Memphis today by an unknown white assassin who escaped in a car. King became internationally known through his *"I have a dream"* speech in 1963.

April 7th: Jim Clark, twice world Formula One champion, was killed instantly at the Hockenheim circuit in West Germany today.

April 11th: Racial tension in America has reached boiling point since the murder of Dr Luther King. There have been riots in dozens of towns and cities.

Alan Knott, 22-year-old Kent wicket-keeper played in all five Test matches against Australia this year, forming a remarkable partnership with Derek Underwood. Knott, who was born in Belvedere made his Kent debut in 1964 and first played for England last year. He is on course for a brilliant career.

May 6th: Following Enoch Powell's *"rivers of blood"* speech on April 21st a Gallop Poll has suggested that 74 per cent of Britons support him.

May 9th: Charlie, Reggie and Ronnie Kray and 18 others have been charged with conspiracy to murder and fraud.

May 10th: A seven-sided 50 New Pence coin is to replace the ten shilling note.

May 22nd: The Manchester United footballer, Bobby Charlton, today scored a record 45th goal for England.

June 6th: Senator Robert Kennedy was killed today in the Ambassador Hotel, Los Angeles, hours after winning the Californian Democratic primary election.

June 7th: A Palestinian Arab immigrant, Sirhan Sirhan, has been charged with the murder of Robert Kennedy.

June 8th: James Earl Ray, the man wanted in connection with the murder of Dr Martin Luther King, was arrested in London yesterday.

June 24th: The comedian Tony Hancock, star of *Hancock's Half Hour,* was found dead in a Sydney hotel room today.

July 1st: 26 nations have signed a Nuclear Non-Proliferation Treaty.

July 5th: Lone yachtsman, Alec Rose was knighted today.

July 6th: Australian Rod Laver today won the men's singles in the first open championship at Wimbledon. Billie Jean King won the women's final.

July 17th: A dinner was held at the Royal Star Hotel, Maidstone tonight to celebrate Colin Cowdrey's 100th Test cap.

July 29th: Pope Paul today told the world's Catholic community that any form of artificial birth control was against the divine will.

August 28th: Basil D'Olivera, England's Cape-Coloured all-rounder, has been omitted from the South African cricket tour, despite an innings of 158 against Australia last week.

September 8th: Virginia Wade, former Tunbridge Wells Grammar School girl, beat Billie Jean King to become the first women's open tennis champion of the US.

September 17th: Mr Vorster, the South African Prime Minister, has cancelled the MCC cricket tour following the news that Basil D'Olivera has been named as a replacement for the injured Tom Cartwright.

Under the Harbours Act of 1964, the powers, duties, properties, rights and liabilities of a number of existing harbour authorities has been transferred to a new body named the Medway Ports Authority.

October 27th: Clench-fisted salutes of the American "black power" athletes brought controversy to the Mexico City Olympic Games this month.

November 3rd: Graham Hill today became the world motor racing champion.

GREAT HITS OF 1968

Wonderful World

I Pretend

April 11th: *A very happy Colin Cowdrey in the garden of his home, Kentish Border, Limpsfield with his wife Penny and his three sons and one daughter. Cowdrey had just returned from the West Indies where he captained England to a 1-0 series win against the mighty Caribbean team skippered by Garfield Sobers. Cowdrey scored two centuries and handled his bowlers brilliantly throughout the tour. His Kent colleague, Alan Knott, played in the last two Tests. The Kent and England skipper is now looking forward to the arrival of the Australians for the Ashes series in England. So are his cricket-mad sons, Jeremy, Christopher and Graham.*

Housing estates mushroom as the cherry orchards vanish

March 29th: If intensive development in the Sittingbourne, Sheppey and Faversham area continues for a few more years the finest cherry orchards in England will disappear for ever, Lord Cornwallis, President of the Kent County Playing Fields Association, said this week.

He was referring to the Buchanan report and South-East study which once again shows that the greatest menace to the survival of the Garden of England is the pressure of population.

"The villages around Sittingbourne contain the best cherry orchards in the world", said Lord Cornwallis. "I was horrified to see orchards already being torn down and built on. The proposed Channel Tunnel may mean about five railway lines through the Weald of Kent, not to mention such things as marshalling yards. If we are not careful we are going to find it tight in Kent for open spaces".

The Kent Playing Fields Association is one of scores of societies in the county now fighting for the preservation of the countryside against the relentless and unceasing pressure of would-be residents, expanding industry, motor traffic and speculators. There is no doubt that the electrification of the railways has brought almost all parts of Kent within commuting distance of London and housing estates are mushrooming everywhere. It is estimated that 15,000 applications for "development" are being considered by each local authority in Kent.

The gradual loss of the cherry orchards and the hedgerows, once rich with wild rose and honeysuckle, is a continuing tragedy for a county that has just become too popular.

The Harrison-Gibson furniture store in Bromley High Street, along with £65,000 worth of stock, has been destroyed in the town's biggest blaze since the war. The fire began at 3 pm on Monday and within minutes sheet flames surged in all directions. With the fire strengthening its hold general manager Mr Frederick Doe went from floor to floor methodically checking that everyone had left, an act of bravery in line with the firemen who fought the blaze. A spokesman for the Army and Navy Stores who are negotiating to purchase the business says the fire has not altered the position.

No literary merit in Blyton's books, say critics

Date: Enid Blyton, the children's author and a household name all over the world has died after a long illness. She survived her second husband, surgeon Kenneth Waters by just a year. She was 71.

The controversy which accompanied her "politically incorrect" books on Noddy has followed her into death and this week critics say there is little or no literary merit in her writing; in fact one writes that "the vocabulary is drained of all difficulty until its achieves a kind of aesthetic anaemia".

Whatever they say there is no doubt that the girl who was educated at St Christopher's, Beckenham, where she became head girl, entertained millions of children. Her output amounted to some 400 different titles, many translated into 20 or more languages. By the 1950's her income was more than £100,000 a year.

Enid lived in the Beckenham, Bromley area from 1897 until 1929 when she moved to Beaconsfield. Here she wrote the *Famous Five* series, followed by the *Secret Seven* and the *Adventure* books and much more. She did not employ a literary agent herself dealing with publishers all over the world.

1968

October 21st: *Sir Alec and Lady Rose today received the Freedom of Portsmouth.*

Heath sacks Enoch Powell over 'rivers of blood' speech

April 21st: **Bexley Conservative Association is giving full support to the drastic action taken this week by their member and opposition leader, Edward Heath, in sacking Mr Enoch Powell from the shadow cabinet over his "rivers of blood" speech.**

Powell, Tory shadow Minister of Defence, said at Birmingham that Britain "must be mad, literally mad as a nation to allow 50,000 dependants of immigrants into the country each year."

"As I look ahead I am filled with foreboding", he said. "Like the Roman I see the River Tiber foaming with much blood".

Although he is aware that the speech expresses the fears of many people, Mr Heath considers it is racialist and inflammatory and that Enoch Powell will have to go.

Alec Rose sails home to a hero's welcome

July 4th: Yachtsman, Alec Rose, aged 59, returned home to a massive celebration today after sailing around the world in his tiny ketch, *Lively Lady.* Among the congratulatory telegrams are those from the mayors of Canterbury, where he was born, Broadstairs where he used to live and the President of the County Society.

A civic welcome also awaits him in Broadstairs in honour of his 28,500-mile adventure which had taken 354 days and included several escapes from possible death.

Mr Rose's second wife is a Broadstairs girl and her mother and three sisters all live in the town.

His first wife Barbara, manageress of a dress shop in St George's Street, has also sent him a telegram: "Nelson, Drake and now Rose". She said: "I met him in Canterbury when he was 19 and the first thing he told me was that he wanted to sail round the Horn."

Alec Rose was born in Canterbury and went to Simon Langton School. During the war he served in North African and Russian convoys with the Royal Navy. Later he ran a nursery business in Littlebourne, then Ash before moving to a shop in Herne Bay and then Portsmouth where he lives.

Medway scare as nuclear submarine blazes

August 17th: Appliances from all over Kent raced to Chatham Dockyard yesterday when fire broke out on *H.M.S.Valiant,* the Navy's first all-British nuclear submarine. As the people of the Medway Towns tensely waited for news of any possible radiation leaks, firemen using breathing apparatus and nuclear experts with geiger counters were eventually able to report that all was well.

Today health specialists will check everyone who went on board the Valiant. A dockyard spokesman said: "We always take the most stringent precautions when an incident of this type occurs."

For the 40 firemen the blaze was difficult to tackle because of the cramped conditions. One crew stayed on duty beside the submarine all night to ensure that flames did not reappear.

The nuclear refitting base was opened at Chatham Dockyard in June. Constructed between the old Numbers six and seven docks, it has been designed for the refit and refuelling of the non-Polaris Fleet class submarines, built at Barrow. It consists of a huge cantilever crane for the removal of used reactor cores, an office block, underground workshops and a health centre.

The complex was opened by Vice-Admiral Sir Horace Law who said: "Nuclear power has given submarines an entirely new dimension — the ability not to come to the surface for air. The Royal Navy is extremely proud of its nuclear fleet and it will not be lost on those present that Chatham is really well in on the support of the navy in years to come. It was an obvious choice to put these facilities on the Medway."

The height of the real Battle of Britain and the pilots find time to relax with a game of draughts before the next order to scramble. Scenes like this are being re-enacted at Hawkinge for the new film.

The Few return to Hawkinge for a re-run of the Battle

August 23rd: The sound of the Merlin engine, the sight of a squadron of Spitfires screaming over the sun-baked runway and the chilling vision of vapour trails in the sky has returned briefly to Hawkinge — for the film *Battle of Britain*, due to be released on the 30th anniversary of the outbreak of war in 1939.

The old forward fighter station has become a gigantic film set. Dispersal huts, GS Belfast sheds and hangars are back in place along with fuel bowsers and oil drums. Spitfires and Hurricanes, ME9s and 10s, Dorniers and Junkers are on the runway with a star-studded cast of actors taking the place of the original crews.

In reality this famous grass airfield has finally gone. The Ministry of Defence could find no further use for Hawkinge and it was offered for auction in 1964 with a further 77 acres offered for sale last year.

Soon a housing estate and a hostel will replace this famous home of the Few.

1968

Marina won the hearts of the people of Kent

A much-treasured family photograph of Princess Marina with her late husband, the Duke of Kent and her eldest children, Prince Edward and Princess Alexandra when expecting her third child. It was taken shortly before the Duke's death in an flying accident in 1942.

August 28th: Princess Marina, Duchess of Kent, former colonel-in-chief of the Royal West Kent Regiment, chancellor of the University of Kent and one of the best-loved and hardest-working members of the royal family, died yesterday Tuesday, aged 62.

Marina was the daughter of Prince and Princess Nicholas of Greece and the grandaughter of King George I of Greece. Her mother was the Grand Duchess, Helen, a cousin of the murdered Czar Nicholas II.

In 1934, at Westminster Abbey, Marina married Prince George, fourth son of King George V and Queen Mary, who had just been created Duke of Kent and rapidly won the hearts of the British people.

She was known for her good taste in clothes, many of which she made herself and won a reputation as one of the best-dressed women of all time. After her marriage her elegance greatly influenced the style and appearance of the British public.

Her husband died tragically in 1942 and her eldest son Prince Edward succeeded as the second duke. Princess Alexandra was born in 1936 and Prince Michael in 1942. In widowhood she took over many of her late husband's duties and her public duties increased, particularly in the county of Kent.

As colonel-in-chief of the RWK Regiment she saw some of its troops in operation against the rebels in the Malayan jungle. She represented the Queen at the independence celebrations in Ghana. She toured Australia, Canada, Mexico and South America and there is no doubt that her charm increased the prestige of the British royal family wherever she went.

Princess Marina died at home in Kensington Palace after a short illness. It is her wish that her husband's body be taken out of the vaults at St George's Chapel, Windsor so they can be buried side by side at Frogmore.

St Clements, Old Romney, badly damaged during the war and almost declared redundant.

The miracle of St Clements

The people of Old Romney, who worship at the little Norman church of St Clements, have just witnessed a miracle.

Some months ago the church's ambitious restoration programme had to be halted because repairs to the tower had completely exhausted all available funds. With an "impossible" £5,000 to raise many thought the only course was for the Diocesan authorities to declare the church redundant. It was a desperate time for all concerned — so the villagers asked God what they should do. They prayed.

A few weeks later the rector received a call from the Rank organisation who wanted to shoot scenes in the church for a film of Russell Thorndike's *Dr Syn* with Donald Sinden — an actor closely associated with the Royal Shakespeare Company — in the title role.

Rank paid for the repairs to the minstrel's gallery, provided a new staircase and left a generous cheque, enabling the remaining restoration work to recommence. Cheques from the Friends of Kent Churches and the Historic Churches Trust followed.

On completion of the restoration this year a thanksgiving service and four-day flower festival of praise will be held. The future of this ancient church, a shrine of faith for more than 800 years, has been safeguarded.

...And a six-minute miracle at The Oval

August 27th: With just six minutes to spare England levelled the series against Australia in the fifth and final Test Match at the Oval today — thanks to an extraordinary spell of bowling by Kent's Derek Underwood, known to his colleagues as "Deadly".

With the Australia score at 86-5 a freak storm flooded the playing area but the ground staff, aided by volunteers from the crowd, enabled play to continue with just 45 minutes remaining. Wickets fell regularly to Underwood and, with five minutes remaining, he trapped Inverarity leg before to return with the figures of 7-50.

In the county championship such feats are commonplace for the 23-year-old from Bromley. He made his debut for Kent in 1963, played his first Test in 1966, regularly appears near the top of the bowling averages and has struck up a superb understanding with the 'keeper, Alan Knott.

Tonbridge, where amphibious vehicles took people to safety. The cellars of the Angel Hotel are badly flooded.

'Tropical' storm brings chaos to Kent

September 16th: Kent today is mopping up following one of the greatest storms of the twentieth century. Right across the county towns, villages and hamlets are under water. Rivers are running wild down the valleys, roads and railway lines are blocked by landslides and lakes spread out over hundreds of acres of Kent's fertile land. In many places vehicles have floated away and helicopters have been employed to rescue people in distress.

The culprit was a rapidly-deepening area of low pressure to the south-west which produced a 'trough' across the south-east. It remained stationary all day on Saturday (14th) and that meant prolonged, heavy rain.

For hour after hour from the early hours of Sunday morning to nightfall, lightning flashed, thunder rolled and the great blackness above released its load in proportions of tropical intensity.

In Tonbridge the River Medway overtopped the town bridge and flood waters swept into the High Street inundating most of the shops. All the factories and works were flooded, Cannon Bridge was washed away carrying with it the town's main sewer.

In Maidstone the Medway lapped the arches of the town bridge. As water filled the pedestrian subway and swirled up the High Street the town was closed and an emergency declared. Boardwalks were erected yesterday by the Royal Engineers. They may have to be extended.

It's the same story over much of low-lying Kent. Along the courses of the Medway, the Stour, the Ravensbourne, the Eden, the Darent, the Swale and all their tributaries flood defences have capitulated and some people are still trapped in upstairs rooms.

The village of Shoreham is cut off. The bridge at Otford has been swept away. Westerham is under water and General Wolfe, sword aloft, looks more like a ship's captain alone on the bridge. Dartford is inundated and, at Edenbridge, drama has followed drama.

Last night in Edenbridge the swirling muddy water was almost at rooftop height and people marooned in their bedrooms. Some tried to swim for safety but were seen being swept from one roof to another. Lifelines were thrown to those in trouble; they were all saved.

From the air today large areas of Kent are waterlogged with factories, churches, oasts and the tops of apple trees floating in the middle. Reception centres have been set up and all voluntary organisations mustered. Police, fire, ambulance services and soldiers are overstretched and undermanned. Kent now faces the most urgent rebuilding programme since the war.

The Sevenoaks rapids. The town is more than 600 feet above sea level but thousands of tons of rain water gathered in Knole Park, burst through the ragstone wall and surged wildly down Seal Hollow Road.

Train crashes in the fog at Marden: 4 killed

January 4th: The driver and three passengers were killed and 11 others injured when the 8 pm Charing Cross to Ramsgate express train ran into the back of a parcels train near Marden on Saturday.

The accident occurred in thick freezing fog when the train was travelling about 75 miles an hour. Eight coaches were derailed, the line was torn up and 170 people were thrown around their carriages like loose pebbles.

Farm workers were quickly on the scene to be joined by police, fire and ambulancemen in a grim battle against thick swirling fog and clinging mud to rescue the injured passengers. They were taken to the West Kent Hospital, Maidstone.

As the weary rescue workers toiled through the night and into the next day they found four bodies, a 12-year-old girl, a British Railways clerk, an RAF technician and, more than 12 hours after the crash, the train driver.

The actual scene of the accident was on a isolated stretch of line at Brook Farm which became a base for rescuers and rescued.

January 5th: Thanks to the quick actions of drivers and signalmen another big disaster was averted on Sunday when a main-line train ran into an obstacle on the line at Folkestone.

A large concrete pillar had deliberately been placed across the track and several hundredweight of ballast across the other three tracks. An alert was issued by the signalman at Cheriton and a down train going at speed just managed to stop

Commuters' 'daily nightmare'

Kent's newspaper editors are united in voicing their concern about the "daily nightmare" which the county's commuters are suffering. They say the tragedy at Marden, the work of evil minds the following day and a whole catalogue of derailments, cancellations, strikes and weather-related scares is causing great stress. Add to that poorly-lit trains, vandalism and British Railways' inability to communicate and "you have a recipe for traumatism".

Among the critics is the *Evening Standard* which says that a passenger "must put his trust in God — he will not get home if he puts it in British Railways".

In reply Southern Region say they run the busiest network in the world. Every day it takes 300,000 people to work. It has 3,000 miles of track, 8,000 bridges and 130 tunnels to maintain with 250,000 miles of wiring.

On average, there is one breakdown every 100,000 miles. It concluded that if 20% of commuters avoided the 8.30-9-0 am peak by 15 minutes there would be seats for everyone.

National Bus Company

January 1st: The National Bus Company came into existence today following the nationalisation of the transport industry by the Labour Government.

This means that London Transport, Maidstone and District and East Kent now control all the major services throughout the county of Kent. As part of a plan to put it under the control of the GLC, the London Country Buses Services Ltd passes to the NBC with headquarters in Reigate.

The new Transport Act also provides financial help in the form of 50 per cent grants towards the cost of new buses and the provision for councils to cover losses on socially desirable services. All the companies are now undergoing major management structure and territorial changes.

Changes on the buses and changes on the rivers. Under the recent Harbours Act, a number of powers, duties, properties, rights and liabilities of existing harbour authorities have been transferred to the Medway Ports Authority.

Four die in Kent blizzards

February 14th: A blizzard which began on Friday night produced more than 12 inches of snow, blocked numerous towns, villages and hamlets in East Kent, paralysed public transport and left many people stranded for the night in makeshift accommodation, including the Tory leader Edward Heath.

The conditions were so severe that four people died in Kent. One was struck by a train near Snowdown attempting to follow the railway line home, one died on an isolated farm at Martin Mill, near Dover, a 13-year-old boy was struck by a car in the blizzard at Kippings Cross and a fourth man collapsed after abandoning his car in the snow. near Deal. An ambulance took more than an hour to reach him.

Seven passengers and three crewman endured an uncomfortable night in a train which was "lost" for the night near Reculver and Mr Heath spent Friday night at the Walpole Bay Hotel after attending the Broadstairs Sailing Club's annual dinner.

'The destruction of Kent cannot go on at this alarming rate. Every day we see mistakes which cannot be altered and we see planning permissions which should never have been given' — Lord Cornwallis.

January 1st: An Australian company, News Ltd, owned by Robert Murdoch, has taken over the *News of the World.*

January 3rd: Violence flared in Londonderry yesterday at the end of a 73-mile long civil rights march from Belfast. A car owned by the Rev Ian Paisley was tipped over at the Guildhall.

January 4th: 50 people were killed when an airliner crashed into houses near Gatwick.

Ferbruary 22nd: BBC today began a new TV series called *Civilisation,* presented by Kenneth Clark of Saltwood Castle, near Hythe. *See page 154*

February 24th: President Nixon and Mr Harold Wilson met for the first time today in London.

March 5th: London's East End twins, Reginald and Ronald Kray, have been given life sentences for murder. The trial heard how these gangland bosses terrorised the east end of London.

St John's Chapel at Swingfield, part of a 13th century Preceptory, has been acquired by the Minister of Works and will be restored.

April 8th: Concorde 002, the British-built prototype of the Anglo-French supersonic airliner, made her maiden flight today with a £365 million investment behind her.

April 25th: The BBC's longest-running radio serial, *The Dales,* ended today after 21 years.

The famous Invicta steam engine of 1825 has been moved to the Dane John Gardens in Canterbury.

Lympne Airport has been renamed Ashford following its acquisition by the Borough Council.It now has a paved runway of 1,350 metres with a passenger lounge and office block on the site.

May 1st: Major James Chichester-Clark, the new leader of the Ulster Unionists, succeeds as Prime Minister of Northern Ireland.

***June:** Art historian Sir Kenneth Clark of Saltwood Castle, Hythe, who has been knighted. His TV series* Civilisation *was broadcast by the BBC in 13 episodes this year.*

June 20th: High-grade crude oil has been discovered on the borders of the British and Norwegian sectors of the North Sea. It is now 10 years since Shell-Esso found a natural gas field off the Dutch coast.

June 22nd: American actress Judy Garland was found dead in her London flat today. She was 47.

June 30th: Four million in Biafra are facing starvation following the Nigerian Government's ban on night flights by the Red Cross.

July 2nd: Rolling Stone Brian Jones was found dead in his swimming pool in Hartfield, Essex.

July 7th: Thieves have stolen ancient silver belonging to the town of Dover, valued at £15,000.

July 12th: Tony Jacklin becomes the first Briton to win the British Open since Max Faulkner in 1951.

July 4th: Ann Jones today beat Billie-Jean King of the United States 3-6, 6-3, 6-2 to win the Wimbledon ladies' singles.

August 1st: *Vortigern*, 4,800 tons, sailed on her maiden voyage from Dover to Dunkirk today. She can carry 1,000 passengers and 240 cars.

Another Kentish vineyard has opened at Biddenden.

August 31st: Rocky Marciano, former world heavyweight champ, today died in a plane crash. He never lost a professional fight.

September 1st: King Idris of Libya has been deposed by a group of revolutionaries led by Muammar Gaddafi.

September 7th: Jackie Stewart, a 30-year-old Scot has won the world motor racing championship.

October 21st: Edward Heath has appointed his friend Margaret Thatcher as shadow education minister.

A new skirt, the "maxi", is proving popular with women of all ages who see it as a warm and attractive alternative to the "mini".

November 18th: The Bowles pursuits centre was opened at Eridge today by Prince Philip.

December 18th: Both Houses have agreed that the law passed in 1965 to abolish the death penalty should continue indefinitely.

December 19th: A sterilisation clinic for men is to be opened in Birmingham. A simple vasectomy operation costs £16.

Former Dartford Grammar School girl Sheila Hancock is making a big name for herself in the popular television comedy series, *The Rag Trade,* showing the hilarious antics and emotions of a group of working class women in a clothing factory. Miss Hancock, who is married to actor John Thaw, was one of the first schoolgirls to obtain a Kent grant for RADA and has seldom been out of work. She is an ardent feminist and works hard for a number of charities.

December 24th: Charles Manson, who runs a commune in Los Angeles and calls himself Jesus, has been charged with the murder of Sharon Tate and six others.

The Kingsnorth Power Station alongside the Medway Estuary near Grain has become operative. At full capacity it will be the largest dual-fired generating station in Europe.

GREAT HITS OF 1969

My Way

Gentle On My Mind

May 2nd: *Master mariner and former merchant seaman, Robin Knox-Johnston of Downe, near Bromley, is seen here at Tower Pier, London. He arrived at Falmouth on April 22nd completing his epic voyage round the world in his famous Bermudian ketch,* Sulhaili. *Knox-Johnston, christened by national newspapers "Round Robin", becomes the first man to sail solo non-stop round the world. His lone voyage was completed in 312 dramatic days and with so many mishaps and adventures provides one of the most exciting true sea stories of a decade that includes similar feats (but not non-stop) by Francis Chichester and Alec Rose. Robin Knox-Johnston kept a diary of his solo circumnavigation and when he has settled down to life on terra firma he will be writing a book. Then he plans to take on more sailing challenges.*

Kent deserted as man sets foot on the moon

July 22nd: The pubs were quiet, the cinemas empty and the streets throughout Kent resembled ghost towns. Practically the whole population was at home, in front of their TV sets, watching one of the most momentous historical events ever known.

The moment they had been waiting for eventually came in the early hours of Sunday morning when American astronaut Neil Armstrong, commander of Apollo 11, stepped off the ladder of his lunar module onto the moon. "That's one small step for man, one giant leap for mankind," he said.

Within seconds Armstrong was joined by fellow astronaut Buzz Aldrin and the two men were soon moving in the moon's low gravity, collecting samples of dust and rock and planting the Stars and Stripes.

One man watching the moon landing with particular interest was Commander H.R. Hatfield of Clarendon Road, Sevenoaks, a member of the British Astronomical Association and the country's leading authority on lunar photography. On the first moon orbit he astounded the scientific world by photographing Apollo as it was venting oxygen and revealed the actual moment of jettison. His photograph has been used in newspapers all over the world.

The Kent branch of Oxfam are not so impressed with the moon landing. A spokesman said this week that the cost of one Saturn 5 booster rocket is more than sufficient to provide primary school places for every Indian child born during the next decade.

A hovercraft leaves Pegwell Bay, near Ramgate, for the journey to Calais. In the background are the distinctive chimneys of the new power station at Richborough.

Pegwell Bay hovercraft competes with Seaspeed

October 21st: Christopher Cockerell's great invention has really taken off in Kent. Yesterday Princess Anne named the second of British Rail's Seaspeed hovercrafts after herself and took a smooth trip to the Goodwin Sands and back. Seaspeed, however, does not have things all its own way. A few months ago Prince Philip opened a new Hoverport at Pegwell Bay, run by Hover-Lloyd which operates a service to Calais. Although Cockerell's first prototype was tested as long ago as 1953 it was only last year that Princess Margaret and Lord Snowdon inaugurated the world's first international hovercraft service between London and Boulogne. Seaspeed can take 254 passengers and 80 cars.

1969

Richmal dies but William continues with his pranks

Miss Richmal Crompton Lamburn, former classics mistress at Bromley High School for Girls but better known all over the world as the author of more than 40 books about the irrepressible schoolboy hero, William, has died at her home in Chislehurst, aged 78.

Richmal who walked with a stick ever since she was struck down with polio in 1923, forcing her to give up teaching, produced a number of light novels, but will always be remembered for introducing William and his badly behaved outlaws.

Her first book was *Just William* which appeared in the spring of 1922. Since then the sales of William books in the English language alone have topped an estimated nine million.

Most of her stories are centred on Bromley and the surrounding villages. She lived in the area from the moment she arrived to teach at the High School in 1917. Her earnings enabled her to buy a big house on Bromley Common in 1927 and she lived there until moving to a bungalow at Chislehurst in February 1954.

December: At the age of 86 Sybil Thorndike has retired from the stage. Her final appearance was at Leatherhead. A few weeks earlier she had given a Dickens reading in Restoration House, Rochester.

Flashback to 1951 when Richmal Crompton opened the junior department of Bromley Central Library.

Life peerage for art historian, Ken Clark

The art historian, Sir Kenneth Clark who lives with his wife and family at Saltwood Castle, near Hythe, has received a life peerage for his remarkable contribution to the interpretation and patronage of the arts.

As director of the National Gallery during the war, Clark was responsible for the evacuation of the entire collection from London into the slate quarries of North Wales. He was also well-known for his critical studies of *Leonardo da Vinci* (1939), *Landscape into Art* (1949), *Piero della Francesca* (1951), *The Nude* (1955) and *Rembrandt and the Italian Renaissance* (1966).

However, he has achieved even greater fame and almost film star status for his brilliant television series *Civilisation* which was broadcast by the BBC in 13 episodes this year. In this he has spread the gospel of art throughout the English-speaking world, making it accessible to a whole generation as no other writer/narrator has been able to achieve. In fact *Civilisation* has been judged the best series ever made for television.

Kenneth Clark is now 66. He purchased the impressive Saltwood Castle following the death of Lady Conway to house his own works of art.

Lord and Lady Clark have two sons, Alan and Colin and daughter Colette, Colin's twin sister.

July 23rd: *A bronze statue of Sir Winston Churchill by the great sculptor, Oscar Nemon, was unveiled on Westerham Green yesterday by Sir Winston's former wartime colleague and Prime Minister of Australia, Sir Robert Menzies —currently Lord Warden of the Cinque Ports. Among the distinguished guests at a moving but simple unveiling ceremony was Lady Clementine Churchill, her daughter, Mary Soames and Captain Christopher Soames, British Ambassador in Paris.*

In a moving tribute to Sir Winston and the British people, Sir Robert said that courage, love of country and the human, sublime, unspeakable humour of the British people were qualities which Sir Winston exemplified.

The plinth on which Sir Winston's statue stands is a gift of Marshal Tito and the people of Yugoslavia. The photograph (right) shows the statue of the great man being lowered into position.

1969

'The destruction of Kent cannot go on'

THIS last decade may well be remembered as the exciting, swinging, liberating sixties but for preservation groups and all those interested in our heritage it may also go down in history as the "decade of the urban vandals". All over the country, centuries-old features have disappeared with a frightening rapidity. And Kent has suffered more than most.

Folkestone is a prime example. In the four years between 1962 and 1966 borough councillors responsible for this major Kent resort approved the demolition of the Pleasure Gardens Theatre, the Bathing Establishment, the Majestic and the Queen Hotels — all fine Victorian heritage buildings. That's not all. Picturesque 19th century properties on The Leas were demolished to make way for the Whitecliffs.

In other Kentish towns, big and small, planners have been accused of capitulating under the relentless and unceasing pressure applied by expanding industry, speculators looking for quick profit, a desire to redevelop and an obsession with road-widening schemes.

In Tonbridge, the urban council dismissed the most vehement pleas to save the elegant buildings just north of the Big Bridge over the Medway which were doomed in the interests of a wider thoroughfare. Town cries reached county hall but to no avail; the County reneged on a promise made in 1928 to the Society for the Protection of Ancient Buildings and took down the 16th-century Angell's Jewellers shop, six or seven other picturesque buildings and Tallyho Alley.

In Ashford there is a blueprint for expansion of the town into a city the size of Liverpool. Opponents to the scheme are fighting the plan for a vast ring road around the proposed "modern atrocities" but to little avail; important buildings are already being demolished to make way for the giant office complex for Charter Consolidated.

In Sevenoaks, the active town preservation society implored the council to save the White House, a neglected Tudor building with a contemporary fireplace and timber framing. They also tried to save an alleyway of weatherboarded cottages and a row of Victorian buildings all earmarked for demolition because of the county's insistence on "satisfactory access" to a new car park. They failed.

Commercial redevelopment and the "desperate" need for more car parking space was the reason why an area of Victorian villas and the attractive Albion Place in Maidstone were converted into offices.

Correspondents to local newspapers are adamant that urban councils have caused more damage than Hitler ever achieved. This outrage has spawned new groups of caring conservationists. Societies for the preservation of buildings, churches and the countryside have appeared in every town. In most cases they are fighting a losing battle.

In Ramsgate they have tried in vain to save the Italianate conservatory in the George V1 Memorial Park at East Cliff. In Rochester there was a wholehearted but fruitless attempt to rescue Nash's Cottage at Chalk where Dickens had spent his honeymoon. In Maidstone conservationists failed in their endeavours to stop the barbarous destruction of the house once occupied by Lawrence Washington, ancestor of George. It was pulled down — to the dismay of thousands of American sightseers.

Five years ago Kent County Council held a conference in Maidstone and invited local authorities, amenity associations and bodies interesting in preserving buildings of historic interest. Lord Cornwallis was one of the speakers. "The destruction of Kent", he said, "cannot go on at this alarming rate. Every day we see mistakes which cannot be altered and we see planning permissions which should never have been given. The county is too popular and the only answer is to build satellite towns and preserve our heritage".

His sentiments were echoed by speaker after speaker most of whom described our age as one of architectural mediocrity and appallingly low standards of sensibility and taste.

continued on next page

Tonbridge High Street as it looked in 1870 above the Big Bridge. John Angell's jeweller's shop is on the right.

Preservation societies are meeting every week to discuss their particular battle strategies. Members know that somewhere beneath all the plans and blueprints and the town consultants' diagrams lie the threatened buildings. Thousands are being cynically destroyed, not because they are beyond repair but simply because they stand in the way of the developer's vision. Their fate has been secondary to the process of rebuilding.

There are just a few examples of conservationists winning the day. In Deal there was a plan for redevelopment which would have completely altered its character and swept away the best old buildings. Public reaction was so hostile that the project was abandoned.

The Sixties have also seen the disappearance and change in ownership of many long-standing Kentish firms — particularly in paper manufacturing, the motor trade, brewing and the food and drink industry. In Maidstone the paper industry declined with the closure of Lower Tovil Mill. Rootes took over Tilling Stevens, only to be taken over by Chrysler in 1967. Foster Clark was bought by Oxo after going into receivership, Sharps merged with Trebor. Mason's waterside brewery closed and so did the Medway brewery following its acquisition by Courage.

Above: The Bathing Establishment was built, in Italianate style, in 1869 and included heated seawater swimming baths. The building was closed in 1958, demolished in 1966 and is now a car park.

DRIVING TUITION

Folkestone, Hythe & District Herald

Chronicle, Observer, Express and Kent Evening Echo.

No. 3825. SATURDAY, OCTOBER 31st, 1964. PRICE 5d.

VISIT TOY FAIR GROUND FLOOR

BLUEPRINT FOR THE FOLKESTONE OF A.D. 2000

Traffic-free shopping precinct in heart of the town

Low level road along The Leas

POINTS FROM THE CONSULTANTS' REPORT

THE long-awaited report of the consultants on the redevelopment of the Town Centre of Folkestone was submitted to the Town Council at a special meeting on Thursday evening. A far-reaching, drastic yet imaginative plan. It is in effect the blueprint of the heart of Folkestone for the next century.

AT this stage the plan is that of the consultants; it has not yet been approved by the Council. It is not a fixed scheme which cannot be amended; the consultants make clear that it can be adjusted as circumstances and conditions in the future require. Here are its main proposals:

Changes in character of certain areas

Two Distributor Roads

Numerous Kent towns have hired town planning consultants to prepare ambitious redevelopment plans "for future prosperity". In many areas, names like Colin Buchanan, Max Lock, Gerald Eve or Charles Holden are as familiar as that of the local MP. But their proposals are not always popular, particularly among members of preservation societies who oppose any scheme designed to alter the character of their town.

Here are details of the blueprint for Folkestone.

Enterprise Neptune adopts the White Cliffs of Dover

May: The White Cliffs of Dover, the sight of which has gladdened the heart of many returning Englishmen, is among the beautiful stretches of coastal scenery to be preserved in an ambitious operation called *Enterprise Neptune.*

A Neptune appeal has been launched by the National Trust in a bid to save more than 900 miles of Britain's coastline. A survey designed to identify the areas of outstanding beauty concluded that one-third of the 3,000 miles was already ruined and one-third of little interest.

The appeal director is Commander Conrad Rawnsley, grandson of the man who helped Octavia Hill establish the Trust in 1897.

Land near St Margaret's Bay in front of the Dover Patrol memorial and the white cliffs below will be among the first coastal areas to be acquired. It will benefit from *Enterprise Neptune* which has just been launched at a luncheon in the Mansion House with a Government pledge of £250,000.

Kent author Arthur Mee wrote: "The loyal Englishman has not been born who can look upon Shakespeare's Cliff without emotion. It stood here when our race began. Through all our ancient story it has guarded our island home".

The new Golden Arrow with its electric engine stands by the side of the old steam engine. Each carries the British and French flags.

No more steam on the 'golden way'

Steam traction on the famous Golden Arrow/Fleche d'Or service between London and Paris has ended. On January 11th, the SNCF Pacific No 231 K82 pulled into Calais Maritime with the final steam-hauled Fleche d'Or to run between Amiens and the French coast. It marked the end of a chapter in railway history.

The Golden Arrow and its French counterpart were the product of the glamorous Pullman era. Introduced in the 1920s to rival the famous sleeping car services which had reigned supreme in Europe before the 1914-18 war, the Golden Arrow was a byword in luxury. To those who could afford first-class comfort the route between London and Paris was to become known as the "golden way".

The Sittingbourne and Kemsley Light Railway has also closed and Bowaters Group plan to hand it over to the Locomotive Club of Great Britain to preserve. Opened in the late 19th century to carry paper mill workers, there were at one time 13 steam locos, one diesel loco and 400 wagons, the line extending for 14 track miles.

'The year 1906 saw a change of Government and it saw Kent win the County Championship. It's now 1970 and what could be more certain?' — Ted Heath at Kent CCC's Centenary Dinner in April.

January 8th: Asian 'flu has now claimed more than 4,000 lives in the UK. It is believed the virus comes from Hong Kong.

February 9th: Employment secretary Barbara Castle's Bill giving women equal pay has passed its second reading unopposed. She said that women will still keep special privileges in some areas.

February 17th: The Russian woman who claims to be Anastasia today lost her 50-year fight to prove she is the daughter of Czar Nicholas II.

February 23rd: In order to develop the RB 211-50 airbus jet engine, Rolls-Royce have asked the Government for £50 million.

March 3rd: The rebel colony of Rhodesia today became a republic.

March 24th: Henry Cooper regained the British heavyweight boxing title today by beating Jack Bodell.

March 23rd: The High Court today awarded damages of £370,000 to 18 children who were born with defects caused by their mothers taking the drug thalidomide.

April 9th: Paul McCartney today issued a writ in the High Court calling for the dissolution of the business known as The Beatles. So ends the most influential partnership of the last decade.

April 15th: A new road bridge across the Medway at Rochester was opened today by Princess Margaret.

April 18th: The Morris Minor, Britain's longest-running motor car will cease production next year, British Leyland announced today.

May 1st: A new car ferry terminal was opened today at Dover by Mr Fred Mulley, Minister of Transport.

Another long-distance footpath is soon to be opened in Kent. Conceived this year by the Ramblers Association it is to be called The Wealden Way and will run from Gravesend to Eastbourne in Sussex. The path will pass through the village of Luddesdowne and by one of the oldest inhabited houses in England.

Christopher Hussey, the architectural historian who inherited Scotney Castle and estate in 1952, has died aged 71. An influential writer with Country Life, *Hussey was the author of a pioneering study of* The Picturesque (1927) *which was inspired by his knowledge of Scotney. The garden had been ravaged by the war years but Hussey decided long-term planning was essential and set out to create one of the most beautiful gardens in England. Today the old mediaeval castle is the romantic ruin that he envisaged. It lies as a backdrop among ornamental trees and shrubs.*

May 22nd: The MCC today cancelled the South African tour of England. The cancellation is a triumph for Peter Hain and his anti-apartheid "stop the tour" campaign.

May 31st: The great racehorse *Arkle* died today.

June 4th: Racegoers hail a new wonder horse, Nijinsky, who won the Derby today in the fastest time since 1936. Lester Piggott was the jockey. Nijinsky has now won eight races in a row.

June 14th: West Germany today beat England 3-2 and so knocked them out of the World Cup.

June 15th: Sir Laurence Olivier has been given a life peerage for his services to the theatre.

June 17th: Rover today launched a new all-purpose four wheel drive car called the Range Rover.

June 21st: Tony Jacklin today becomes the first Briton to win the US Open Golf Championship for 50 years. He joins two other golfers to have won the British and US Opens in the same years, Bobby Jones and Ben Hogan.

June 22nd: It has been announced that women may soon be able to become full-time ministers of the Methodist Church.

June 26th: Kent police are desperately seeking new recruits who should be between the ages of six and 18 months and enjoy biscuits. Established seven years ago Kent's Police Dog section needs more to replace those nearing retirement.

July 20th: Iain Macleod, Chancellor of the Exchequer, died suddenly tonight in Downing Street after a heart attack.

August 12th: Dame Sybil Thorndike today opened the Young Vic theatre.

August 20th: England's soccer captain Bobby Moore has been cleared of charges of stealing an emerald bracelet from a shop in Bogota, Columbia in May.

October 9th: An arsonist today set fire to the Photo Productions Laboratory, Gillingham and destroyed millions of greeting cards. 16 appliances and their crews fought the blaze for 12 hours.

October 10th: A new cult television comedy programme, similar in humour to radio's Goon Show, is winning many admirers. Starring John Cleese it is called *Monty Python's Flying Circus.*

October: A clinker-built boat (Viking or Saxon) has been discovered during the widening and deepening of Hammond's Drain on the Graveney Marshes. The boat, largely intact, was originally 40 feet long and 10 feet wide. It has now been successfully excavated and will be reassembled, piece by piece, in the National Maritime Museum at Greenwich.

November 27th: The Gay (Good As You) Liberation Front held a demonstration in London today, urging homosexuals and lesbians to express their feelings openly and without shame.

November 26th: The first year of Mr Heath's Government has been hit by more working days lost by strikes than at any time since the General Strike of 1926.

GREAT HITS OF 1970

In The Summertime
Yellow River
The Wonder Of You

Of all the photographs taken during the recent filming of The Battle of Britain, *this is one of the most remarkable. It shows Lord Dowding, former Commander-in-Chief of RAF Fighter Command, with a few of The Few who are gathered around in the semi-starched formality of a school photograph taken with the headmaster. The names of those who epitomise the courage shown by so many at the time are (l to r): Al Deere, Tom Gleave, Robert Stanford-Tuck, Ludovik Martell, Douglas Bader, Boleslaw Drobinski, Johnnie Kent and Peter Townsend.*

Lord Dowding dies at Tunbridge Wells aged 88

February 3rd: Air Chief Marshal Lord Dowding, who led Fighter Command to victory in the Battle of Britain 30 years ago, died at his home in Calverley Park, Tunbridge Wells yesterday aged 88. With his second wife Muriel he had moved there only a few months before from Darnley Drive, Southborough following a fall at the Air Marshal's Club which had left him incapacitated.

Since 1940 and that famous battle in the skies above Kent, Dowding has been a legendary figure, particularly to the Battle of Britain pilots who regarded him so highly. One of his proudest moments was when he received a standing ovation from his "chicks" at the premiere of the film *Battle of Britain* in 1969.

Lord Dowding's first wife died in 1918. In 1952 he married Muriel Whiting whose husband, Pilot Officer Max Whiting had been killed in 1944 when his Lancaster bomber failed to return from a mine-laying raid on the Kiel Canal. They met through his interest in spiritualism and his concern for the families of hundreds of young men who died under his command.

In retirement, Dowding devoted himself to a study of spiritualism and theosophy and he published many books on the subject. He wrote articles for newspapers, gave lectures on occult subjects, gave up shooting and became a vegetarian. Muriel shared his beliefs.

Many tributes have been paid to Lord Dowding by pilots who recall his single-mindedness and, in particular, his appearance at a Cabinet meeting on May 15, 1940, when he set out the stark issues of survival or immediate defeat and insisted that no more fighter squadrons should leave the country.

The Battle of Britain was his finest hour. The deployment of his forces, his rotation of squadrons, his regard for reserves of aircraft and personnel were accompanied by an overall mastery of the air weapon. He commanded and won the struggle for air superiority over south-east England.

After the battle Dowding was physically and mentally exhausted but his replacement as Commander so soon after the victory appalled most members of Fighter Command. He was eventually persuaded by the Prime Minister to visit the United States on behalf of the Ministry of Aircraft Production. Dowding's funeral will be at Tunbridge Wells. His ashes will be interred in Westminster Abbey.

This scar across part of the most sensitive countryside in Kent is now part of a four lane bypass around Sevenoaks.

By-pass relief for our choking towns

The traffic jams and appalling road accidents which have plagued Kent for many years have been considerably reduced by the opening of many vital bypasses in the last few years.

Prominent among these is the new road bridge at Rochester, opened on May 15th by Princess Margaret who had earlier visited the Letraset factory at Ashford.

Other completed projects include a new approach to the city of Canterbury, an east link road at Tonbridge and the long-awaited but highly sensitive Sevenoaks bypass which cuts through the attractive Whitley Forest.

More road-building projects are under way. The Dartford diversion (A2) — seven miles across Dartford Heath, the Tonbridge bypass and the Ditton bypass (M20) are due to be completed in 1971.

1970

June 12th: *The fire which raged out of control on Herne Bay Pier today (see above) is just one of many conflagrations to keep Kent's firefighters as busy as they have ever been. The fire accidentally caused during repairs, completely destroyed the pavilion. A few weeks earlier, Ramsgate's biggest fire since the war devastated the town centre. A public house, four shops and a supermarket as well as a block of flats were extensively damaged. It took 20 appliances several hours to control the blaze and cool down premises not yet affected by the intense heat.*

Fire engine hits tree and explodes: 8 men injured

September 2nd: Eight firemen have been taken to hospital, two are critically ill in the intensive care unit following the horrific crash of an appliance on its way to a fire in Maidstone. The vehicle skidded, hit a tree, exploded into flames and was left perched 12 feet in the air against the broken trunk.

With their uniforms blazing three firemen fell to the ground and rolled in rainwater puddles to smother the flames. The other five men were trapped in the blazing vehicle, desperately trying to claw their way through windows and jammed doors.

Other firemen and four ambulances arrived on the scene and the driver Roger Lynn, who was trapped in his cab, was the last to be rescued. He had to have his leg amputated.

The other members of the crew, Malcolm Farrow, John Page, Albert Foreman, Albert Bray, Alan Bush and Leading Firemen Peter Whent and Donald Bates are suffering from varying degrees of serious burns.

Welcome, BBC Radio Medway,

December 19th: "This is Henry Hall speaking and this is Radio Medway". With these words at 6pm yesterday evening, the BBC's new local radio station for North and West Kent finally hit the airwaves to the delight of hundreds of people.

The station frequency is VHF 97 and the veteran broadcaster had the honour of introducing the first voices of Radio Medway on *Gala 97*, from Broadcasting House, Chatham. Guests included Peter Brough and Archie Andrews, Franklin Englemann, Vera Lynn, Ray Moore and Tessa O-Shea. It was followed at 8.45 with Trevor Taylor's story of the River Medway in words and sounds and then a "singalong" from the Community Centre of St Matthew, Wigmore.

The introduction of BBC Radio Medway — "the voice of a friendly neighbour, welcoming you as we hope you welcome us"— launches a new era for both entertainment and local information and the station's team includes Harold Rogers (manager), Langley Brown (news editor), Jimmy Mack (breakfast presenter), George Pixley (sports editor), David Cornet and John Greenslade.

Broadstairs musician sails into Number 10

NE 22 1970 INEPENCE

THE TIMES

Mr. Heath's first Sunday as Prime Minister. He lunched with Lord Aldington (not in picture) and Lady Aldington (centre) a Knoll Farm, Aldington, Kent. Also in the picture are Mr. William Heath, the Prime Minister's father, and Mrs. W. S. Deedes, wife of the M.P. for Ashford.

Cabinet gets its first call to 10 Downing Street

By DAVID WOOD

Mr. Heath is calling the first meeting of the new Cabinet at 10 Downing Street tomorrow morning. The first task to which

Service heads of Whitehall departments.

Mr. Heath has already seen senior civil servants, including Sir William Armstrong, Head of the Civil Service, and Sir Burke Trend, secretary to the Cabinet,

part, he has taken over a Government machine designed by Mr. Wilson to carry out socialist policies, and some fundamental alteration is made necessary by the reversal of the policies. There is, for instance, to be much less

with Mr. Wilson's 21. It is the smallest Cabinet since Mr. Harold Macmillan was Prime Minister, but still rather larger than Mr. Heath had hoped. The size of his Cabinet has been governed to some extent by his

Orpington hero is given the boot

Six of Kent's seven Labour MPs lost their seats to Conservative opponents leaving only Mr James Wellbeloved of the pre-election Socialist members with a return ticket to Westminster from Erith and Crayford.

The hero of the Liberal revival of 1962, Mr Eric Lubbock, was defeated at Orpington and Dame Patricia Hornsby-Smith recaptured Chislehurst which she lost in 1964.

The biggest surprise was at Rochester and Chatham where Mrs Peggy Fenner turned Mrs Anne Kerr's 2,246 majority hold from the last election into a safe Conservative margin of 5,341.

The other Conservatives gains were at Dover, Faversham, Gravesend and Dartford, where the loser was Mr Sydney Irving, the Deputy Speaker.

Edward Heath promises to install Steinway in White Drawing Room

June 20th: The small boy who grew up in Broadstairs to win a musical scholarship to Oxford's Balliol and develop a love of sailing is Britain's new Prime Minister. With most of the general election results in, the Tories are back in power and Edward Heath firmly installed at Number 10.

Most of the opinion pollsters had signalled an easy Labour victory but the final tally looks this this: Tories 330 seats, Labour 287, Liberals 6, Others 7.

Mr Heath appeared on the doorstep of Number 10 and promised a strong government. He attacked Labour as "men of straw, trampled over by greedy, strike-prone unions responsible for rising prices".

His many friends and admirers on the Isle of Thanet were recalling today how Ted Heath, aged nine, was introduced to a Thornton Bobby piano costing £42. It became the love of his life, led him to the choir at St Peter's Broadstairs and then on to Balliol. The piano has served him well but Mr Heath has always said that if he could occupy Number 10 he would have a Steinway installed in the White Drawing Room, overlooking Horse Guards Parade.

At Oxford, Ted Heath organised a Town Carol Concert which became an annual event. He became President of the Oxford Union and, encouraged by his tutor, A.D. Lindsay, developed a new interest in politics.

A keen sailor and member of Broadstairs Sailing Club, Ted Heath has ocean-going skills. As skipper of the Tory Party his greatest mission on the not-too-distant horizon is to lead Britain into the Common Market. Many say it will not be plain sailing.

Kent wins the championship in centenary year

September 10th: Kent Cricket Club, bottom of the County Championship in July and severely reprimanded by their manager Les Ames, have just completed the greatest comeback in their history. Yesterday, at the Oval, Cowdrey scored a century and helped his side acquire eight bonus points. That clinched the issue — Kent had won the title for the first time since 1913.

In the end the margin at the top of the table was 17 points and there were jubilant scenes at the Oval. Prime Minister Edward Heath joined the players in a glass of champagne and reminded the players they had achieved cricket's greatest prize in their centenary year.

The great charge came after Ames' dressing-room conference at Mote Park. In 13 games, seven were won and 20 or more points achieved on four occasions with a record 23 points in the last home game against Leicestershire at Folkestone.

Luckhurst and Denness provided magnificent starts. Asif Iqbal, John Shepherd, Bob Woolmer and newcomer Graham Johnson provided all-round support and when they were not on Test duty, Cowdrey, Knott and Underwood showed why they played for England.

The most exciting game was at Folkestone's Cheriton Road against Notts for whom Garfield Sobers scored a chanceless century . In the second innings Kent were set 282 to win in three hours and, thanks to the exhilarating batting of Denness, Luckhurst and Asif and the coolness of Knott, in mounting tension, Kent won with eight balls to spare.

September 13th: To round off a good season Kent has finished second in the John Player Sunday League — a 40-over bash introduced for the first time last year. The attendance at Kent's eight Sunday home games was 25,151, just a few spectators below the 29,328 who watched 36 home championship days.

Marianne and Mick on cannabis charge

January 26th: Mick Jagger, the former Dartford Grammar School boy from Wilmington, better known as pop's wildest prodigy, has again been in trouble for taking drugs. Today he was fined £600 for possession of cannabis but his girlfriend, singer-turned-actress Marianne Faithfull, was found not guilty.

Jagger lives with Marianne and her three-year-old child Nicholas by her first marriage. They own a dignified terraced home in London overlooking the river and two homes in Berkshire.

The couple like to travel. Jagger says: "It's satisfying to be able to go where I like so I get out of England every month."

When in London, Jagger, the front man for the Rolling Stones, works very hard. He is the songwriter with Keith Richard and organises the group's recordings and rare appearances.

The Queen meets the churchwardens, verger and choir of St Mary's Church, Ashford. With her is Prince Philip and the vicar, Canon Neville Sharp. Princess Anne is in the background.

10,000 Catholics honour St Thomas the Martyr

July 16th: Canterbury Cathedral has seen many stirring occasions but this was one of the most impressive — the sight of 10,000 Roman Catholics in the Precincts last week celebrating High Mass with the Dean.

They were commemorating the death, 800 years earlier, of Archbishop Thomas Becket who was murdered on December 29th, 1170 by four knights who had heard their King call out in despair: 'Who will deliver me from this turbulent priest.'?

Within three years Rome had made him St Thomas the Martyr and the pilgrimage to his shrine began. By the time of Chaucer they were arriving "from every shires end of Englelond to Caunterbury" — and they kept on coming in greater and greater numbers from further and further afield.

There have been many celebrations to mark the octocentenary. A national service was held in the Cathedral on Wednesday (July 15th) attended by the Queen Mother and by prelates of churches all over the world. During this month, T.S. Eliot's *"Murder in the Cathedral"* will be performed again and a Son-et-Lumiere staged at Green Court throughout the summer.

Today the Canterbury Pilgrims still arrive daily but their method of transport is rather more modern. Sadly, the marvellous shrine of Thomas Becket is no more; that wondrous thing of gold and rubies has perished in the dust of ages.

Morning Service for the Queen

December 13th: The Queen and Prince Philip together with other members of the royal family attended morning service at Ashford Parish Church today. The visit commemorates the 500th anniversary of the rebuilding of St Mary's by Sir John Fogge who lived at Repton House.

This is the third royal visit to the town in recent years. In April, Princess Margaret visited the Letraset factory on the Kingsnorth Industrial Estate and early last year Prince Philip attended the 100th Ashford Fat Stock Show to present prizes to the winners.

'The most potent weapon in the hands of the aggressor is the mind of the oppressed' — Steve Biko, South African black leader in a speech this year.

January 1st: A new divorce law, introduced today, makes "irretrievable breakdown of marriage" sole grounds.

January 2nd: Sixty- six football fans were crushed to death as crowd barriers at the Ibrox Park stadium in Glasgow collapsed.

January 20th: Kent's postmen today joined their colleagues throughout the country for the first postal strike ever known. The postmen want a 19.5% pay rise.

February 4th: Rolls-Royce today declared itself bankrupt.

February 5th: Two astronauts have walked on the moon after Apollo 14 made a safe landing.

February 9th: A British soldier was shot dead during rioting in Ulster today — the first soldier to be killed since troops moved into the province in August 1969.

February 18th: Australian tycoon, Rupert Murdoch, has been told he cannot take control of London Weekend Television as well as run a national newspaper.

February 20th: Uganda's dictator, Idi Amin, promoted himself to general and president just one month after seizing power.

March 6th: 4,000 women marched from Hyde Park to 10 Downing Street in support of the women's liberation movement.

March 8th: The *Daily Sketch* closed today after 62 years of publishing.

Arthur Plewis, the only practicising wheelwright in England, has closed his workshop in High Halstow after 50 years to live in retirement in Lower Stoke.

March 29th: The Government has plans for 60 commercial radio stations.

April 15th: The go-ahead has been given for the building of a £15 million arts centre at the Barbican in London.

April 17th: It is believed that more than 7,000 people have died in the civil war in East Pakistan.

It was in this Swiss chalet in 1870 that Charles Dickens wrote his last words. There was a communicating tunnel under the road to the chalet which stood in the grounds of Dicken's home at Gadshill for many years It was bought by been Rochester City Council a few years ago and completely restored.

April 19th: Unemployment has reached a record level of 814,819 — the highest since May 1940.

April 24th: Sir Leslie Doubleday, president of Kent Cricket Club today accepted the County Society's Gold Medal on behalf of the club.

May 8th: Arsenal has won the FA Cup to go alongside the Football League title. It is only the second "double" this century.

May 10th: 100 Labour MPs have defied party policy and signed a declaration supporting British entry into the EEC.

May 12th: Mick Jagger, former Dartford Grammar School boy, today married Bianca Perez Morena de Macias in St Tropez.

May 21st: Chelsea beat Real Madrid 2-1 today to win the European Cup Winners' Cup.

June 19th: Hughie Green's *Opportunity Knocks* is Britain's most popular television show with a weekly audience of 6.6 million.

July 2nd: A 19-year-old half-aboriginal girl, Evonne Goolagong, has won the women's singles title at Wimbledon.

June 24th: Prince Philip today visited Templar Barracks at Ashford, Trinity Homes for Retired Mariners at Walmer, the Coastguard Stations at Deal and Folkestone. Dungeness Lighthouse and the Trinity House Experimental Station.

July 6th: From today crash helmets will be compulsory for motor cyclists.

July 19th: John Jacob Astor, Lord Astor of Hever, second son of William Waldorf Astor and formerly MP for Dover, has died aged 85.

July 25th: South African surgeon Christian Barnard claims he has performed a combined heart and lung transplant.

August 11th: In a massive crackdown on terrorism in Ulster, 300 suspected IRA supporters were arrested in dawn raids yesterday. The introduction of internment prompted immediate riots.

September 1st: One penny and three-penny coins cease to be legal tender.

The Kent Messenger newspaper group has acquired the *Kentish Express* from the British Printing Corporation.

September 24th: Ninety Russian diplomats have been expelled from Britain for spying.

October 30th: An opinion poll today says most Britons oppose entry into the Common Market.

November 8th: Princess Anne opened the West Hill outpatients department at Dartford Hospital.

November 10th: Two women in Belfast are tarred and feathered for dating British soldiers.

November 23rd: Continuing clashes along the border between India and East Pakistan are threatening to erupt into a full-scale war.

December 31st: Crown Courts have been set up at Maidstone and Canterbury to replace the Assize Courts and Quarter Sessions which date back to the 14th century.

GREAT HITS OF 1971

Maggie May

My Sweet Lord

A mediaeval wall painting, above the piscina in the south aisle of St Augustine's Church, Brookland, has been fully uncovered and cleaned. It was first discovered in 1964. The painting depicts the martyrdom of Saint Thomas à Becket and the armour of the knights is of special interest. Brookland is one of Kent's oldest churches. It was built in the mid-thirteenth century and little has changed structurally. The lead font, first used for the baptism of children more than 600 years ago, is considered the most important of the lead fonts in England and the church still retains its original drain.

Roman house uncovered in Dover

Archaeologists have unearthed a Roman house in New Street, Dover, which is believed to be the most perfect example in the world outside Italy.

The house — under a permanent modern building — once stood outside a third century fort and is built of brick and flint with two main rooms which are about six feet in height. These are plastered and painted with superb pictures dating from about 200 AD.

The larger rooms have a hypocaust system and the floors are of red mortar. It is hoped the painted house can be preserved and opened to visitors.

Kent homes rock as tanker explodes at sea

January 15th: Eight Italian seamen, including the Master, were killed when a Panamanian tanker, delivering a cargo of petroleum to Canvey Island, was in collision with a Peruvian vessel, seven miles off Folkestone. It was one of the worst peacetime disasters in the open waters of the English Channel this century.

The next morning, a Hamburg-Amerika Line ship with a German crew struck the wreckage and a further 21 seamen died including two stewardesses.

The first impact occurred at 3am on the morning of January 11th. It tore the tanker in half and caused an explosion which shook houses all the way down the east Kent coast. There was no time for a Mayday message to be sent; within minutes the bridge and bow section of the 13,604-ton tanker — the *Texaco Caribbean* — had sunk.

On the 9,481-ton vessel, the *Paracas*, the bow suffered severe damage but the crew were uninjured. The Master immediately called for tugs to assist her.

Although the Deal Coastguard Station had heard the explosion, the first Mayday message came into the North Foreland Radio Station from a fishing vessel off Folkestone.

Lifeboats were launched at Dover and Dungeness and numerous ships converged on the scene. They found the stern section of the *Caribbean* afloat but listing precariously. Several men were in the water and others in the ship's lifeboat.

The Norwegian *Bravour* picked up 22 of the crew and transferred them to the Dover lifeboat. The little fishing vessel which had reported the explosion, the *Viking Warrior,* found the injured boatswain in the water gripping a piece of wood. Although his clothes had been blown off he was alive.

The *Paracas* was towed to Hamburg but there was no hope for the *Texaco Caribbean* which was disappearing slowly into the sea. Yet the drama was not over.

Just before 8 am, the *Brandenburg* (2,695 tons), struck the wreckage and listed within five minutes. Again there was no time to send a Mayday message and no time to launch the lifeboats. The crew of 32 were in the water.

The *Viking Warrior,* still in the area, saw a number of the men clinging to wreckage and made a second distress call. She helped to pick up 11 men and seven bodies. There was no sign of the 14 still missing. The wreck of the *Brandenburg* was later located with a gash 100 feet long in her port bridge.

Desperate to prevent further disasters occurring Trinity House has marked the wreck zone with painted buoys and placed a light vessel in the area. There are reports, however, of ships passing unnervingly close. The situation is tense.

May: Hot pants are the latest female fashion craze to sweep the country and the girls say they are really cool. So put away those mini and micro-skirts — they're out of date. Our model with the cricket bat is lovely Hilary Ambrose of Bourne Close, Tonbridge, who just can't wait for the summer to arrive.

Tristar contract bankrupts Rolls Royce

February 4th: A disastrous contract to manufacture the RB211 jet engine for the new Lockheed Tristar has bankrupted Rolls-Royce, which is still considered to be the symbol of British engineering excellence. The company is now in the hands of the receiver.

The company was formed at the beginning of the century by Charles Rolls, Kent's great pioneer motorist and aviator and Henry Royce of Manchester.

More lives lost at sea and on the railway

February 26th: An express train from Victoria failed to stop at Sheerness yesterday, ran through the buffer stops and the booking hall and came to rest in a taxi rank outside the station. A woman, Miss Joyce Carr, who was buying a ticket was killed and nine people injured.

It is believed the driver suffered a loss of consciousness while approaching Sheerness. He said today that he had a good run to the Isle of Sheppey with satisfactory brakes and remembers applying them at he approached the station. The next thing he recalled was coming to while leaning over the controls.

The station's old timber buildings have been badly damaged and there will be a temporary replacement.

February 27th: *There has been yet another tragedy in the Dover Straits. A Greek vessel,* Niki *(2,371 tons), with a cargo of rails struck the wreckage of the* Brandenburg *today and sank very quickly. Once again the Dover and Dungeness lifeboats were launched, a Shackleton aircraft dropped flares and many ships converged on the area.*

To no avail. On this occasion only bodies have been found and it is believed the crew of 21 and the wife of the Chief Engineer have all perished.

The accident brings the total of lives lost in this area of the Channel to 51 since January 11th. Trinity House is preparing to send another lightship to the area.

June 11th: Three passengers were killed and 126 injured when a diesel-hauled "party special" returning from Margate left the rails at Eltham Well Hall where there was a speed limit of 20-miles an hour over a sharp curve.

Among those killed was the driver who had been drinking heavily before he took over the train. Three times the legal limit of alcohol was found in his blood.

An inspecting officer will tell an inquiry that the derailment was caused by the driver's failure to brake sharply on the steeply-falling gradient before Eltham Well Hall in readiness for the speed limit.

1971

February 16th: Between 50 and 60 chanting demonstrators carrying placards marched from Penchester Gardens, Dover to the Town Hall on Saturday where Mr Enoch Powell was speaking to the local Conservatives about the situation in Britain following the collapse of Rolls-Royce. The demonstrators arrived in two buses from the University of Kent. There were no arrests.

March 5th: The sudden appearance of Russian ships in the Atlantic means a huge disappointment for about 200 Chatham girls. They were looking forward to a dance at Chatham Town Hall to welcome Medway sailors from the ships of six different countries, representing NATO's standing force. With the arrival of the Russians, however, the dance has been cancelled.

March 16th: Henry Cooper, the most successful British boxer of postwar years, has announced his retirement from the ring after losing his British, Commonwealth and European title to Joe Bugner. Cooper held the British heavyweight title for an unbroken spell of ten years and five months since winning it from Brian London in 1959. He lost it briefly in 1969 when beaten by Jack Bodell but won it back again.

May 1st: The Daily Mail, the newspaper founded by Alfred Harmsworth of Broadstairs in 1896 and known as the pioneer of popular journalism, appears as a broadsheet for the last time today. Tomorrow Viscount Rothermere, nephew of Harmsworth (later Viscount Northcliffe) and now chairman of the company will launch the first tabloid edition. Next week, the Daily Sketch, Britain's oldest tabloid newspaper, will close.

March 26th: *Forty men were thrown into a jangled hell of 1,200 tons of concrete when the new bridge over the M20 Ditton by-pass collapsed on Monday (March 22nd). Hundreds of tons of steel scaffolding then crashed on top of them. Ambulancemen raced to the scene expecting to cut living men out of rapidly hardening concrete but they discovered, almost miraculously, that only one man had been killed although 15 were injured. The men, employed by Richard Costain Ltd, were constructing the bridge when an earth movement caused one of the bridge pillars to slip. The complex 220-foot long structure, along with the boxes into which the concrete was being poured groaned, then capsized — almost in slow motion like a ship going down.*

The accident, the first of its type on all bridges over British motorways, will now be the subject of an inquiry carried out by the South East Road Construction Unit. Whitehall experts are already sifting through the tangled steel, wood and now hard-set concrete to find the vital clue which leads to the reason for the structure's collapse. Civil engineers all over Europe anxiously await the result of their findings. The bridge, when rebuilt. will carry an 18-foot carriageway over the Ditton end of the Maidstone bypass.

***August 11th:** Edward Heath, the sailing Prime Minister — pictured here at Broadstairs in 1967 with his "Snipe" class racing dinghy Blue Heather (his initials are E.R.) —yesterday led a British team to victory in the Admiral's Cup — sailing's most prestigious prize. All three British yachts completed the Fastnet Race which is considered to be the most gruelling test of ocean racing. Heath was skipper of the sloop* Morning Cloud 11, *a successor to his previous boats and last of the victorious team to finish after losing part of her spinnaker gear off the Scillies. They were all well ahead of their nearest rivals. Mr Heath, who learned to sail when he lived in Broadstairs and now plans to write a book about his favourite sport, has been criticised for putting the race ahead of the Irish crisis in the list of his priorities.*

Decimal currency: old folk say —'what's the point'

February 12th: Shopkeepers, publicans and their customers throughout Kent are predicting this week that prices of most products (perishable and otherwise) will rise dramatically with the introduction next Monday (Feb 15th) of decimal coinage.

Many more people, particularly the old, say they will find it hard to adjust to the concept of a 10 pence coin which equals a florin and the fact there will no longer be 240 pennies in the pound.

There is plenty of help. Pamphlets have been issued by the Decimal Currency Board and local authorities. Officials have offered to visit homes to explain the system.

So next Monday is D (for decimal) Day. After centuries of dealing with pounds, shillings and pence the old illogical but lovable system will change.

People will just have to accept that a 'p' replaces a 'd', that 1/- now equals 5p and the half-crown piece has disappeared.

This is all that remains of the New Theatre which was opened in 1947 by Queen Mary. The first theatre in Bromley High Street was built in 1899 as a multi-pupose hall to house banquets and civic functions as well as stage presentations. Under the floor it also had a swimming pool which was never used because all the water seeped away before the opening ceremony. Seven years later the name was changed to The Lyric and then The Grand Electric Theatre showing moving films with lectures and lantern slides. During the war it became a warehouse and air raid shelter. In December 1947 a syndicate sponsored by J. Arthur Rank renovated the theatre as The New, a repertory playhouse.

Bromley's New Theatre destroyed by fire

May: The 900-seat New Theatre, Bromley, has been completely destroyed by a mystery blaze which could be seen for many miles. More than 100 firemen with 15 appliances were called to the scene and managed to prevent the flames spreading to other buildings in the High Street but they were unable to save one of the south-east's most popular theatres outside London.

Today specialist fire prevention officers will sift through the still-smouldering ruins to find a reason for the outbreak. The auditorium and stage is just a shell but some of the dressing rooms are intact and valuable costumes worn in the current production have been saved.

The blaze was discovered at 4 am by two resident members of the theatre staff who were awakened by the noise of falling timber. By that time flames were leaping through the roof.

The New Theatre, opened in 1947 by Queen Mary, was in the last week of a three-week run of *The Heiress* starring Patrick Cargill and Anne Stallybrass. Cliff Richard was due to appear next week in Graham Greene's *The Potting Shed.*

In September 1958 the owners of the theatre applied for permission to demolish the building to make room for development, which did not include a theatre. There was a public outcry leading to the presentation of a petition with a massive 37,000 signatures. Because of this, permission was refused.

The following year plans for a new library and theatre were put forward to Bromley Town Council. These recommended the retention of the old theatre with an improved and modernised foyer and individual shops facing the High Street. The new complex, now in the ownership of the Bromley Theatre Trust and controlled by the Council, was due to open in two years' time.

CENSUS 1971

Gillingham regains top spot as Kent's biggest town

The way in which ribbon development and the spread of outer surburbia is eating into the heart of Kent's countryside is clearly reflected in the latest census figures for the county. New brick buildings now pepper many of the villages and more and more bungalows can be found in the holiday conurbations of the coast. The Thamesside and Medway towns are growing rapidly and the population of Maidstone has increased by more than 20 per cent since 1961. Here are the Kent towns, in order of size of population — minus the London boroughs.

GILLINGHAM	*86,862*
MAIDSTONE	*70,987*
CHATHAM	*57,153*
ROCHESTER	*55,519*
GRAVESEND	*54,106*
MARGATE	*50,347*
DARTFORD	*45,705*
TUNBRIDGE WELLS	*44,612*
FOLKESTONE	*43,801*
RAMSGATE	*39,561*
ASHFORD	*35,615*
DOVER	*34,395*
CANTERBURY	*33,176*
QUEENBOROUGH	*31,590*
TONBRIDGE	*31,016*
SITTINGBOURNE	*30,913*
NORTHFLEET	*26,718*
DEAL	*25,432*
WHITSTABLE	*25,449*
HERNE BAY	*25,198*
BROADSTAIRS	*20,048*
SEVENOAKS	*18,247*
FAVERSHAM	*14,818*
HYTHE	*11,959*
SOUTHBOROUGH	*9,755*
SWANSCOMBE	*9,206*
TENTERDEN	*5,950*
SANDWICH	*4,490*
LYDD	*4,315*
NEW ROMNEY	*3,447*

The gentle star of Dracula takes a morning dip in the North Sea

Peter Cushing —not all Hammer House of Horror!

November: Early every morning fishermen at Whitstable Harbour, preparing for a day's work, will see a tall, upright man in his late fifties walk briskly along the sea front and then plunge into the "invigorating" waves of the North Sea. A few minutes later they will see him striding smartly back to his home near the Sea Wall for a healthy breakfast. It is a routine that continues most days of the year.

The country's cinemagoers know him as Frankenstein, or Dracula — the monstrous star of Hammer films who has terrified millions of people for many years now.

In Whitstable, however, he is Mr Peter Cushing — the gentle, kind neighbour who has just lost his wife Helen after a long illness.

Mr Cushing has made over 70 films and they are not all the grisly, macabre stories for which he was nearly typecast. He has played Sherlock Holmes, appeared in *Dr Who and the Daleks* and enjoyed great success as *Hamlet* and the *Man in the Iron Mask*. In 1955 he was named Television Actor of the Year for his portrayal of Winston Smith in George Orwell's *1984*.

He and Helen moved to Whitstable some years ago and fell in love with the town and its long street of old houses, the tiny shingle beach, the harbour and its fishing fleet and the bracing air.

He nursed his wife through her illness and her death is a bitter blow. He intends to busy himself painting and reading, collecting cigarette cards and model figures (his greatest hobby). For these he has built a working theatre which contains 10 scenes all from different plays and periods. Meanwhile this star of 90 films is keeping fit with his long morning walks and the dip in the sea.

'Wherever he goes he is welcomed with Kentish fire and from his example he is known as the Spirit of Kent' — Roy Pratt Boorman on Lord Cornwallis who has retired as Lord Lieutenant.

January 9th: The miners' strike began today with the government urging shops to ration coal supplies.

January 13th: Naval officer David Bingham is jailed for 13 years for supplying secrets to Russia.

January 30th: British paratroopers opened fire on civil rights marchers in Londonderry's Bogside killing 13 men and youths and injuring a further 17. The killings are being described as mass murder. Newspapers have tagged the event 'Bloody Sunday'.

January 22nd: Britain, together with Ireland, Denmark and Norway, today signed the Treaty of Brussels. They will be members of the European Community as from next year.

February 16th: Electricity blackouts lasting more than nine hours have been imposed over the whole country. Since last week industry has been working a three-day week as the miners' pay dispute deepens.

February 22nd: President Nixon today urged China to join the United States on a "long march together" by different routes to world peace during a banquet in the Great Hall of the People in Peking.

In an IRA bomb attack on the 16th Parachute Brigade at Aldershot, six civilians and a priest were killed in a revenge attack for last month's 'Bloody Sunday' battle.

March 19th: Bangladesh today signed a friendship treaty with India.

March 25th: The Stormont Parliament of Northern Ireland is to be taken over by the British Government and the province administered from Whitehall. Mr Heath said direct rule will last for about a year to get both sides working together for peace.

April 27th: Women will be admitted for the first time to five of Oxford's 27 all-male colleges.

Bromley Borough Council is to buy the South Camp, the operational part of Biggin Hill airfield and maintain it as an airfield, encouraging small business aircraft and executive jets to fly alongside the many flying clubs. The cost is believed to be a snip at £450,000. The North Camp of the former front-line fighter base is now the headquarters of the Officer and Aircrew Selection Centre. On September 15th, as usual, the RAF will stage its spectacular At Home display which draws huge crowds from all over the world. The North Camp also houses St George's Chapel as a permanent memorial to those who gave their lives flying from Biggin Hill.

May 28th: The Duke of Windsor who gave up the throne to marry "the woman I love", died today in France. He will be buried in English soil at Frogmore.

June 17th: Police arrested five men today in the Democratic committee's offices at Watergate in Washington. They are accused of attempting to bug the building.

June 18th: 118 people aboard a BEA Trident were killed today when the airliner crashed in a field near Staines.

July 27th: The Sheerness Harbour extension was opened today by Princess Alexandra.

July 28th: A nationwide dock strike began today following the jailing of four dockers for contempt of court.

July 30th: Dame Sybil Thorndike today visited Aylesford — the village where she was born and married to open a community centre.

August 3rd: A car ferry terminal has been opened today by Mr John Peyton, Minister of Transport . The service between Folkestone and Calais is inaugurated by two ships, *Hengist* and *Horsa.*

August 14th: Edward Heath has opened the new village hall at St Peter's, Broadstairs, where he had learned to play the church organ.

September 5th: Nine Israeli hostages, taken from the Olympic village near Munich, were killed today as German police mounted a rescue attempt. In the gun battle four Arabs and one policemen also died. The hostage-takers are members of "Black September," a band of Arab Guerrillas and they were demanding the release of 200 Palestinians held in Israeli jails.

September 11th: Britain has won gold medals in yachting and eventing in the Olympic Games at Munich, which has just ended. It will be remembered for the attack by terrorist gunmen and also for the extraordinary perforamnce of Mark Spitz who won seven swimming golds for the United States.

September 20th: A memorial service was held at Canterbury today for Lord Fisher of Lambeth, Archbishop of Canterbury from 1945 to 1961.

September 21st: The first Ugandan Asians to arrive in Kent are staying with relatives in Gravesend. The Sharma family say they were subject to more than eight hours military interrogation at Entebbe Airport and are almost penniless.

October 10th: John Betjeman has been appointed poet laureate.

November 6th: Prime Minister Edward Heath has placed a 90-day freeze on wages, prices and rents.

November 7th: Richard Nixon was re-elected President of the United States by a huge majority.

November 17th: The *Sunday Times* has been banned by the High Court from publishing articles about the drug thalidomide.

GREAT HITS OF 1972

Amazing Grace

Puppy Love

E.M.Forster's *Maurice* is published at last

January: A manuscript written by the brilliant novelist, Edward Morgan Forster and rejected because of its frank portrayal of homosexuality, has been published at last — to great acclaim.

The book, partly autobiographical, was completed in 1914 and told the story of homosexual love and the future of England as a classless society through the love of a stockbroker, Maurice and a gamekeeper, Alec. It is called *Maurice.*

When suppressed by the censor, Forster had it circulated privately and then later said he would write no more. The long silence lasted 40 years and Forster died last June aged 91.

Despite his small output, the former Tonbridge schoolboy who lived in Tunbridge Wells for many years has been acknowledged among the two or three major novelists of his time.

Where Angels Fear to Tread, his first novel, was followed by *The Longest Journey* (1907), *A Room with A View* (1908) and *Howard's End* (1910). After publication of his volume of short stories, *The Celestial Omnibus* (1911) he visited India where he closely observed the British colonial attitudes. His final major work was *A Passage to India* in 1927.

Forster's finest achievements were his novels, in which character and the clash of ideas overshadow plot. His narrative point of view was normally that of an outsider, and his novels, especially *A Passage to India* and *Howard's End*, are sad examinations of the social codes and barriers that thwart communication and frustrate feeling.

Obituary

RICHARD CHURCH

Richard Church, poet, essayist and novelist died at his home of four years, The Priest's House, Sissinghurst Castle, just three weeks before his 79th birthday.

He was the author of more than 50 books and had been an editor for Dent's, the publishers for more than 20 years. He was responsible for publishing works by the poet Edward Muir and did much to secure the publication of Dylan Thomas's first collection.

Church was best known for his books about Kent. He loved the villages and, in particular the luxuriance, beauty and culture of The Weald. Critics have said that he was to Kent what Hardy was to Dorset.

In the 30s he wrote a trilogy of the Civil Service entitled *The Porch* which was greatly acclaimed. In 1955 his biography of childhood *Over the Bridge* was followed by the award of the CBE. He leaves a wife, three daughters and a son and 14 grandchildren.

RUSSELL THORNDIKE

Russell Thorndike, the brother of England's leading dramatic actress, was brought up in the shadows of Rochester Cathedral, where his father was a minor canon, and then moved to Aylesford when dad became vicar of that lovely village church. He made a name for himself as actor and producer but never achieved the international reputation enjoyed by Dame Sybil. He died aged 87.

After one successful book, Thorndike created his *Dr Syn,* a respectable Christian pastor by day and mysterious smuggler by night, known as The Scarecrow. The book was a sensation and Thorndike became a best-selling author. *The Scarecrow* was made into a film with Peter Cushing in the title role and it is said that Thorndike's fee for the film rights disappeared in one glorious pub binge.

June: The highlight of this year's Kent County Show at Detling on July 14th will be the appearance in the dressage and show jumping events of Princess Anne, now one of Britain's finest all-round riders.

Late last year Princess Anne was named Sportswoman of the Year by the British Sportswriters Association. She comfortably headed the poll ahead of the world showjumping champion, Ann Moore and Tunbridge Wells' tennis player, Virginia Wade.

The Princess, now 21, won the European Three-day Event championship on her horse, Doublet, at Burghley.

Carmelite brothers' goodbye to Father Lynch

May 5th: Father Malachy Lynch, who took his brothers of the Carmelite Order back to their monastery at Aylesford in 1949, has died. He was the inspiration behind the restoration project at Aylesford Priory.

The Carmelite Order also owns Allington Castle, on the banks of the Medway near Maidstone. It was purchased in 1951 from George W. Horsefield, son-in-law of the late Lord Conway and is used as a "desert house" for Carmelite sisters.

After a year in Allington, where they wear the brown Carmelite habit, the sisters return to their professions, carrying with them the spirit of prayer and contemplation developed in their "desert year". They then return to Allington for 40 days each year,

July 31st: *Lord Astor of Hever, seen here with the Queen at Fort Halstead, Sevenoaks, is the new Lord Lieutenant and Custos Rotulorum of Kent following the retirement of Lord Cornwallis who has served his county in that capacity for 28 years. Gavin Astor was born on June 1st, 1918, the first child of Major J.J. Astor, later first Lord Astor of Hever. He went to Eton and New College, Oxford, joined the army at the outbreak of war and, in 1940, was commissioned in his father's old regiment, the Life Guards. In 1944 he was taken prisoner by the Germans in Italy. Returning home, he married Lady Irene Haig, daughter of the Field Marshal. They have two sons. From 1959 to 1966 he was the chairman of The Times Publishing Company.*

Tributes are flooding in this week to Lord Cornwallis whose CV includes a post as Aide-de-Camp to Field Marshal Haig, Chairman of the County Council, president of the County Society, captain of Kent Cricket Club and Pro-Chancellor of the University of Kent.

Kemsley Mills fire the greatest ever known

June 11th: No firefighter in Kent has ever experienced a blaze as furious as the one which has just destroyed the Bowater Kemsley Mills at Sittingbourne; in fact it is believed to be the biggest blaze in the Brigade's history.

Called out soon after midday on June 8th the men were faced with flames that were shooting so high in the air they could be seen in Canterbury. Scores of stations were alerted and hundreds of thousands of gallons of water poured onto the flames.

By the time the fire was under control after 48 hours, 330 officers and men had been involved at the scene and 60 appliances and 40,000 feet of hose employed. Damage is estimated at a massive £500,000.

1972

Kent miners celebrate an "epic victory"

March 26th: More than 2,000 Kent miners and trade unionists gathered in the Winter Gardens at Margate today to celebrate the most epic victory in their history. With the Deal Girl Pipers providing a rousing battle sound, the miners toasted the success of a class struggle that had lasted seven long weeks and brought the country to its knees.

A few days earlier the miners, along with their colleagues across the country, had voted to accept the pay settlement recommended by the Wilberforce Court of Inquiry.

Jack Dunn, general secretary of the Kent Area of the NUM described the strike as a unique battle "fought — not only for a decent living wage— but for a livelihood. We had been told", he said, "that our labour was no longer necessary for the British economy and pits were to be phased out in this age of oil and nuclear power. The three remaining Kent pits at Betteshanger, Snowdown and Tilmanstone were among those under threat".

The bubble of unrest which has simmered for many years burst completely in January when miners walked out of the coalfields and imposed a total blockade on the movement of coal and allied fuels. They were supported immediately by railwaymen, seamen, dockers and lorry drivers. In Kent, the entire mining community was put onto a war footing.

The tradition of industrial militancy has been a feature of the Kent pits since the Great Strike of 1926 and Betteshanger today is renowned throughout the country as "the most militant in the British Coalfield". In the 1938 Betteshanger strike the colliery band toured the Medway and Ashford area to raise money for food for the striking men. Later 1,200 miners with banners and band marched down to St George's Hall, Deal, to accept "indoor relief" in the workhouses of Kent until they had won their case. In 1961, 140 Betteshanger men were given redundancy notices and, in retaliation, 127 organised a stay-down strike in the pit. For six days they lived at the coal face and food came down from the colliery canteen where the girls had declared their full support. The men were also given books, cards, dominoes and even an old record player. The strike was successful; the NCB agreed to open a new seam at 1,900 feet and the future of the colliery was secured.

By the beginning of February the crisis had deepened. Power stations had been forced to close, electricity blackouts lasting up to nine hours were imposed over the whole country, householders were asked to heat only one room and industry was working a three-day week.

Led by Jack Collins, national delegate for the area, the 3,500 Kent miners looked after the picketing of 150 miles of coastline and the biggest concentration of power stations, coal wharves and depots in Britain.

After the recommendation had been accepted Jack Dunn said: "We carried the struggle to unprecedented heights and have played our part in history. We took over the NUM offices in London, and other picketing organisations, we organised flying squads to picket in London and the south coast, we held hundreds of meetings large and small with demonstrations and parades, we have humiliated the Tory Government and we have received an offer beyond the realms of optimism of four months ago...Our members with the support of millions of trade unionists have shattered the Tory wage restraint policy...We have forged a new political and class consciousness throughout Britain."

See page 187

Film and TV contracts for the countryside author

October: A selection of short stories written by the novelist, Herbert Ernest Bates, are to provide the basis for several new television plays. The series will be called *Country Matters* and many of them will feature strongly the Kent countryside where "H.E." lives with his wife Madge.

Most of the stories were written before the war soon after the couple came to live at the Granary in Little Chart Forstal.

Bates is delighted with the television contract and also with a film contract from Sir Alexander Korda, the Hungarian film producer, who gave him a phenomenal salary, "until", said Bates, "I woke up to the fact that, thanks to tax, all I got out of every pound was sixpence".

Korda's film director David Lean has now bought the film rights for *Fair Stood the Wind for France, The Cruise of the Breadwinner* and *The Purple Plain.*

There is a strong possibility that the short novel *Darling Buds of May,* which was written by Bates in 1959, will also be converted to television. Encouraged by its success, Bates provided the Larkin family with several more adventures in *A Breath of French Air, When the Green Woods Laugh, Oh! To Be In England* and *A Little of What You Fancy.*

In his recently-published autobiography, which appears in three parts, H.E. Bates admits there is something of himself in Pop Larkin — "a passionate Englishman, a profound love of nature, a hatred of pomp, pretension and humbug, a lover of children and family life and a flouter of conventions".

He says: "The only things I don't share with Pop are a business ability to sell junk at a profit of 300 per cent or to avoid the payment of income tax."

A distant view of Maidstone from the North Downs Way at Blue Bell Hill. Below this escarpment and to the right is the prehistoric monument, Kits Coty which consists of three upright stones with a capstone on top.

Ramblers can take the high road to Dover

October: **The first 43-mile section of a long-distance footpath which will eventually follow the chalk downs from Dover through Kent and deep into the Surrey countryside was opened today.**

The North Downs Way was one of the recommendations to arise from the publication of the 1967 Countryside Bill — which also allowed local authorities to set up country parks. For Kent's many ramblers and for London's city dwellers, bursting for an excursion into the countryside, this is good news.

The first section runs from Dover to Hollingbourne but, when completed, the North Downs Way will be just under 200 kilometres in length. It follows areas of outstanding beauty, keeping to the Weald side of the downs for most of its way and, on occasions, converging with the Pilgrims Way. An acorn is used as a waymark to guide the walkers.

The route was actually surveyed by the Ramblers' Association who also suggested an alternative loop from Wye to Canterbury.

November 30th: *This bronze, imaginative larger-than-life statue of Sir Winston Churchill was unveiled today by his grandson Winston in the Pine Gardens at St Margaret's-at-Cliffe. The gift of Mr Fred Cleary, the statue was designed by Oscar Nemon and erected by the St Margaret's Bay Trust in the setting of specimen trees, a lake and a waterfall.*

Archaeological corps 'rescues' manor and castle

March 23rd: For several months the newly-formed Archaeological Rescue Corps, assisted by the West Kent and Reculver excavation groups, have been keeping a non-stop watch on a massive pipe-laying operation in the Darenth Valley in the hope that important archaeological sites will be revealed.

They have not been disappointed. Eleven sites, including Neolithic, Iron Age, Romano-British and Anglo-Saxon, have been discovered at Darenth. A hitherto unknown Roman villa site has also been found at Horton Kirby which was saved from destruction by instant action in a matter of just 15 hours.

This week produced the most exciting find of all. A giant mechanical excavator cutting a sewer trench at Farningham stopped dead when it hit a masonry wall, 14 inches thick. It has now been identified as the site of Farningham Manor and Castle, similar to the one that still survives at Eynsford.

The full-time CIB Archaeological Rescue Corps was created last year when 10 members gave up their careers in order to survey, excavate, record and publish sites threatened with destruction. They are assisted by more than 300 volunteers. The Department of Environment has provided headquarters in disused buildings at Dover Castle.

The newly-revealed archaeological sites in the Darenth Valley are causing great excitement particularly among those who recall the "rediscovery" in 1949 of the Roman Villa at Lullingstone.

Today, it is one of the most visited sites in Kent. It stands on the banks of the River Darent and dates from about AD 90, probably as the home of a farmer and later expanded as the country residence of officials.

The central room has a mosaic floor which was laid two centuries later. There is also a "deep room" with a well and above it, a Christian chapel. The Lullingstone Roman Villa is still considered to be one of the most important archaeological discoveries in Britain since the war.

September 28th: *This photograph of four smiling Asian girls was taken at West Malling airfield this week. The girls are sitting on a see-saw, which is fairly appropriate because they have just been whisked from one extreme to the other. They also look happy, rather than confused, which certainly pleases the authorities.*

The children and their parents are among the thousands of Asians expelled from Uganda by General Idi Amin. They arrived at Heathrow airport and have been accommodated temporarily in the disused airmens' huts at West Malling before dispersal to other parts of England.

Just over a week ago General Amin declared that 50,000 Asians with British passports were to leave immediately. Most of the families had been settled in East Africa for more than a century and formed the most prosperous community in Uganda. They were given no choice.

Reporters from Kent newspapers interviewed some of those who came to West Malling. They spoke of assaults, plundering, threats and bullying by Amin's soldiers. Most of them were penniless as every last shilling had been taken when they boarded the plane to London.

1972

David Bowie returns from US tour 'on top of the world'

Bromley boy, David Bowie, in his new platform shoes.

October: Yet another Kent boy has become a pop icon with adoring followers all over the world. His name is David Jones but in order to avoid confusion with the David Jones of The American Group, *The Monkees,* he has changed it to David Bowie.

Well known in Bromley, where he lived for a number of years, Bowie has just returned from a highly successful tour of the United States. There, he won unanimous praise from critics for his dazzling performance as a mythical rock star, Ziggy Stardust. Wearing a tight, glittering metallic costume, with high laced hunting boots and orange-tinted hair he looked as if he had just come from outer space.

This sensational extra-terrestrial image followed the release of his hit single *Space Oddity* which benefited from the first landing on the moon more than two years ago. He followed that with the *Rise and Fall of Ziggy Stardust* and *Spiders From Mars.*

Bowie was born in Brixton and attended Stockwell Infants School but his father, unhappy about the number of West Indian immigrants living in the area, moved to Canon Road, Bickley and later to a larger Edwardian house at 23 Clarence Road, Bromley. John and Peggy Jones sent David to Raglan Infants where he joined the 18th Bromley Wolf Cubs and played baseball with the Beckenham Blue Jays. His second school was Bromley Technical High in Oakley Road where he was a rebellious pupil who refused to work hard and was perhaps better known for his unusual hairstyles and recalcitrant nature. He left with one 'O'Level in art.

David Jones' (Bowie's) decision to be a singer-guitarist came at an early age. "I saw a cousin of mine dancing to Elvis' *Hound Dog* and I had never seen her get up and be moved by anything. The power of music really impressed me".

He learned to play the guitar and the saxophone and helped form a local band called the Konrads who played in church halls in the district. One regular venue was Cudham village hall. Gathering place for the group and other musically-minded friends was Vic Furlong's record shop near Bromley South Station which was their equivalent to London's Tin Pan Alley.

David was writing original material before he took his first job as commercial artist. He continued performing with local rock groups until 1968 when he recorded his first album, *Love You Till Tuesday*. It made little headway so he changed his name and in 1969 recorded two successful LPs, *David Bowie* and *The Man Who Sold The World.* This latter album included a style known as glitter rock or glam rock.

Space Oddity followed and with this big success Bowie acquired his weird extra-terrestrial image. The song introduced Major Tom who, Bowie says, will return one day in a new single.

Many critics are suggesting that Bowie — who is married but also admits to being bisexual — must curb his controversial public persona, which includes wearing dresses, and supposed Fascist sympathies. In rock music production, however, he is a talented musician and plans to continue using science-fiction themes starring himself in various androgynous personae.

'It was as if a sleeping giant had come awake. The miners left the coalfield in their thousands to invade the industrial nerve centres of Britain' — Malcolm Pitt, ripper at Tilmanstone, on the miners' dispute.

1973

January 19th: A British super tug was sent today to protect fishing boats from Icelandic gunboats.

January 23rd: President Nixon announced today that fighting in Vietnam will stop at midnight next Saturday. Within 60 days, he said, all American troops and military advisers will be withdrawn.

February 1st: Women were today allowed on the Stock Exchange floor for the first time.

February 7th: A general strike in Ulster today hit power supplies, commerce, industry and transport.

February 14th: Joe Bugner was beaten by Muhammad Ali (formerly Cassius Clay) on points after a blistering 12-round contest.

The exchange of prisoners of war taken on the battlefields of Vietnam began today when 20 men returned home to California.

March 16th: The Queen today opened the new London Bridge.

March 26th: Noel Coward died at his home in Jamaica, aged 73. Coward, who lived in the Romney Marsh area for many years, will be remembered as playwright, actor and cabaret performer who personified a witty and often outrageous way of life.

March 31st: Red Rum is the Grand National winner in a record time of nine minutes 1.9 seconds.

April 1st: The Government today introduced Value Added Tax (VAT).

April 8th: Pablo Picasso,91, arguably the most influential painter of the century and the most prolific, died of a heart attack at his chateau at Mougins.

April 30th: Four of President Nixon's top aides have resigned over the Watergate scandal. Nixon has denied any personal involvement in either the break-in or the cover-up.

Mike Denness (left) took over the captaincy of Kent only last year but has already won a hatful of trophies and received the ultimate reward — the England captaincy in the West Indies. Opening the batting for Kent with Denness is Brian Luckhurst, whose England career began with two centuries against Australia in the 1970-71 series. This season he played against West Indies but misses out on a trip to the Caribbean. Both Denness and Luckhurst have proved to be prolific scorers for Kent and form the best opening partnership in the County Championship.

May 5th: Second division Sunderland beat Leeds United 1-0 to win the FA Cup today.

May 24th: Earl Jellicoe and Antony Lampton, two government ministers, have resigned after admitting they associated with prostitutes.

May 29th: The Queen's only daughter, Princess Anne, is to marry Lieutenant Mark Philips, aged 24, of the Dragoon Guards, it was announced today.

July 3rd: Elizabeth Taylor says she has separated from her husband, Richard Burton.

July 30th: After an 11-year-fight, thalidomide victims have been awarded compensations totalling £20 million.

August 29th: President Richard Nixon refuses to hand over tapes of White House conversations.

September 7th: Jackie Stewart, the most successful driver in Formula One history, has announced his retirement with his third world championship assured.

September 17th: A government report entitled Equal Opportunities for Men and Women proposes that an Equal Opportunities Commission be set up and so end the discrimination against women in employment, training and education.

September 28th: The poet, W.H. Auden, died in Vienna today aged 66.

October 8th: A new commercial radio station, the London Broadcasting Company (LBC), went on the air today, breaking the BBC's 50-year radio monopoly.

October 17th: England fail to qualify for the World Cup soccer finals after drawing 1-1 with Poland.

October 17th: The oil states have increased prices by 70 per cent and cut back production in protest at US support for Israel in the Yom Kippur war. In one of the fiercest battles since the Second World War, Egyptian and Israeli troops are fighting in the Sinai desert.

October 26th: US forces throughout the world are on military alert over the Soviet Union's plan to send forces to support the Egyptian Third Army trapped in the Sinai desert.

November 11th: Israel and Egypt sign ceasefire agreement in the first-ever pact between the two nations.

November 13th: A state of emergency has been declared in Britain as power workers and miners begin industrial action.

November 14th: Princess Anne and Mark Philips were married today at Westminster Abbey.

November 26th: Secretary for Trade and Industry Peter Walker said today that the Government is printing 16 million petrol ration books. Drivers will be able to collect them from post offices.

Kent's municipal borough and urban councils are making arrangements for the introduction next April of the two-tier system of local government, which has caused great controversy in many areas. Many corporate towns will lose their self-governing status.

GREAT HITS OF 1973

Tie A Yellow Ribbon
Welcome Home

Flashback to 1880 when work began on one of the many Channel tunnel schemes. This was the scene at Abbot's Cliff, Dover, where the project was eventually abandoned.

Objections pour in as Channel Tunnel wins Government approval

Calais could be 'a great British hypermarket'

September 12th: Work is to begin once more on building a tunnel under the Channel to link the white cliffs of Dover with Sangatte in the Pas de Calais. The Government today approved the 32-mile link for a rail tunnel costing an estimated £468 million and says a start can be made by 1975 with possible completition in 1980.

Accompanying the promise of "special provisions" to soften the impact of the Channel on Kent come all the old arguments about the fear of invasion, the likelihood of rabies, the sacrifice of many acres of heritage coast and the damage to the county by the traffic that will stray off the exisiting motorways.

If the project wins Parliamentary sanction it will be the third time this century that engineers have started exploratory bores and contractors been invited to submit option designs.

This year already five million passengers, one million cars and two million heavy lorries have crossed the Channel and those figures are rising by 10 per cent annually. Dover Harbour Board has spent £8 million in the last eight years to treble its cross-Channel capacity.

British and Continental shipping and harbour officials believe that a long railway tunnel will not be seen as an attractive alternative by the majority of travellers — and that a passenger war is certain to erupt.

Bigger and better ships, improved harbour facilities, lower fares and ferry services only a few minutes slower than the proposed tunnel times, will be their objectives as soon as the rail link is officiallly sanctioned. There will be plenty of time for the people of Folkestone, Frogholt, Newington and Cheriton to voice their objections to the effects of the terminal construction in the area and to demand the payment of compensation. Many people are very worried.

The French apparently do not share our fears. For over a century they have dreamed of ways of turning Britain into an extension of Europe. Their reasons are economic as they see British money reviving the flagging fortunes of Northern France, turning Calais and Boulogne into Great British Hypermarkets and ending Kent's long domination of the Channel ferry scene.

The pros and cons of the Channel Tunnel project have been the greatest talking point of Kent's recent history. This time it looks like becoming a reality.

Dame Edith Evans as Lady Bracknell.

Kilndown's Dame Edith Evans celebrates 60 years on the stage

Celebrating 60 years on the professional stage is one of Britain's best-loved and most versatile actresses, Dame Edith Evans who has lived in an Elizabethan manor house at Kilndown, near Goudhurst, for many years. Best known for her role as Lady Bracknell in *The Importance of Being Ernest,* Dame Edith has played more than 150 different roles in the course of her long career and, at 85, has no thought of retiring.

The daughter of a minor civil servant, Edith Mary Evans was indentured as a milliner in London and made her debut on the stage as an amateur in the role of Viola in *Twelth Night* in 1910. By 1913 she had made her first professional appearance in Cambridge and was quickly engaged at the Royalty Theatre, Dean Street, London on a contract with a salary of £2. 10s. a week.

Since then she has performed without a break. "God has been very good to me", she once said. "I don't think there is anything extraordinary about me except this passion for the truth".

She was appointed DBE in the New Year Honours of 1946 but remained untouched by fame, always retiring to her wonderful garden at Kilndown to "recharge my batteries". Dame Edith was married for 10 years and her husband George (Guy) Booth died in 1935. The couple had no children.

Three trophies and England captaincy for Mike Denness

September 29th: It's been another great season for Kent Cricket Club — in fact one of the best in the club's long history. Kent won the Benson and Hedges Cup, the John Player Sunday League Cup, took fourth place in the County Championship, reached the quarter-final stage of the Gillette Cup and then won the Fenner trophy at Scarborough this month. In fact, for several weeks of the season there was talk of the Grand Slam.

Mike Denness said that he inherited a great team from Colin Cowdrey and spoke highly of team spirit and the strength in depth of the playing staff, despite the handicaps.

Alan Knott, Derek Underwood and Brian Luckhurst all played for England and Bernard Julien, Kent's overseas signing was making his mark as an all-rounder with the West Indies. With so many absentees the burden of scoring runs was left to Denness, Graham Johnson, Asif Iqbal, John Shepherd, Bob Woolmer and, of course, Cowdrey.

For Denness, the crowning moment of the season came with his appointment as England's captain in the Caribbean. His appointment was announced during the first game of the Folkestone Week. In the second game Kent played Leicestershire, captained by Ray Illingworth — the skipper England had just sacked!

There have been many more improvements to the Canterbury ground; sadly the club made the decision not to play any more first class games at Gravesend, Blackheath or Gillingham where car parking and spectator comfort is rather inadequate. There is also talk of eventually dropping Hesketh Park, Dartford, the Crabble, Dover and even the Municipal Ground, Folkestone, where there are no parking problems. That will leave just St Lawrence, Canterbury, Mote Park, Maidstone and The Neville, Tunbridge Wells.

Next year, 1974, will be the final season for Leslie Ames as manager of Kent and the boys hope to give him the best farewell present of all — the County Championship pennant.

Some of the exhibits in the Lashenden Air Warfare Museum at Headcorn aerodrome

A new hobby emerges — digging up the battle wrecks

Although the Battle of Britain was 33 years ago hundreds of crashed German and British aircraft still lie buried in the Kent countryside, prompting enthusiasts to group together and search for the more interesting wrecks.

This resurgence of interest in the greatest aerial combat ever known is shown particularly by former schoolboy witnesses to wartime crashes. Many have vivid memories of precise sites and incidents and are keen to add to their original collection of memorabilia.

Led by such people as Dennis Knight, Steve Vizard, Christopher Elliott, Peter Foote and Ken Anscombe, these aviation archaeologists are forming groups and even museums. Among the best known are the Ashford and Tenterden Recovery Group (Brenzett Museum), the Halstead War Museum, the Kent Battle of Britain Museum and the London Air Museum.

The Kent Battle of Britain Museum opened at Chilham Castle this year and its curator is Mike Llewellyn who has already investigated hundreds of crash sites and excavated Rolls-Royce Merlin engines, fuselage, propellers, blades, tail wheels, parachutes, airframes, maps, personal photographs, bullets and other fragments.

Earlier this year they found a Hurricane which had crashed in the Harty Marshes at Sheppey on September 7th, 1940. The pilot was a Czech, Sergeant Koukal who had baled out grievously burned. On landing a local resident tore the burning clothes from his body and gave him first aid. Koukal spent two years in East Grinstead Hospital under Archie McIndoe undergoing 22 operations and eventually returned to Czechoslovakia.

Sergeant Koukal heard about the successful excavation of his Hurricane and visited the Kent Battle of Britain Museum where he met Mrs Carrie Wright whose husband had helped to save his life. By way of appreciation the former Czech fighter pilot presented Mrs Wright with his pilot's badge, now in the care of the museum.

November 26th: **Sixteen million petrol ration books are to be printed immediately, Peter Walker, the Secretary for Trade and Industry said today.**

The Government has not yet decided that rationing is necessary but they must act quickly in view of the Middle Eastern crisis and the world-wide shortage of petroleum products.

Already 200 petrol stations have had to close in Britain including several in Kent. The last time petrol was rationed was during the Suez crisis of 1956.

With petrol supplies running perilously low, Kent's garage proprietors are welcoming the introduction of rationing. They have also appealed to customers not to abuse staff during this grave situation. "I have never been called so many four-letter words in my life," said an attendant at the Iden Park garage in Cranbrook.

Queen Mother's racehorse trainer dies at Fairlawne

May 29th: Mr Peter Cazalet, renowned the world over as the Queen Mother's racehorse trainer, and a former High Sheriff of Kent died today at his home, Fairlawne, Shipbourne, near Tonbridge. He was 66.

Mr Cazalet grew up at Fairlawne, a great mansion on a hill with 1,500 acres and stables that housed some of the greatest jumpers in England. He was one of National Hunt racing's most famous names and trained more than 1,100 winners — of which 250 carried the blue and buff striped colours of the Queen Mother.

Peter Cazalet pictured in 1950.

In his younger days he was an outstanding sportsman, playing racquets, cricket, tennis and squash, but his greatest love was racing. He competed in the Grand National five times until a fall put an end to his career in the saddle in 1938.

He took up training horses and will be best remembered for his greatest disappointment. This was in 1956 when the Queen Mother's *Devon Loch* inexplicably collapsed less than 100 yards from the winning post. *(see page 54)* Subsequently the nearest he came to winning jumping's biggest prize was when he saddled Gregory Peck's *Different Class* to finish third in 1968.

However he did win the Mackeson Gold Cup in 1956 with Col Whitbread's *Dunkirk,* the Hennessy Gold Cup three years later with *Border Mask* and the King George V1 Chase on four occasions.

Until his recent illness, Peter Cazalet appeared in the stable yard at 6.30 every morning to inspect every horse. At 7.0, whatever the weather, he would join the jockeys, stable lads and "bumpers" (amateur riders) on their ride up the windy gallops, carefully scrutinising every rider and horse.

Kent faces the challenge of a three-day week

December 17th: As the miners continue with their overtime ban, Edward Heath is facing the greatest crisis of his premiership and may soon be forced to call a general election to seek an answer to the question: "Who rules the country — an elected government or the unions?"

Today, Anthony Barber introduced his crisis budget by cutting a massive £1,200 million from public spending, limiting industry and commerce to five days' electricity consumption in the fortnight to December 30th and three days a week in the New Year and closing all TV services at 10.30 pm.

New rotas for electricity cuts in Kent have been published in all local papers by Seeboard to give the public a chance to see when power is to be cut off.

Kent's newspaper editors are united in describing the approach of 1974 as one of the most challenging moments known in peacetime. "None of us knows what lies ahead", says the *Kent Messenger.*, "We can only be sure that we face difficulties, inconvenience and real hardship. Let's meet the challenge together and show the world that we believe in one special union — the union flag."

One announcement comes from the management of Trebor-Sharps toffee factory in Maidstone. The 400 women are to receive a pay rise of £1.45p a week as a reward for their efforts during last week's power emergency.

1974

Charles and his wife-to-be may live at Chevening

May 22nd: Prince Charles — pictured here with Lady Sarah Spencer with whom he is romantically linked — may soon take full possession of the great house of Chevening, near Sevenoaks which has been beautifully restored to its former glory.

When the last owner of the house, Lord Stanhope, died in 1967 he left Chevening to the nation in the wish that the "Prime Minister, or cabinet minister, or lineal descendant of King George V1" would make it into a family home.

To the delight of local people, the Board of Trustees of the Chevening Estate today nominated Prince Charles as the occupant, in the hope that the future King of England will enjoy the peaceful atmosphere, magnificent gardens and treasures housed in the mansion — much of it designed by Inigo Jones.

Princes Charles, now 25, is often seen in the company of Lady Sarah Spencer who attended West Heath School, Sevenoaks, with her sisters Lady Diana and Lady Jane. He has visited Chevening often and is well-known in the nearby village of Chipstead, whose residents are optimistic that the Prince will settle down at Chevening with his future wife and family.

This is just what the late Lord Stanhope would have wished for his stately home. The Trustees have preserved the house and estate in the manner which he requested. The house, beautiful now, was very dilapidated in 1967.

Lady Sarah Spencer, the daughter of the 8th Earl Spencer of Althorp, is seen here with Prince Charles at a polo match this year. With her two sisters, Jane (older) and Diana (younger), she attended West Heath School, Sevenoaks and is familiar with all the villages around Sevenoaks.

'We are all minorities now' — Liberal leader, Jeremy Thorpe, after the first general election of 1974 had ended in stalemate.

January 10th: A train drivers' strike today paralysed the UK.

February 4th: The Brazilian Government has refused to extradite the Great Train robber Ronald Biggs, who escaped from jail in England, because he has a Brazilian child.

A bomb exploded on a coach on the M62 near Bradford today killing, it is feared, 11 people. Bodies were thrown 250 yards.

February 11th: Four star petrol today rose to 50p a gallon, the fourth rise in a year. Inn keepers are also predicting a 50p pint of beer is not far away.

March 1st: Prime Minister Edward Heath sought Liberal support today as neither the Tory nor Labour parties could command an overall majority after the general election. Labour won 301 seats, Tories 397 and the balance of power is in the hands of 14 Liberal and nine Scottish and Welsh Nationalist MPs.

March 3rd: It is feared that all 344 passengers on board a Turkish Airlines flight from Paris to London have died in the world's worst air disaster.

March 6th: The miners' strike has ended with a 35 per cent pay increase. Britain will now return to a five-day working week.

March 15th: A federal grand jury said today that President Nixon was involved in a conspiracy to cover up White House involvement in the Watergate burglary of 1972.

March 20th: A gunman attempted to kidnap Princess Anne today in the Mall. He was arrested in St James' Park but shots were fired and a police bodyguard, the Princess's chauffeur, a policeman and a taxi passenger who attempted to tackle the man were all wounded.

March 30th: Red Rum won the Grand National today for the second time.

***May 14th:** Archbishop of York, Dr Donald Coggan (left), aged 65, has been named as new Archbishop of Canterbury in succession to the retiring Michael Ramsay. Educated at Merchant Taylors' and St John's College, Cambridge, Dr Coggan is married with two daughters.*

A 50 mph motorway speed limit has been imposed on Britain's motorways.

April 1st: Only 10 of 45 English counties and one of the 13 Welsh counties survive unchanged after the local government bill became law today. Cumberland, Rutland, Huntingdonshire and Westmorland have disappeared altogether. Kent survives but Sussex is split into two counties with the county towns at Lewes and Chichester.

May 1st: Sir Alf Ramsey was sacked today as England's soccer manager.

May 18th: India detonated her first nuclear device today and attracted world wide criticism because 200 million Indians live below the poverty line.

June 2nd: In a massive explosion at Flixborough, a Humberside chemical plant, 29 people are feared dead.

June 21st: According to figures published today inflation is running at 16 per cent, a post war record.

June 17th: Eleven people were injured today in a bomb explosion at Westminster Hall. It was planted by IRA terrorists who breached the high security arrangements.

July 1st: Senora Isobel Peron became the first woman President of Argentina today following the death of her busband, Juan Domingo. She does not have the popular support enjoyed by his first wife, Evita.

July 5th: Don Revie has been appointed England's new soccer manager.

July 6th: 21-year-old Jimmy Connors and his 19-year-old girlfriend Chris Evert are the new Wimbledon champions.

August 8th: President Richard Nixon resigned today. He now faces impeachment by Congress for his involvement in the Watergate scandal. Gerald Ford is the new President.

October 1st: A hamburger restaurant, owned by McDonald's, has opened in south London. The company plans to open more in Kent and London.

John Conteh of Liverpool today became the first British holder of the world light-heavyweight title since Freddie Mills 25 years ago.

October 5th: Five people were killed today by IRA bombs in two Guildford pubs.

November 7th: One person died and 28 were injured when an IRA bomb was planted in a pub at Woolwich.

December 24th: Labour MP and former Postmaster General, John Stonehouse, whose clothes were found on a Miami beach, was in custody today in Australia.

December 31st: Vigorous price rises and wage increases have pushed the cost of living up by 20 per cent. Much of the country's industry is reeling under crippling wage demands.

GREAT HITS OF 1974

Seasons In The Sun

Billy Don't Be A Hero

47 into 14 equals confusion — and inflation

March 30th: The system of local government set up in Kent 86 years ago has been scrapped. Next week council officers and staff will arrive at work to find a new bureaucratic machine in place — and some unhappy, confused people.

Reorganisation has been preceded by months of planning and many arguments. The passing of the Local Government Act has been described as "bringing local government nearer to the people" but many see it as a modern indignity that "will never work as well as the present municipal set-up".

The county of Kent retains its old boundaries but the County Borough of Canterbury, 19 municipal borough councils, 10 urban district councils and 17 rural district councils have disappeared.

The 47 councils have been merged into 14 district councils. Some have applied for borough status and appointed a mayor. Others have established town councils and elected a mayor with minimal powers. But for the first time ever, town and country will be run by the same council.

Sadly, reorganisation has coincided with an unfortunate, almost desperate, economic climate. There will be massive rises in county and district spending and both businessmen and householders face the biggest rise in rates ever known. Of the £148 million KCC budget, more than £13 million will be used on covering increases caused by inflation.

Nowhere has the argument against "local reform" been greater than at Canterbury which fought unremittingly to keep its status as a county borough. However, the new unit, by Royal Charter, has taken the title City of Canterbury and can become the custodian of the old traditions. With Herne Bay and Whitstable now included, the new administration has a population three times greater than that of the old city.

Sheerness, too, is unhappy. Having long lost its own MP (now shared with Faversham), the new Act has stripped the town of its municipal status, sold the Guildhall and made it part of Swale District Council, centred at Sittingbourne.

Many other administrations are furious at the way "alien" districts have been dumped upon them. Sevenoaks, for example, takes part of the old Dartford rural area which includes Swanley — a London overspill. Tonbridge is paired with Malling and Tunbridge Wells takes over Cranbrook Rural.

New names have been introduced. Rochester and Chatham become Medway, New Romney, Folkestone and Hythe is Shepway, Sittingbourne and Sheppey is Swale, Gravesend is Gravesham.

March: The Dartford warbler, one of the smallest and rarest birds in Britain, is faced with extinction following the recent disastrous moorland blaze in Dorset which has destroyed its main breeding ground.

Almost as small as a wren, it was first identified by Dr Lathan among the heather and gorse on Dartford Heath in 1773. Then an entirely new species to Britain, he named it after his town and saw it thrive. As people, buildings and roads began to arrive so the Dartford warbler moved on to more isolated areas in Dorset and the West Country. The recent fire has destroyed 600 acres which is 10 per cent of the warblers' few remaining breeding grounds.

Ornithologists say the bird is never still for a minute, throwing itself into various attitudes, erecting its tail and crest, frequently rising into the air with fantastic movements and catching insects on the wing.

PM calls election as miners strike again

February 7th: Prime Minister Ted Heath today announced a General Election would be held on February 28th. It follows another miners' dispute which has escalated into a full confrontation between the Government and the trade union movement.

In the Kent coalfield, as a result of an overtime ban, Tilmanstone has been locked out for three weeks. Yet again the mining community has balloted for strike action in support of a wage claim in opposition to the Government's incomes policy. They are preparing to picket power stations and coal depots in the south-east.

Mr Heath has unsuccessfully appealed to the miners to call off their strike for the duration of the campaign. Harold Wilson has accused the Prime Minister of making a "run for it" in the hope that the strike will divert voters from the Government's economic failures.

Defeated Heath seeks solace in Kent

'I will not resign', says troubled leader

October 13th: Ted Heath intends to remain as Leader of the Conservative Party following his narrow defeat in Thursday's General Election — the second this year.

Labour won by the narrowest of overall majorities — just three seats — and the final tally today is Labour 319, Tories 276, Liberals 13, Nationalists, 14 and Others 13. "It is a viable majority and my Government can endure," said the Prime Minister, Harold Wilson.

Mr Heath spent the weekend among his supporters in East Kent. He stayed at the home of Lord and Lady Aldington at Knoll Farm, Aldington and today visited his 86-year-old father in Broadstairs.

When he arrived at his father's home in Dumpton Gap a crowd of more than 200 cheered and shouted encouragement. "Don't resign," they shouted. "Stay on, Ted".

The Tory leader intends to, although he is now in trouble with his own side, many of whom believe a change is necessary after four of the most difficult years in the history of politics.

In the year's first General Election on March 1st, only four seats divided Conservative and Labour; Mr Heath, acting within his constitutional rights, told the Queen he would negotiate with Liberal leader Jeremy Thorpe for support.

Mr Thorpe declined the coalition so Harold Wilson began his third term as Prime Minister. His first act was to end the miners' strike by conceding to practically all their pay demands.

Arthur Scargill, the NUM executive who organised the flying pickets during the dispute of 1972 is pictured at Snowdown Colliery with Kent miners. Mr Scargill has persistently warned of likely pit closures.

Peggy Fenner is only Tory casualty

Only one Kent seat changed hands during the double-election campaign. Mrs Peggy Fenner, Rochester and Chatham's Conservative MP since 1970 and Kent's only woman MP was ousted (in October) by her Labour opponent, Bob Bean, who won with a 2,418 majority.

The other successful Labour candidates are John Ovenden, who held on to Gravesend, and Sydney Irving, who increased his majority at Dartford.

The safest Conservative seat in Kent is now Canterbury where David Crouch has a majority of 13,755 followed by Sevenoaks with an 11,605 majority for Sir John Rodgers.

Kent's MPs are as follows: Maidstone, John Wells; Rochester and Chatham, Robert Bean; Gillingham, Freddy Burden; Gravesend, John Ovenden; Faversham, Roger Moate; Thanet East, Jonathan Aitken; Thanet West, William Rees-Davies; Folkestone and Hythe, Albert Costain; Dover and Deal, Peter Rees; Sevenoaks, Sir John Rodgers; Tonbridge and Malling, John Stanley; Tunbridge Wells, Patrick Mayhew; Ashford, Keith Speed; Dartford, Sydney Irving; Canterbury, David Crouch.

'Loveliest castle in the world' left to the nation

With the death this year of the Hon Lady Olive Cecilia Baillie, the magnificent Leeds Castle — once described as 'the loveliest castle in the world' — has been left to the nation in perpetuity. This was Her Ladyship's final and dearest wish and it is accompanied by a massive endowment of £1,400,000.

Leeds rises from a lake created by the damning of the River Len and is revealed as a traditional mediaeval castle, although much of it was built in different periods. The romantic effect is a credit to the skill of successive owners and especially Lady Baillie who devoted her life's work to restoring the building and landscaping the surrounding park.

Lady Baillie lived at Leeds longer than any owner in history and her work there ranks with that of Edward I and Queen Eleanor, Edward III, Henry VIII and Mr Fiennes Wykeham-Martin whose family sold it in 1926.

Under her care Leeds became one of the greatest castles in England and a centre of brilliant hospitality. She frequently entertained the Prince of Wales, later Edward VIII, Prince George, Duke of Kent and Princess Marina as well as ambassadors, politicians and princes from all over Europe.

The Hon Lady Baillie with her daughters Susan and Pauline.

During the second world war Leeds became a military hospital and Lady Baillie set up a convalescent home for badly burned pilots who had been treated by the famous plastic surgeon Sir Archibald McIndoe at East Grinstead.

Lady Baillie, who was 74 when she died, decided some years ago that she would like to establish a charity with wide duties, if funds permitted, to encourage other charitable activities.

She set up the Leeds Castle Foundation in the hope that medical and nursing conferences would be held there, along with research seminars, arts events and conference venues for visiting statesmen.

Dorothy Squires' Bexley mansion destroyed by fire

Dorothy Squires in happier times.

October: Tragedy has struck again for Dorothy Squires, the popular Welsh singer who was once married to actor Roger Moore. Her mansion home at St Michael's Mount, Bexley — where she and Moore entertained so regularly and lavishly — has been destroyed by fire. Friends say it was badly underinsured.

Miss Squires met Roger Moore in 1952 at a party in Bexley. She then had assets valued at almost £3 million and he, 12 years her junior, was a struggling actor who made a living as a male model. He left his Streatham flat, moved into her mansion, divorced his wife and married Dorothy in 1953.

She was then at the height of her fame and well-known in Hollywood which she visited often with her husband, meeting such friends as Gary Cooper, Grace Kelly, Shirley MacLaine and Doris Day.

Back in Bexley the Moore's gave so many parties that Dorothy tried to have it registered as a club but the local authority turned it down.

Problems, however, were not far away. As Moore became increasingly successful, with title roles in *The Saint* and *Ivanhoe*, her career slumped. Friends say it was her heavy drinking which caused the marriage to collapse. The couple were divorced in 1961.

Still in love with her ex-husband about whom, say friends, she had pathologically jealous feelings, Dorothy tried several comebacks including a one-woman show at the London Palladium which she hired herself in 1970.

Last year she was accused of bribing Jack Dabb, the producer of *Family Favourites*, to play her records. She admitted paying his hotel expenses but said they were a gift. Although she was cleared earlier this year the scandal has adversely affected her career.

Now Dorothy is without a home.

__April 28th:__ Although Dartford Football Club's dreams of a league and cup double were cruelly shattered yesterday when the Southern League champions lost in the FA Challenge Trophy final at Wembley, the team has returned to a heroes' welcome. An open-top bus took manager Ernie Morgan and the players on a triumphant tour of Dartford through streets packed with banner-waving supporters. Behind them travelled a cavalcade of hooting, ribbon-bedecked cars. This was followed by a civic reception in which councillors said the players had captured the hearts of the town during a magnificent season. It didn't matter that they had been beaten by Morecambe 2-1 in the trophy final. The Darts had given the town a new era in football and there was now every chance that this former money-troubled club would receive civic backing for its Welling Street ground.

__November 12th:__ The funeral took place today of Medway firemen, Holley and Bell who were killed earlier this week in an explosion in the Royal Naval Barracks at Chatham. Four other firemen were badly injured. They were responding to a call following the discovery of a fire in a three-storey building used as stores and sleeping accommodation. Holly and Bell, both wearing compressed air breathing apparatus, entered with a charged line. The explosion followed trapping both men inside.

Why not join our subscribers for Volume Four?

THE fourth and last volume of this **Kent Chronicle of the Century** will be published in October 1999, covering the last 25 years of the twentieth century. It will be identical in format and, as explained on page 200, available in hardback and paperback with a special limited number of boxed sets.

We thank our subscribers, whose names are printed on pages 198 and 199, and hope you have enjoyed this volume enough to place an order for the fourth.

As well as tracing the still-remarkable story of Kent through the closing years of the second millennium, the final book in the series will contain many special features, fascinating statistics and a list of larger historical places, mentioned in the series, which are open to the public. It is also hoped to include a prediction of what Kent may be like 50 years hence.

The last five years or so of the century will make an interesting comparison with the first five, when the great railway network was seen as the only real catalyst for social and economic change, the internal combustion engine was a toy for the rich only, the flying machine just a far-off pipe dream and electricity in its infancy.

In those early years London had not opened her great suburban jaws to swallow huge areas of north west Kent; the commuter society, attracting residents without roots, had not evolved and visitors arrived only for the traditional two-week summer holiday or, perhaps, a railway outing.

The next volume will include the building of the M25, the Channel Tunnel, the QE2 Bridge, the introduction of the Internet and other technological revolutions. It will show how the unthinkable happened and the Kent mines and Chatham Dockyard closed for good. It will describe the horrors of Zeebrugge and the IRA bombs at Maidstone and Deal and it will outline the increasing threat to the countryside and, in particular, the ongoing Battle of the Green Belt.

If you would like to subscribe to the final volume (or place an order for earlier volumes), please write or telephone to the address below for details. There will be a reduction for subscribers and names will be printed in the book. We will, of course, require a deposit followed by the balance just prior to publication. All subscribers will receive signed copies.

Froglets Publications,
Brasted Chart, Westerham,
Kent TN16 ILY
Tel: 01959 562972
Fax: 01959 565365

BIBLIOGRAPHY

In writing this book I have referred to a variety of pamphlets, newspaper articles and miscellaneous documents kept in the Centre for Kentish Studies and various libraries throughout the county. Prominent among these is the monthly journal *Bygone Kent* published by Meresborough Books. I have also referred to the following books: *Memory Lane*, James Cameron. *The Motor Bus Services of Kent and Sussex,* Eric Baldock. *King's England,* Arthur Mee. *Kent Women,* Bowen Pearse. *The World on Their Backs*, Malcolm Pitt. *The History of Kent Cricket Club,* Dudley Moore. *Tales of Old Tonbridge*, Frank Chapman. *Churchill,* Martin Gilbert. *Romney Marsh,* Anne Roper. *To Fire Committed,* Harry Klopper. *Spirit of Kent,* Henry Pratt Boorman. *Kent Police Centenary*, ed R.L. Thomas. *Kent Weather Book,* Bob Ogley, Ian Currie and Mark Davison. *Hidden Kent,* Alan Major. *Kent Cinemas,* Martin Tapsell. *Chronicle of The Century,* ed Derrick Mercer. *Biggin On The Bump,* Bob Ogley. *National Trust*, Merlin Waterson. *Portrait of Canterbury,* John Boyle. *Kent,* Richard Church. *Kent Bibliography*, T.A.Bushell. *When the Coloured People Came,* Selwyn Gummer. *Teller of Tales,* Pat Davis. *Kent People and Places,* Pat Davis. *Kent*, John Vigar. *Test Pilot,* Neville Duke. *A Kentish Lad*, Frank Muir. *Macmillan,* Harold Macmillan. *The Ripening World,* H.E. Bates. *Gypsies, Didikois and Other Travellers*, Norman Dodds. *Archaeological Excavations in the Darenth Valley,* Brian and Edna Philp. *The Pleasant Town of Sevenoaks,* John Dunlop. *Ashford's Progress,* Henry Pratt Boorman. *Hopping Down in Kent*, Alan Bignell. *History of Southern Railway*, Michael R.Bonavia. *Portrait of Medway,* Roger Penn. *History of Maidstone,* Peter Clark and Lyn Murfin. *Guinness Book of Records.*

INDEX

INDEX

Index (cont)

SUBSCRIBERS

The following kindly gave their support to this book

Mrs P. Abraham
Doreen Allibone
L.F. Ambrose
Charmian Amos
Iain H. Anderson
Sally G. Anning
Jim Armstrong
E.R. Arnold
Roy Arnold
Brian Ashby
Vic Ashlee
Mrs F.E. Austen

Mrs W.J. Baigent
J. Balcon
Mr and Mrs
O.C. Baldock
Charles F. Baldwin
Kathleen and
Tony Ball
R.A. Barham
Megan Barnett
R.A.S. Beck
Heather Bell
Francis Bellingham
H.L. Belsey
D.E. Bengeyfield
Dick and
Pamela Bennett
Eric Bennett
M.E. Bishop
Shirley Blake
Karl Bloomfield
Mr R. Bolton
Miss M.V. Borner
Paul M. Boulton
B. Bowman
G.R. Boxall
Violet Brand
Wendy Brazier
W.J. Brenton
Mr and Mrs
M.A. Brett
The Briers family
Peter T. Brown
Mrs Rosemary Brown
Mrs Anne Buckett
Jean Bunnett
Mary C. Button
Sidney W. Burvill
Carol Bush
Mrs A.K. Butcher
J.J. Butcher

Mr Robin Carden
Joan Carlier
Mrs E. Childs
Janet Chambers
C.A. Chapman
Christopher Chase
Betty J. Church
Mr and Mrs
T.C. Churcher
Mr M.A. Churches
Dennis Clare
Florence Clarke
Roy Cleveley
M. and S. Cliffe
Arthur Clipstone
Marjorie Cocker
Rodney J.D. Collins
Mr N.R.H. Cole
Beryl Cook
Miss J.M. Cook
Mr G.A.P. and
P. Coombs
E. Craker
C.J. and I.B. Crane
Mrs Jean Crisfield
Mrs M Cronk
Richard P. Cross
Ivan Curtis
Jean Cust

Stan Darnell
A. Davidson
Mr R.S. Dawe
John Dawson
Alan Deares
V. Dennett
Clare Dennis
Harry Dobbs
M.J. K. Dodsworth
John F. Dorling
Mr J. Dorman
Mr Clive Douglas
N.O.Durdant-
Hollamby
Mr A.J. Dutton
Mark Dutton
Mr D. Dykes

Eric Edghill
Bernard M. Edwards
D.K. Elliott
Douglas Elks
Rachel and
George Elvery
Evelyn M. Evans
Barry Everett
Jennifer and
David Eyre
Richard Ewing

Mr and Mrs M.
Feltham
Mrs Melanie Felton
Denis R. Fentiman
Harry Fenton
The Finney family
Edgar Fitzgerald
Dr Jim Flegg
Mr N. Folkard
Bill Foster
Christiane P. Foster
Mr C. Fox
Mrs Emerald Frampton
Valerie Fry
Mr B.L. Fuller
Doug Furrents

Edwin and
Gloria Garrett
Mike Godfrey
M.H. Gosby
Mrs Iris Gosling
Richard Griggs
Eileen Gunnell

Yvonne and Terry
Hagreen
Marion Hall
K.W. Hammerton
Alan Hankinson
Barrie and Angela
Harber
Muriel Emma Harker
A.V. Harlow
Alan Harmsworth
R.C. Harris
Sheila Harris
J.C. Hart
J.W. Haslam
Ken Hayes
Marie Hazelwood
Alan and
Marian Healey
M.G. Hewett
J. Hickling
E. Hickmott
Joyce Hickmott

SUBSCRIBERS

George R. Higgs
Neil Hilkene
Guy Hitchings
David Thomas Hobbs
Angela and
Barrie Holness
Brian A. Holyland
Jim Homewood
Bryan Hopkins
Mrs Doreen Hopkins
Mrs Edith Hopkins
Molly Horn
Miss A.E.Horner
M. Hover
John Howcroft
Mr Peter Hughes
Sue and Chris Huke
Alan Humphrey
Maureen Humphrey

Elizabeth Jaecker
Mr H.W.M. James
Maria J Jarvis
Gary & Bobbie Jarvis
Mr A. Jeffreys
Jean and Tony Johns
Mrs J. Johnson
Mrs M.L. Johnson
Mrs C.L. Jones
Paul and Julie Jones
Ray and Brenda Jones
Mr T. I. Jones
Lynn Jung

Alan M. Kay
Bernard Keeling
Derek Kemp
Mrs Maureen Kessel
E. Keys
Peter Kiff
Sue Kirkham

A.J. Ladd
The Langridge family
Angela Legood
Mr David Lewis
Stella Lewis
J. Lindsay
Mrs Linton
John London
Gary Long
Gordon Luck

Philip Macdonald
Timothy F.P. McGrane

Pat Marshall
Ian Martin
Peter Martin
David J. Mason
E. Mason
B.L. and J.F. Matthews
Colin P. Matthews
C.S. Matthews
P.W. Maytum
Mrs P. Meridew
Beryl Miles
John Miskin
Caroline Mitchell
Brian Mole
E. Moody
Mrs A.T. Morgan
Peter J. Morgan
W. Morton
Alan Mount and
Anne Rickard
P.E. Murphy
Tony and
Maralyn Mulcuck

Brian and Muriel
Neal
Mr R.A. Newport
Frederick G. Neville
Brian Nobbs
Mr D.C. Nowers
Pam Nye

George and Sheila
Obermuller
Tony O'Farrell
Len Olive
Peter O'Sullivan
Mr W. Owler

Mrs E. Palmer
H. and R. Parkes
Mrs Lilian M. Parish
G. Parsons
Mr and Mrs B.B.
Payne
Allan Pearce
Miss M. Pearce
Reg and Gwen Pearce
L. Peatfield
Alun Pedler
R. M. Pendleton
John S. Penn
Brian, Kathryn and
Pauline Phillips
B.T. Philpot

Donald Pickering
Marge Piddock
Cyril Pile
Robert Piper
G. John Pluckrose
F.M. Pollard
Mr Chris Porteous
Mrs M.E. Potter
Jan and Chris Powis
Donald Pritchard
Sharon Proudlove
Hugh Pryke

Mrs L. Raeburn
Janet and
Alec Ramage
Mrs E.I. Rand
Paul and
Denise Rason
Paul C. Rayner
Linda Read
David C. Redman
Colin Reffell
Kevin F. Reynolds
Mrs I.C. Rhodes
Pam Ridout
Trevor Robbie
Vera Roberts
Roger, Agnes, Louise
and Declan Robinson
Roy Rofe
Margaret Rogans
Peter Rogers
Mrs W Rolfe
Frank and Joyce
Rooney
Malcolm Round
Mrs Bertha Rose
Colin W. Rumley
R. Ruston
R.D.H. Ruston

St Michael's School,
Otford
Joan Evelyn Sale
Mrs C. Samarasinghe
Mrs E.L. Sands
Mrs Kay Saunders
Brian A. Sayer
Rocky Scurr
Janet Seeley
Mrs J. Sharp
Mary and
Annette Shaw

Tessa and Mike
Sheeres
Maurice G. Short
Ron Sinclair
Jean Sitton
Alan Smith
M.J. Smith
Mr Steve Smith
A.J. Spelman
Roy and Freda Spivey
Joan W. Spreyer
Louise Spreyer
D.G. Stevens
Keith Stevens
June Stigwood
(née Marshall)
Mr James Stock
Mr M.G. Stocker
Ronald H.H. Stokes
Mrs Ivy H. Streeting
Mr S.J. Stringer

Mrs Joyce
Frances Tapsell
Mr C.H. Taylor
George Taylor
Dr H.W Taylor
Kath E. Taylor
Mr S.E. Taylor
Maureen Thatcher
Valerie Thatcher
Mrs Hilda Thickins
Frank M. Thirkell
Mr A.G.W. Thomas
R.G. Thomas
Mr Troye R. Thomas
E. Thompson
Paul Thompson
Miss A. Thorn
Mr E.A.B.
Thorneycroft
Graham Tippen
John R. Toms
Michael J. Tong
Eunice D. Towersey
Norma Towler
Colin Towse
Mr Robin Tregunno
Vivienne Tremain
Miss J. Tresize
Mrs Eve Tucker
Mike Tuckey
Gordon C. Turner
Ron and Doreen
Turner

Audrey and John
Tutton
Mrs Stella D.
Underwood
Mr B.M Vinall
Marshall Vine

Mrs D. Walford
Mr B.A. Walker
David John Walker
Mr P.D. Walker
Philip Wanstall
John H. Warner
M.J. Waterhouse
Mrs I. Watkins
Alexander Webb
Sue Webb
Alan Weeks
Mr S.L.Weller
Alan R. Wells
Keith Wells
Colin Westmancott
Eileen and Ian
Whitehead
Gillian and
Chris Whittingham
David Wickenden
Terry A. Wickens
Simon Wickens
Don Wiffen
A.R. Wilkinson
Geoffrey E. Williams
John and Wendy
Williams
Sidney G. Willson
R.A. Wilson
V.F. Wilson
George and
Mary Winton
Mr P.F. and
Mrs S.M. Winton
David Witherspoon
Christopher Wood
Denzil, Susan, Jane
and James Wood
June R. Wood
Lionel J. Wood
Sylvia Wood
Pat and
Ron Woodgate
Miss Wootton
John Edward Wratten
Mrs P. Wright
Chris Wyer

Kent Chronicle of The Century: Attractive boxed sets of all four volumes will be available.

The details of ***Kent Chronicle of the Century Volume Four (1975 — 1999)*** can be found on page 195 along with information for, present and would-be, esteemed subscribers.

They, and many other readers, may also like to know that all four volumes — ***1900-1924, 1925-1949, 1950-1974 and 1975-1999*** — will be obtainable in both paperback and hardback in a special boxed set, ideal as a prestige present for anyone interested in the history of Kent. The boxed sets, in an attractive cover, will be available only in a limited number, so we urge you to place your order as soon as possible. Subscribers will be offered a box, for their set, at cost price.

If you would like a boxed set, each book signed by Bob Ogley, please write, telephone or fax Froglets Publications for details. Price to be confirmed.

FROGLETS BOOKS

COUNTY WEATHER BOOK SERIES

by Bob Ogley
Ian Currie and Mark Davison

The Kent Weather Book
ISBN 1 872337 15 X........................£10.99

The Sussex Weather Book
ISBN 1 872337 13 9...........................£10.99

The Norfolk and Suffolk Weather Book
Paperback ISBN 1872337 99 6............£9.95
Hardback ISBN 1 872337 98 8..........£16.95

The Hampshire and Isle of Wight Weather Book
ISBN 1 872337 20 1 ....£9.95

The Berkshire Weather Book
ISBN 1 872337 48 1............................£9.95

HURRICANE SERIES

In The Wake of The Hurricane
(National Edition) paperback by Bob Ogley
ISBN 0 9513019 1 8.............................£8.95

Surrey in The Hurricane
by Mark Davison and Ian Currie
ISBN 0 9513019 2 6..........................£8.95

London's Hurricane
by Mark Davison and Ian Currie
Paperback ISBN 0 9513019 3 4 ....£7.95
Hardback ISBN 0 9513019 8 5......£11.95

Eye on The Hurricane (Eastern Counties)
by Kevin Reynolds and Bob Ogley
Paperback ISBN 0 9513019 6 9........£7.95
Hardback ISBN 0 9513019 7 7.......£11.95

King Oak of Sevenoaks A children's story
by Ron Denney
ISBN 1 872337 00 7.............................£6.95

WAR AND AVIATION SERIES

Biggin on the Bump
the most famous fighter station in the world
by Bob Ogley
Paperback ISBN 1 872337 05 8...........£9.99
Hardback ISBN 1 872337 10 4.........£16.99

Doodlebugs and Rockets by Bob Ogley
The battle of the Flying Bombs
Paperback ISBN 1 872337 21 X........£10.99
Hardback ISBN 1 872337 22 8.........£16.95

Flying Bombs over England by H.E. Bates
The 'lost' manuscript
Hardback ISBN 1 872337 04 X........£16.99

Kent at War 1939-1945 by Bob Ogley
Paperback ISBN 1 872337 82 1........£10.99
Hardback ISBN 1 872337 49 X........£16.99

Surrey at War 1939-1945 by Bob Ogley
Paperback ISBN 1 872337 65 1.........£10.99
Hardback ISBN 1 872337 70 8.........£16.99

OTHER FROGLETS BOOKS

Westerham and Crockham Hill in theWar
by Helen Long
ISBN 1 872337 40 6............................£8.95

Underriver: Samuel Palmer's GoldenValley
by Griselda Barton and Michael Tong
ISBN 1 872337 45 7............................£9.95

Tales of Old Tonbridge
by Frank Chapman
ISBN 1 872337 55 4 ....£8.95

CHRONICLE SERIES

Kent — A Chronicle of The Century

Volume One 1900-1924
Paperback ISBN 1 872337 19 8...... £10.99
Hardback ISBN 1 872337 24 4......... £16.99

Volume Two 1925-1949
Paperback ISBN 1 872337 89 9..........£10.99
Hardback ISBN 1 872337 84 8.........£16.99

Volume Three 1950-1974
Paperback ISBN 1 872337 11 2...........£10.99
Hardback ISBN 1872337 16 3............£16.99

Bob Ogley, the author of the majority of Froglets books, was born in Sevenoaks and is proud to be a Kentish Man. He has travelled extensively in pursuit of information and photographs and is in great demand across the south-east to tell the unique story of how he became an author. A former editor of the Sevenoaks Chronicle, Bob was a journalist for more than 30 years before he left his newspaper to concentrate on writing books and giving talks. He is also a regular broadcaster on BBC Radio Kent.

FROGLETS PUBLICATIONS, BRASTED CHART, WESTERHAM, KENT TN16 ILY
TEL: 01959 562972 FAX: 01959 565365